Depr_

Oil Trading &
A Mind At War
With Itself

MW00464466

Jonathan Ford

chipmunkapublishing
the mental health publisher

Published by
Chipmunkapublishing
United Kingdom

http://www.chipmunkapublishing.com

Copyright © 2016 Jonathan Ford

ISBN   978-1-78382-267-6

For my children

Jonathan Ford

Introduction
"Life is the sum of all our choices" Albert Camus

As I confidently pronounced the above quote, wrapping up my best man speech at the wedding of my best mate from College, Dave, and his new bride, Jenny, little did I realise its prescience in relation to my own life. Over the next 25 years, which I refer to as my 25 years of purgatory, every choice or major decision that I made, whether through fear, self-loathing, anxiety, weakness or depression led to disaster upon disaster that led my life into a downward spiral, plumbing depths of misery and hopelessness that I had never imagined possible.

My speech was greeted with raucous applause with many wedding guests commenting it was the wittiest and best they had ever heard.

At this time, March 28, 1990, I was working as an oil trader for Vitol in Geneva: but more of that later.

Early childhood
"Children begin by loving their parents, after a time they judge them: rarely, if ever, do they forgive them". Oscar Wilde

My first memory of childhood, or actually my third or fourth, found me lying on my back in the kitchen of the small hotel that my parents ran in the British Channel Island of Jersey. I had a sharp kitchen knife in my young hands, its point gently pressed between my ribs above where I assumed my heart to be. I was fascinated by the fact that were I to push the knife down hard I would cease to exist. I chose not to press. For most of the last 25 years I wish that I had.

My actual earliest memories stem from a brief period when I was 3 or 4 years old living in Whitley Bay, in the North East of England near Wallsend, a small, largely shipbuilding and coal mining town so named as it sat at the Eastern end of Hadrian's Wall, near Newcastle. My mum had grown up here and, after marrying my father, they decided to try life here before moving to Jersey, where they had met a few years prior.

I had one brother, Duncan, some 17 months my senior, with whom I was very close throughout my childhood and early adult years. I always felt that he was the perfect and favoured child to whom I must live up to. Much later in life he confided that he had felt similarly about me. Duncan must have been about 4 and a half when he was enrolled in his first school, Monkseaton Grammar, where doubtless, were we to stay in the North East, I would soon follow. Daily he would head off usually with me in tow, resplendent in his purple blazer and matching cap and tie. On occasion I would crawl out of my dad's open car window while he was walking Duncan to the school gate and sometimes I would be returned to the car by a kindly teacher, holding my hand, back to the car. The actual thought of school terrified me: I had no idea how to use a camera so how could I do photography. My brother had actually been talking about geography but the only word I knew that ended in "..raphy" involved the bewildering world of cameras.

Even at that age I was a serious child. One Christmas I was absolutely incensed when Duncan received a shining new tricycle with actual pedals while I was given what I considered a pathetic little contraption named "Jolly Jumbo" which had two tiny pedals attached to its front wheel. How I hated this thing and all that it represented. I would hurl it about the house yelling and screaming that I wanted a big boy tricycle like Duncan's even though my feet would not be able to touch the pedals.

In order to mollify my fury Duncan kindly offered, under the watchful eye of my mum's sister Aunt Ivy, to tie the two tricycles together. He would jump on the jolly jumbo and tow me down the hill of terraced houses where we lived. So off we went. However, we soon picked up excessive speed such that my brother flung himself from the jolly jumbo leaving me to go hurtling out of control down the hill and to knock down a poor old lady walking the other way. Abandoning the tricycles Duncan, my Aunt and I ran to our house and hid under the bed until the coast was clear.

In Whitley Bay we lived a few short miles from my mum's parents who still resided in Wallsend. My grandfather entertained Duncan and me, in his strong Geordie accent, with stories about his life in the coal mines and later the Swan Hunter (or Swine and Grunter as he called them) shipyards. Though he volunteered to join the Army during the War he was deemed essentially employed as a shipyard worker and therefore never left civilian life. On his fourteenth birthday he had been put to work down one of the local coal mines. He had a cart strapped to his back in which he hauled coal through shafts too tight for the pit ponies to pass through. My grandfather also had a great love and knowledge of horse racing and enjoyed a weekly flutter as well as a few bottles of Newcastle Brown Ale, delivered to his house in an old milk crate. The father of the singer, Sting had been a milkman I believe in Wallsend or very close by, and I used to tell people that he delivered my grandparents' milk: I suspect that this was not quite so.

My grandmother was a kind, sickly and tiny little lady, the youngest of about eight children, whose duty it had been to stay home and look after her tyrannical mother. She lost several brothers and uncles in the Great War.

Being a shipbuilding town, Wallsend was a strategic target for the German bomber command during the war. My mum told us how every day they would have to take a gas mask to school and had frequent air raid drills as many times the Germans would bomb at night and it was pure chance as to whose house was hit and who died. If there was insufficient time to get to the air raid shelter my mum and her family would simply all hide under the kitchen table and hope for the best. When the whistling of a V1 rocket flying overhead stopped they knew it was about to land and explode in very close proximity. I am convinced this terrifying period in my young mum's life shaped her personality greatly. To this day she has remained extremely nervous at the slightest out of the ordinary noise and I suspect she has suffered all these years from post-traumatic stress disorder. One evening she has recounted how, hiding under the stairs, her family was terrified by an extremely loud and incredibly close explosion that made her jump in fear and set a ringing in her years that is still with her today. She has always said that she thought silence had a background noise to it: it appears she has suffered from tinnitus since that frightful night. Her mental state could not have been helped by a tragic incident in which her cousin, several years her senior was killed. My mum, maybe aged 5 or 6 was walking home holding the hand of her older and taller cousin when suddenly a horse drawn cart unexpectedly reversed crushing her cousin against a wall. The cart passed harmlessly over my mum's head but she recalls grabbing the handle of a gate in the wall and, to this day, not knowing if she could have opened it and enabled her cousin and her to escape injury. Fatally wounded, her cousin was taken to my mum's house where she soon passed away. My poor mother, barely five or six was twice questioned by the police as to whether she had tried to open the gate. To this day she does not know but felt in some way the police were almost blaming her for the death of her beloved cousin.

My mum was a good student and after doing her GCE O Level exams at the local grammar school she became a nurse and soon advanced to staff nurse and mid-wife, frequently driving through the night with the doctor on call, delivering babies in their homes.

Nursing offered an opportunity to move away from the depressed North East of England. Even as late as 1952 food was rationed as England struggled to recover from the war. She and her close friend Betty decided to emigrate to either Canada or Jersey. They chose the latter for the better wages and supposedly sunny weather. It was here that she met my dad.

My dad, two years older than my mum, was barely educated at all. In fact his first language was Jersey French, an old fashioned French patois that today has all but died out. Born in 1931 he was 9 to 14 years old when the Germans occupied the Island. The Germans insisted that all children attend school and learn German but my dad rarely went preferring to spend his time running with his mates through the local woods and annoying the German soldiers. He often told us of how they would unlock the hand brakes on German trucks and watch them go hurtling down a hill, the Germans running behind. On one occasion he told of how he and his friends visited a local farmhouse to listen to the news from London on an illegal crystal set. Suddenly there was a loud noise at the door of the farm and in walked two German soldiers. The locals were terrified but the soldiers merely took off their helmets and sat down to listen along to the news.

After the War and the massive D-Day celebrations on May the 9th 1945 when Churchill uttered his immortal words "...and today our dear Channel Islands shall be set free..." my dad became an apprentice car mechanic. A few short years later he met a young English nurse named Olwyn and they were married in Wallsend, in a double ceremony involving my mum's younger sister, Ivy, and her husband George, an Engineer in the Merchant Navy. Ivy and George never had children and George had an annoying habit of making Duncan or me sniff pepper after which he would roar with laughter as we cried and spluttered uncontrollably.

Shortly after the tricycle incident we moved back to Jersey. As we left Whitley Bay I recall being heart-broken at being forced to leave behind my now much loved Jolly Jumbo, previously the target of much anger and hatred. I was four or five. My dad missed the island greatly and he and my mum were to manage a small hotel that offered bed, breakfast and evening meal to about 16 guests. My mum ran the business side of the hotel whilst my dad served in the bar at night, an ideal job for an alcoholic.

Being six, Duncan was soon enrolled in the local Catholic school, De La Salle, staffed by a handful of mostly elderly Catholic Brothers and a majority of lay teachers. I would have to wait another year before I could attend. At the age of five my mum enrolled me in a small local church school where on day one it became apparent that I was more than up to speed with the other pupils. However, I did not like being told what to do by the teacher so on day two I was sent home early for kicking the poor lady in the shins.

Having turned six the time had come for me to go along with Duncan to De La Salle. I recall blubbering sadly with my parents at my side as I arrived for my first day.

Duncan has already established himself as a star pupil and I therefore assumed it was my duty to do likewise, which I did. However, in my first year I was with children a year older than me so I was not "top of the class" in every subject as was my brother. However, once I was placed in the correct age group I assumed my rightful place atop the pile of students in every subject apart from art, which I did not count. Basically my brother and I were top of the class in every subject all the way through our schooling to age 18, apart from my suffering a brief interlude when my position was usurped by a tall, pale boy named Stephen Taufer. "A new broom sweeps clean," commented my teacher as I had to come to terms with coming second. The following year I was back in pole position where I stayed. Stephen was a very quiet, studious boy who I believe committed suicide in his early adult years.

Our school was composed roughly of 90 students per year, split into 3 classes of 30, until year 10 when numbers tapered off dramatically and pupils left school for the working world. Duncan and I soon enjoyed playing football and as we became slightly older, cricket, and after the age of 11, rugby. Cricket was, and would continue to be, my best sport. I was regarded as a pretty scary fast bowler and used it as an outlet for my internal anger. I would try equally hard to get the batsmen out as to injure them. On one occasion when about aged 12 I splattered a boy's nose whilst practicing in the nets which were not really suitably safe for a bowler of my pace. I felt pride rather than remorse.

Before attending school Duncan and I would be very excited when visited by our Aunt Ivy who was usually gallivanting around the globe with her chief engineer husband, George. She would take us to the beach where we would spend hours scouring rock pools for fish, shrimp and crabs. One day, with two shrimps in a bucket in one hand and holding the hand of my Aunt with the other we ran into Jimmy Saville who asked what I had named my shrimps. "Don't be stupid," I countered. "You don't give shrimps names" and stormed off. It was shattering some 45 years later to learn of the heinous crimes committed by this celebrity who most people thought was an eccentric who worked tirelessly for charity.

At school my best friend was Simon who lived barely a quarter of a mile around the corner from our small hotel, The Cornwallis. Simon and I would enjoy going into the hilly gardens that overlooked the seaside promenade below and throwing clumps of soil (ground bombs) onto the promenade and possibly people below in an effort to give them a "diarrhoea hair colour". The manager of a nearby pub once saw us in action and told my dad who gave me a thorough and probably well-deserved spanking.

The Cornwallis had a car park across the street that directly accessed the promenade of Havre des Pas beach. The "prom" was adorned with strings of coloured lights as was typical of most British seaside towns. I became quite adept at popping the bulbs by throwing stones and once as our family got out of the car I told my dad, "Look, watch". With my first throw I smashed a bulb. For some reason I expected my dad to be as proud as I was but another well-earned spanking ensued.

From the car park Simon and I would at times amuse ourselves by throwing stones at passing cars. Quite why we did this I do not know but one driver took exception to his car door being slammed with a rock. He stopped his car and quickly bolted after us. He caught Simon who pointed his finger in my direction as I ran along the sand. The man soon caught up with me and grabbed me by the scruff of the neck, yelling, but was soon scolded by nearby adults and the situation was defused.

It appears that the memories that have stayed with me from childhood are primarily of destruction from which I must have gathered some sense of joy. I was deeply serious and rarely laughed or smiled.

When Simon's divorced mother remarried they moved out to the countryside near the airport, all of about 5 miles from our house. I was a frequent visitor and we would play in the open fields nearby where we stumbled upon a derelict old farmhouse adjoining a graveyard. I immediately took it upon myself to start hurling large stones through the as yet unbroken windows. The pastor next door soon came out to see what on earth was going on so once again Simon and I made a swift escape.

At such a young age I was unable to identify the source of my anger but believe it may have been related to the fact that the atmosphere in our household was usually tense, for reasons unbeknownst to me. When out buying shoes in the St. Helier town centre I recall leaving the store and telling my mum I had just wanted to overturn all the shoe racks and throw all the shoes around. Quite why I do not know. Perhaps it was the pressure I felt of always having to live up to my brother's achievements. Nonetheless I possessed some serious, heavy anger.

My parents liked to keep us busy so we joined the Cub Scouts, soon to graduate to full scouts and played chess both at school and at The Jersey Chess Club sometimes twice a week. We were both pretty strong players and in 1973 my brother and I, as the headline above our photo in the local paper read, finished first and second in the Island Under 11 Chess Championships. Of course next year I was the red hot favourite to win. However, in the final round of six I made a dreadful blunder to lose a rook and quickly the game. I ran out of the hall bawling inconsolably. This was the first time I felt total and utter devastation. My parents did their best to console me but the depth of my feelings of failure which I have had to deal with for all of my life were totally gut wrenching and all consuming.

My mother had basically decided to dedicate her life, so it appeared, to raising her two boys and guaranteeing their academic success. After a few years running the Cornwallis we bought our own guest house in town, Kia-Ora, and at the same time my dad opened up a small shop where he would repair or recondition washing machines and vacuum cleaners. From our new house my brother and I were able to walk or cycle the 2 miles or so to and from school. Unfortunately the 19% mortgage rate my parents were paying on the Guest House meant that turning a profit was almost impossible so we actually swapped the property for a terraced house in town where we lived for perhaps the next five years. The family who took over the guest house were also unable to make it a success and the father, an alcoholic, was one evening seen flat out in the middle of a road, unconscious through drink, and was put out of his misery by an oncoming vehicle.

Usually on Sundays we would pay a visit to my dad's parents who lived in an old ramshackle farmhouse in the country Parish of St. Martin. My dad had been born in this house which was rented from the Lord of the nearby Rozel Manor. The house did have electricity but no running water. Rainwater was collected off the corrugated iron roof into a large tank, complete with gaping hole, and was, I believe, boiled before being consumed. There was no toilet or bathroom merely an old stall consisting of a large plank of wood with a hole in the centre next to some old, derelict pigsties. I do recall, with a semblance of joy, Duncan and me spending hours on an old go-kart on the stoney hill outside the farmhouse. My grandparents would speak in Jersey French to my dad who would answer in English for the benefit of the rest of us. Regardless of language Duncan and I could barely ever understand a word my grandfather spoke. He was heavily arthritic and we rarely saw him rise from his old blanket-covered couch in the corner. I believe my grandparents never really forgave my dad for marrying an Englishwoman as opposed to a "good Jersey girl". They refused to help my parents in any way with regard to a loan to buy a house or in any other capacity. Though they lived like peasants tending a handful of cows and growing potatoes they were far from broke.

During much of my early childhood I suffered from stomach pains, the cause of which was never ascertained. Perhaps it was stress related. Anyway, I spent a week in hospital under observation but no diagnosis was forthcoming. I hated this week, being away from home, and frequently would cry, telling the nurses that I was convinced I had cancer, to which they would respond with reassurance that I absolutely did not. I think I had learnt about cancer from watching a documentary on TV about the British Olympic runner, Lillian Board, who had died from cancer at the age of 22.

Throughout my childhood I was very thrifty to the point of basically saving every penny I was ever given. One of my happiest memories was the annual pilgrimage to the local Trustee Savings Bank when I would see how much "interesting interest" I had earnt that past year. By the time I was 18 I had saved fully 110 pounds and was very proud of the fact.

As a pre-teen I recall thinking how I little I knew my Dad. He worked the standard nine to 5 in his shop which he now shared with his elder brother, Ralph, would come home for dinner, read the paper and then go out to the nearby pub.

His favourite haunt was "The Temple," named due its close proximity to the Masonic Temple. One night he told us that he had seen the actor, Oliver Reed, raucously arm wrestling with all comers on the bar.

My brother and I were usually busy with homework in which my mother took great interest. It was always somewhat of a relief to receive our end of term glowing report cards from school detailing what wonderful students we were. However, the slightest and mildest criticism in those reports was always highlighted. At the end of year school Awards ceremony my brother and I would always come away with a number of academic prizes (books) and even the Sportsman of the Year Trophy, or similar. This, however, was not celebrated but merely accepted and expected.

My dad was heavily involved with the local football (or soccer) team, St. Paul's, for whom he had played in his younger days: this was a reason for his often being out in the evening, and, as far as I became aware, drinking excessively. St.Paul's FC was actually where Graeme Le Saux, famously later of Chelsea and England, cut his footballing teeth. According to my Dad, John Hollins, the Chelsea manager, was the guest of honour at a local football club dinner at which several rather inebriated St.Paul's officials pestered him relentlessly to give Graeme a trial. Eventually Hollins agreed, seemingly just to get some peace: I'm sure Graeme was immensely thankful for the persistence of his friends. At home, there was palpable tension in the air between my mother and father but I was not sure of the source. Duncan and I at this age never discussed it, but I think Duncan knew that my dad was drinking, and perhaps this contributed to his going to the toilet to pee sometimes as many as 20 times before finally going to bed. He would also often go into my parents' bedroom complaining that he could not sleep. Obviously this annoyed my parents, and on one fear-filled occasion my mother rushed yelling into our bedroom and proceeded to bounce frantically upon his bed shrieking "I can't sleep, I can't sleep," her enormous breasts breaking out of their nightie in the frenzy. Many nights I would go to sleep to the drone of their clearly agitated voices downstairs. Never could I make out a word or indeed did I want to but all was not well and it was with a heavy sadness that I would drift off to the escape of slumber.

"Educating the mind without educating the heart is no education at all". Aristotle

After age 11 when I entered, "Senior School" I was able to join in the annual De La Salle Island walk. This involved a walk of 36 miles in March around the island with checkpoints every three miles. If you were to complete the walk in under 10 and a half hours you received a plaque or small trophy: I desperately wanted one of these. Duncan had earnt one the year before and had numerous chess trophies whilst I had very few. My first year of the walk, which was sponsored to raise money for charity, was a dreadfully wet day during which it rained almost constantly. After about 24 miles I was suffering with large and extremely painful blisters. I plodded on in great pain for another 6 miles but at the 30 mile point I could go no further. I broke down in tears at my disappointment. I recall my parents driving us home and then carrying me into the house as something that felt like rigor mortis had set in throughout my body. My mood was slightly lifted as I smelt the roast chicken, chips and peas which I covered in malt vinegar that my mother had prepared. I can smell that meal as I write.

Almost everything I can think of my school years had academics and seriousness as its focus. Joy, if it existed, was to be found in learning, or serious reading or learning a musical instrument. When about eleven years old, against my wishes, I was entered by my mother in the local Eisteddfod where I had to recite a long poem, suitably inflected, in French. I came in second, not that I cared. I can still recite the poem to this day. It was "The frog who wanted to be as big as an ox," by La Fontaine.

It must be said, however, that my mum worked tirelessly in her efforts to keep us well fed and well educated. My dad always came home from work to a cooked lunch and my mother did all the domestic chores, other than the dishes, by herself. Even years later when we came home from College, over the various end of term breaks, she would eagerly cook for us and any of our visiting friends and still do all of the household chores. Basically for our entire childhood life my brother would have a cup of cocoa and I a cup of milky coffee, made lovingly by my mother of course, every night. When we were studying quietly at home she would also at regular intervals quietly bring us a piece of home-made cake and coffee or some other form of sustenance.

Obviously we had library time at school and I read one or two ghost stories but my mother considered such reading frivolous. Reading should enhance one's knowledge. In a spare moment you should read an encyclopaedia or a reference book though you could perhaps be permitted something satirical and critical of the modern world such as "Animal Farm" and "1984" by George Orwell and

Aldous Huxley's "Brave new World". I found this infuriating and I rebelled by not reading anything. I did, however, often skip through the dictionary for new words as words fascinated me.

My life must have had some moments of joy but they are simply hard to remember. In all the photos of my childhood I have not found one in which I was smiling. Neither can I remember being hugged by my parents or hearing the words "I love you" in our house. On the latter two points I have sought to almost overcompensate vis a vis my own children so that they are not infected by the insidious sadness and negativity with which I have seemingly forever been tormented. Not that this one step alone is responsible but I believe it plays its part.

The Teen Years
"All happy families are alike; each unhappy family is unhappy in its own way". Tolstoy

At the age of 15 I began to be acutely more aware of my dad's excessive drinking and the effect it was having on my mother, not to mention Duncan and me. We sold our house in town and moved to a large old Jersey Farmhouse in the Parish of St. Mary that we rented from the National Trust for Jersey. The house was of historic significance and in return for our living there at a modest rent my parents were expected to maintain the large front lawn, the spacious walled-in garden with its old apple and pear trees and to clean the offices of the National Trust which occupied the two large front rooms on one side of the house, known as The Elms. The National Trust would hold monthly meetings in these rooms. The house was adjoined by a working farm where a farmer and his family lived raising cows for milk and growing potatoes.

My parents seemed delighted to be moving to the "country". For sure my dad was as he had a large area in the walled-in garden where he could indulge his passion for growing vegetables from potatoes to radishes and carrots to lettuce. My mother also seemed to enjoy working in the garden but at the same time my dad's drinking seemed to become heavier and heavier. My brother and I did not share their enthusiasm for moving to the country as we were no longer within walking distance of school or perhaps more importantly any of our friends' houses. We felt a definite sense of isolation and when my dad would come home from work or the pub drunk the atmosphere at the dinner table was utterly pathetic and close to intolerable. My mother did her best to hide her disgust and sadness as my father, spectacles askew across his face, stumbled and struggled through his dinner. My brother and I would eat as quickly as possible and then escape to the adjoining family room where we would do our homework while watching TV. My dad may then go out to the pub or he and my mother would simply argue in the kitchen. This is what I remember most of my teen years, and very unhappy years they were.

At this time, in addition to a heavy homework schedule, my parents had us involved in extra activities as much as five days a week which I think by anyone's standards is a little excessive. Mondays we had our Duke of Edinburgh Award Club meeting which Duncan and I attended with my best friend Steven and his brother Robert. Tuesdays were chess club to which I would usually wear an overly warm high neck sweater that my mother had knitted. Wednesdays were typically a Duke of Edinburgh Award service night when we had to do something of benefit to the community to earn the award. Thursday was free until my parents decided to enroll us in the local canoe club in which we had zero interest but reluctantly went along. We initially learnt to canoe in the large Fort Regent swimming pool but both Duncan and I were pretty shy and introverted and I recall sitting in my swimming trunks, waiting for our turn in the canoe, with barely a word being said all evening. Friday was either an after school chess match against another school or we would attend yet another chess club. At the weekend during term time we would typically have at least one football or rugby or cricket match which at least got us out of the house. After a long week at school I would both look forward to and dread the weekend. Why could we not have a normal, "Happy," home life? In many ways I hated going home. I spent quite a bit of time in town at the house of my best friend Steven where the atmosphere was always light and jovial and somewhat chaotic given that he had four siblings. Steven's mother was to remark a few years later when meeting me on a trip home from College that I seemed so much happier compared to when I was a child.

When my brother turned 17 my dad taught him to drive and he was allowed to share the old Morris 1100 my dad used to drive to and from work every other week. On the other week my dad would have the shop van which he shared with his brother: they would alternately do one week on the road making house calls for repairs and one week in the shop in town. This meant every other week my brother would drive the two of us to and from school but the other week my dad would take us and then we would wait in the library doing our homework until he picked us up at about 5.15pm. During this time my dad had a couple of famous customers namely Alan Whicker of "Whicker's World" and Jack Walker who was the owner of Blackburn Rovers Football Club in England. Jack also lavished money on the main rivals of St. Paul's, First Tower United, much to my dad's dismay.

To my mother's credit she did strive hard to give our family life a semblance of normalcy. We would often on a Sunday morning cycle as a family a few miles along the country roads and share a picnic. We would also often play tennis at the school tennis courts, my mum having been a keen player in her youth. My dad had been a good table tennis player and played tennis as such while my brother and I had decent hand-eye coordination and could therefore play reasonably adequately. However, tennis brought back the demons of my anger. After hitting a few balls out or into the net I would totally lose my temper and begin to curse and swear and hit balls deliberately over the boundary fences. I simply could not handle not making the perfect shot all the time which of course was utterly ridiculous yet my outbursts were filled with fury so much so that I am amazed my parents continued for quite some time taking us to play. Similarly if I played pitch and putt golf, something for which I had never had a lesson, I would immediately lose my temper in a rage and start slinging clubs. Usually at that point my friends and I would call it a day.

From the age of 14 our all boys Catholic School began to share some lessons with the girls from the Girls' Catholic School just a few hundred yards down the road. My brother and I had never had much to do with girls and were very shy in their presence. In fact all the while he was at school, i.e., living at home, my brother never went out with a girl though he did attend 6th form parties where drinks were copiously available. I think, in addition to his natural shyness, he had worked out to go out with a girl would not be worth the domestic strife. I on the other hand thought I would give it a try so I asked a girl when I was 17 if she would like to go and see a movie that so happened to be "Apocalypse Now". She agreed and so it was arranged that our respective parents would drop us off and pick us up. During the 25 or so minute drive to the cinema with my parents you could hear a pin drop. My mother's face was rigid with disapproval. As we approached the cinema she asked "Do you at least know what apocalypse means?". "Great disaster," I answered. After that I came around to my brother's way of thinking: it really was not worth the pain, anguish and embarrassment that we were forced to feel over something so entirely normal and trivial. Another hurtful issue was that of praise. Essentially we were expected to always be top of our classes and get excellent grades in our exams, which we did, but if ever we expressed pleasure or pride in a sporting achievement, for me cricket comes to mind, my dad especially would put us down or tell us "not to be too big for our boots". I think my dad's father had done similarly to him even to the point of hoping he would lose his football matches and laugh when they did.

Unlike today parents rarely came to watch their children play and it was almost considered odd to have your parents watching. My parents would often pull up in their car to watch me bowl in a cricket match, as I swore and muttered my way through my performance, being angry at myself, the world, the batsmen or nothing in particular. The anger drove me to bowl as fast as I could. Turning 17 was of course a huge milestone for all teens as it meant you could learn to drive and consequently, have a degree of freedom. When it was my turn my dad agreed to teach me and he was indeed a very capable and patient instructor. Only once, as I drove down the driveway of our house straight into a large pothole that sent the car bouncing violently did he say, relatively calmly, "Mind the fucking potholes". It was the first and only time I can recall he used the F word.

Being 17 meant I was in my penultimate year of school and my brother in his last. We had both excelled at the extremely arduous GCE O Level exams that we took at the end of year 10, both of us oddly enough achieving 11 grade As and one Grade B. We also both elected for our final two years of studying for our A Levels Mathematics, Physics and Chemistry. I must confess we found these subjects pretty easy and we had a great deal of free time both at school and at home. For some reason my brother agreed, at my mother's prompting, to take a night class and study for an A Level in French. Though she suggested I do the same the following year there was no way I was going to assume that unnecessary workload and I was tired of being compared to Duncan.

My dad's drinking of course continued. My mother would have periods of depression and even on occasion Duncan would lose his temper and fling some insult or put down in the general direction of my dad. We had a pool table in the house and would frequently play with my Dad, usually when he was drunk, when he would giggle and act like a silly schoolboy. This was very sad. At times my poor mother was beside herself. She essentially had no friends of her own, only one or two acquaintances and wives she knew of friends' of my dad's. So desperate was she for some relief that she managed to obtain some "Antabuse," a drug used to treat alcoholism. The idea being that the person taking the drug would feel so dreadful should he or she drink alcohol that they would resist the urge. However, she did not tell my dad but simply put it into his food. He could not understand why he had agonising stomach aches and other dreadful symptoms but he was an unbelievably tough man and came through this episode unscathed. I am not sure what it was my mother hoped to achieve by this: it could not possibly have any positive benefit if my dad were not aware that he was taking it. Perhaps she was trying to kill him.

Jersey has one of the highest, if not the highest rates of alcoholism in the UK. Most of my dad's football drinking pals were probably alcoholics. One guy gave his wife an especially torrid time and kept a mistress in town. Both his teenage children killed themselves when they were about 18.

As my brother entered his final year of school it was time to think of University and our School Deputy Headmaster, Mr. Sankey, who himself had gone to Oxford, decided that my brother should try and do likewise. No student from our school had ever gone to Oxford or Cambridge for about 50 years. My brother was a little reluctant at first thinking that even if he were to be accepted he would be totally out of place as he would be stuck with a bunch of toffee nosed Public School kids. This was a common misconception made all the more so by a visionary Physics Tutor at Hertford College, Oxford, Dr. Neil Tanner, who decided to make a special effort to reach out to schools who had talented pupils that would ordinarily not even consider applying for Oxford or Cambridge. And so it was to Hertford College that my brother applied in the autumn of his final year. After two interviews and a successful written examination he was given an unconditional offer, i.e., he simply needed to pass two of his three A Levels to gain admission. The school and the family were all rightly delighted, so much so that the school presented him with the prestigious Brother Dennis Lawrence Memorial Medal, given only to those who had performed an extraordinary feat. The last recipient had swum the English Channel. Of course the pressure was now on yours truly.

Throughout our later teen years Duncan and I remained extremely close, sharing many common friends and spending most of our time together at home. This helped us cope I believe with the domestic situation in which we found ourselves. Of course, when he left for College I would be without my partner, as it were.

By the time you had reached 18 at our school you were basically in a class of less than 20 students. This contrasts dramatically with some US schools where you could be in a "graduating" class of over 800 as indeed were my eldest two children. Graduating is a word we use in the UK for successfully completing college and not for finishing high school let alone Kindergarten.

"I am not young enough to know everything".   Oscar Wilde

As school Head Boy, Duncan, along with the other prefects, was invited to a party at the girls' Catholic school with their equivalent pupils and a certain number of staff. Alcohol was served. I so happened that afternoon to be at Steven's house in town. Around 530 pm my brother knocked at the door, totally out of breathe. We quickly realised that he was totally plastered and had run all the way from the party to Steven's house. Shuffling him up the back stairs out of site to Robert's bedroom we pondered our next move. Duncan managed to clog the sink with his first alcohol induced vomit. Less than twenty minutes later the door bell rung and my parents stood furiously at the front door. Duncan and I silently and sheepishly got into the back seat of our car and we started the five mile or so drive home in total silence. About one mile from home my brother suddenly urged my dad to stop the car as he felt sick. "Oh no," my mother exclaimed, "he must be car sick". "I'll give you car sick" my dad muttered as he did as asked and my brother took care of matters. Soon we arrived home and my brother went straight to bed. I on the other hand decided to watch some TV but my still furious parents told me that I could not go out as previously planned the following night to a school party. I never was quite sure what I had done to deserve that. I must say, I did often feel that many of my parents' decisions made no sense, but what did I, a mere teenager, know. The next day things had calmed down a little and my mother had decided that her precious son had been duped by some other nasty pupils who had spiked his drink with vodka. What joy!

My brother's final year at school swiftly passed and he sailed through his A Levels with ease achieving three A grades, which was pretty typical for someone going to Oxbridge. That summer we played a lot of cricket and spent a fair amount of time at the beach. But soon he would be gone. Oxford's academic year consisted of 3 very short eight week terms but Duncan went up a week early, as most students did, to get the lay of the land and to join the College football team who had quite intensive training the week before the academic term started.

With my brother at College I entered my final year of school but was now exposed alone to the harsh realities of my home life. My dad was seemingly always drunk and my parents forever arguing. If I went to a school party at the weekend my dad would typically pick me and a friend who lived nearby up and bring us home as we of course did not want to drink and drive. He of course could and would drink and drive to his heart's content. It was terribly embarrassing being driven by your father hunched over the steering wheel, like a giggling teenager, somehow driving us safely home though he did typically put the headlights on full beam when a car approached and dipped them when there was no car approaching. We never did crash or indeed somehow he was never caught drink driving by the police though in all likelihood he would have known the honorary (unpaid, civilian volunteers) policeman and would have been let off. His drinking was very much centred around his football club but he would also keep a few bottles of whiskey under the car seat for emergencies and even stashed a few in suitable hiding spots in our walled-in garden. He also had an odd habit of burying wads of cash wrapped in cloth in odd places around the garden and at times he was either unable to locate them or would accidentally stick a pitch fork through the entire bundle which would lead to my very embarrassed mother having to take the damaged notes to the bank and request new ones. I am not sure how she explained those situations.

It was during this final year at home that I really felt the heaviness and intensity of my domestic situation. Once again I wanted to go home after school or at the weekend but at the same time I dreaded it. I was aware that I was very unhappy. This was a critical period as I had to prepare for my Oxford interviews and if needed, examination. I studied extremely intensively before my interview in October of my final year and actually did pretty well in three quite daunting interviews with eminent professors in the City of Dreaming Spires. The College reported back to my school that they were pretty much set on taking me but just to make sure they wanted me to sit the entrance exam. To have been accepted without doing the exam would have been a dream but I had not quite made it. I now had to study up on physics and mathematics especially as Physics was to be my chosen subject at College, just as it was for my brother. Now, whether this is an excuse or not, I am not sure but at this particular time my dad's drinking had really reached a crescendo. In fact he would cry to me that I (and the cat) was the only one who understood him and my mother and brother were against him. I did not know what to make of this but it made me feel utterly empty. I totally flunked the entrance exam but was at least given the consolation of a follow-up interview and the chance to redeem myself.

The second interview was set for early December just after term had ended. My brother was still in College so I slept on his sparse college room floor. Oxford was adorned in snow as we experienced a winter so cold that it has only been surpassed last year by that of 2014-15. We strolled into the Parks where the River Cherwell was frozen solid: the ice was so thick it resisted all our attempts to break it by hurling large stones onto it with great gusto. On the morning of my interview we awoke to the news that John Lennon had been shot dead outside the Dakota building in New York. I was never a fan of the Beatles.

The interview appeared to go reasonably well but not well enough and I failed to be accepted. After my chess debacle this was the second time in my life I felt devastated and had failed to live up to my brother and to my own expectations. I had an unconditional offer in hand from Imperial College, London, which was hardly Bognor Poly (if there is one) but I had my heart set on going to Oxford. Everything I saw and all that I heard from my brother was what University life was meant to be: I was not going to get to experience it.

My parents made the trip from Jersey to Oxford via car and boat to pick us up as they often did at the end and beginning of term. I had not yet officially received the result of my interview and still had a couple of weeks of school left before the 3 week Christmas break. Every year I looked forward eagerly to Christmas as I loved the season with all the smells and tastes and traditions yet every year it degenerated into a massive disappointment due primarily to my dad's drinking. For some ridiculous or masochistic reason my brother and I would almost always buy my dad a bottle of brandy for Christmas. What on earth were we thinking?

On the day that school "broke-up" for the Christmas break we would leave at lunchtime after the entire school attended mass. As we were not Catholic my brother and I did not take Communion but I was always fascinated by the fact that all the thugs and trouble makers at school were good Catholics.

My habit was to then go home and take out our simple silver tinsel Christmas tree that we used year after year and to decorate it. My mum would cook lots of special items like mince pies and sausage rolls and my dad would either be at work or in the pub.

One evening in the days just before Christmas, my mum and drunken dad were doing the dishes in the kitchen while Duncan and I watched TV in the adjacent room. The door was open to the kitchen and I happened to glance towards the sink where I saw my mum brandishing a large bread knife in the direction of my dad. With the foolishness of a drunkard, my dad grabbed the blade of the knife with his bare hand. Blood was everywhere. I was amazed his fingers were not severed or surely some tendons must have been, at the very least. In spite of our efforts at persuasion, my dad refused to go to hospital for stitches, preferring just to wrap his hand in an old cloth. As I have said, he was extremely tough and resistant to pain as exemplified by the following story some 14 years before: I recall my dad limping into our bedroom to say goodnight to my brother and me after he had suffered an injury playing football. The next morning he finally agreed to go to hospital to have his leg examined. He drove himself to the Emergency Room (or A&E) where the staff were in absolute disbelief as his Achilles tendon had totally ruptured and his calf muscle was balled up under the back of the knee. How on earth he managed to tolerate the pain all night and then drive a manual car the next day is beyond me. That was my Dad.

The next six months I focused on my looming A Level exams in June. I did my best to survive the domestic bliss of my household; I did have the benefit of my brother back home for about 5 weeks over Easter. Finally the exams came and went and I was finished with school. In those days, and I suspect even now, there was no such thing as a "high school graduation". Everyone just finished their last exam and headed home, or to the pub.

In the middle of August the Deputy Headmaster phoned to ask my family to come up to the school to get my exam results. When we arrived his sanguineous bald head was beaming as he said, "Amateur Athletics Association, just like his brother". I had achieved 3 A-grades, for what it was worth. He then, to my total surprise, said that Dr. Tanner at Hertford College, Oxford, had told him, after I was rejected, that they would accept me the following year, if I wanted to take a so-called gap year between school and College, were I to achieve 3 A-grades in my A Levels. Why on earth he had not told me that months earlier I don't know, but I had set my mind on going to College that autumn and so Imperial College of London University, it was to be.

College Life
" Education is the most powerful weapon which you can use to change the world"
Nelson Mandela

As October approached my anxiety increased as I thought about leaving what I knew for the great unknown. Furthermore it was not Oxford and this disappointment still lay heavily in my heart. My parents and I took the overnight car ferry from Jersey to Weymouth and drove up to London. Imperial College is in one of the nicest parts of the City but still it was not what I wanted. We had a cup of coffee at the Serpentine cafe in Hyde Park as I faced my future. Who was to know that a few short years later I would be working just over a stone's throw from the Serpentine.

I had been allocated a shared room in an enormous town house, one of many that the College owned, in Evelyn Gardens, South Kensington. The thought of sharing a room with a total stranger turned my stomach: you did not do that at Oxford. My roommate was a puny, long haired kid from Plymouth who was into heavy metal and I soon realised drugs as he took to chewing some very odd looking substance that looked like gooey chocolate. At least he offered me some but I refused. I quickly met a tall, muscular guy I had previously met at my Oxford interviews. He had a huge protruding chin that made him look like Desperate Dan. Frank Brufton from Sheffield he was, and we soon became close friends. His mother, I learnt, had taught cookery at school to the two female vocalists in the Human League. Frank and I soon befriended a tough looking Northern Irish guy, Laurie Duffy, who was not quite as fearsome as his cold stare and harsh Northern Irish brogue would have you think.

I immediately set about joining the College football club. They ran about seven teams and after attending trials I found myself in the centre of the third team defence. It seemed so alien to me to have to take the tube all the way to East London or goodness knows where to play our games. Again, this was not how my brother had explained his life in Oxford where all the football pitches were a short cycle ride from College. I found the work reasonably easy and did well. My brother and I both received a grant from our local authority, Jersey, with our parents being expected to supply a relatively modest amount of about 200 pounds each per term. Being thrifty I spent as little as possible on food and even managed to save some money. Towards the end of the first term I was still not happy and Oxford gnawed inside me. I decided to ask my mum to call the deputy headmaster and have him ask Dr. Tanner if I could drop out of Imperial and attend Hertford in Oxford the following year, as he had suggested. The response I received was not what I expected but was good enough: Dr. Tanner explained that were I to drop out of Imperial essentially a University place would be lost to the system and thus it was not possible for me to do this and then go to Oxford the following year. I would have in essence taken two University places. However, one of the Physics students at Hertford had decided after one term to transfer to Zoology and therefore, in theory, I could go to Hertford in January and complete the remaining two terms of my first year. There was the small matter to overcome of an arcane Oxford University by-law that stated in order for a student to graduate with a degree he had to be in residence in Oxford for nine terms. This would not be possible for me. Undaunted Dr. Tanner explained that he could seek special dispensation for me to circumvent this requirement but it would require a special ceremony and a specific decree to be granted by the University. I cannot express my gratitude enough to Dr. Tanner for taking on this task and making my transfer possible. As the end of term approached in London we had our end of year exams and I came 6th out of about 200 which was not bad at all. The Head of the Imperial Physics department called me in for a chat and asked if I was sure that I wanted to transfer. After all, Imperial had a stellar reputation in the sciences and a First Class Degree in Physics from Imperial was certainly within my sites. I understood but explained, since my brother had gone to Oxford, my heart had been set on going there and it was absolutely what I wanted. And so the wheels of change were set in motion. That Christmas I made my own way home by train and boat and when I turned up at our front door my mother gasped as I looked dreadfully gaunt and drawn having lost about 16 lbs, primarily due to my desire to save money rather than spend it on food. I believe I tipped the scales at around 160 lbs a full 90 lbs less than I weigh now.

After another pretty miserable Christmas at home my parents drove us both up to Oxford in mid-January. I was both nervous and exited. Would I be good enough academically to hold my own? How would I cope with the fact that I had missed an entire term's work on thermodynamics which was going to be the subject of a paper taken at the end of the first year exams, known as Honour Moderations or Mods? Dr. Tanner was already ahead of me. Though Mods required our taking six papers there were more than six subjects to choose from and the work that I had done at Imperial made me a perfect candidate to sit the Atomic Physics paper instead of the thermodynamics one. Over the next couple of years I would have to bring myself up to speed on thermodynamics but there was plenty of time for that.

So, on the Saturday before term began, I found myself decked out in my cap, white bow tie, black suit and short commoners' gown, sitting in a small room in the stately Sheldonian Theatre where the

English Parliament had actually sat during part of the English civil war. There were several other mostly foreign students present along with many august looking tutors and Professors decked out in splendid robes of various colours and decorated with fur. After a brief ceremony conducted in Latin, of which I did not understand a word, I was accepted into the University. I was effectively matriculated and was even the subject of a bulletin in the University magazine. Apparently the last time such special dispensation was granted to a student to allow him to graduate with just eight terms of residence was about 40 years prior and the lucky student was the celebrated author, Auberon Waugh.

So began what were probably the best two and a half years of my life, not to sound too clichéd. All first years, or freshers as they were termed, were housed in College but because of my late arrival I was put in a College house, Abingdon house, about a mile away filled with second years, a couple of which I already knew having met them when visiting my brother. I was thrilled. I joined the College football and rugby clubs and played for the 2nd XI at football but was surplus to requirements to the rugby team.

As was pretty common at any University much of the social life centred around the College Bar and the numerous pubs in the City. Some of these were amazingly historic such as the Bear and the Wheatsheaf and the King's Arms, the latter right next to Hertford. It so happened that my 19th birthday on March 5, 1982, was also the date of Hertford's Commemoration dinner. I was not sure what exactly it commemorated, my birthday perhaps, but it involved a relatively fancy meal in the Dining Hall followed and preceded by copious amounts of drinking. During the dinner I suspect I engaged in my favourite party piece of urinating in the coffee pot and then putting it back on the table for others to enjoy. Unbeknownst to me a couple of second years, Andy Beverly and Dave Adams, who lived in Abingdon House had taken it upon themselves to get the new kid well and truly plastered. I think they somewhat underestimated my capacity for alcohol and toward the end of the evening the three of us were singing rugby songs in the College bar each with a toilet seat draped proudly around our necks. I have little doubt that towards the end of the evening I would have been "talking to God on the big white telephone". Interestingly, Dave Adams after College became a journalist. His father worked for Reuters so it was in his blood. Dave happened to be about the only Western journalist in Panama City when the Americans invaded Panama to capture Noriega so he was in great demand and his articles were all over the front pages of the British broadsheets and his voice on the BBC World service. Andy, next year's rugby Captain, did a stint in the Army during which he saw active service in Northern Ireland before making his fortune with Morgan Stanley in the City and spending his cash on high-end racing cars and a pheasant shooting lease.

Unfortunately the College Dean did not take too kindly to the damage caused that night and that was the end of the annual Commemoration dinner.

Unlike most Universities, Oxford, composed of over thirty colleges, worked on a tutorial system. There were lectures every morning but these were usually not synchronised with the work you were assigned by your college tutors. As a result I think I went to all of two lectures during my three years and basically my week consisted of two one hour tutorials which I shared with another student and three hours of practical laboratory work. Otherwise the time was yours to do with as you saw fit. However, the tutors assigned a lot of complex work and though they explained it during the tutorials you all but had to teach it to yourself from textbooks. In this department I had my brother in the year above me as a terrific resource. For my first two terms, despite the occasional binge drinking session usually followed by a curry I actually worked very hard as I wanted to be certain that I would do well in the coming Mods. I did have an unpleasant tendency to get belligerent and angry when I drank to excess.

Breakfast, lunch and dinner were available in the student dining hall, ours being a modest and smaller imitation of the Christ Church Hall in which the dining scenes in the Harry Potter films were shot. Christ Church in fact was such a grand College that its chapel was a full blown Cathedral. Every day but Sunday two dinners were served: the regular casual dinner at 6pm and then "formal hall" at 730pm. For formal Hall you had to wear a jacket and tie and your gown. On Sundays there was only the formal option so my friends and I usually attended this meal after which my brother and I made the weekly pilgrimage to the nearby phone box and called our parents. At Formal Hall there were certain rules such as no talking about work, women and not looking at the portraits on the wall. If caught breaking such a rule another student could "sconce" you. This involved the Hall Porter bringing up to you a large silver double-handled flagon containing about two and a half pints of beer. The idea was for the person challenged to drink the entire contents without stopping, or he could simply refuse the challenge and pay for the bill. Many of the people challenged ended up throwing up either in the Hall or just outside and that resulted in failing the challenge and thus having to pay the bill. One quiet Sunday evening, luckily with no pressing work to be done, I was sconced. I casually quaffed the beer and then comfortably sat and finished my meal before heading off to the College bar to make a complete evening of it.

Summer, or Trinity, term in Oxford was a terrific time: punting on the Cherwell, long summer evenings, first-class cricket in the Parks where many a famous cricketer had earned his Blue, the most recent being Imran Khan, one of the world's greatest all-rounders and now a significant figure in Pakistani Politics. I, however, focused primarily on my work and I recall studying late at night in my little attic room in Abingdon House and then listening to the news on the radio before turning in. I particularly remember being haunted by the terrible news one night that HMS Exeter had been hit by an Exocet in the Falkland Island campaign resulting in dozens of dead and horribly wounded. Many students, as you can imagine, were deeply against this military campaign and indeed against everything the Thatcher government did including the breaking of the Unions and the decimation of Britain's centuries old coal mining industry. As depicted in the terrific film, Billy Elliott, many communities were ruined and, rather like Reagan in America, Thatcher seemed to usher in a new period of "me first" capitalism as she sold off many of our Nationalised industries and lowered taxes on the wealthy. Arguably this is when the seeds of the great income disparity we now see on both sides of the Atlantic were sown. I however, had little time or interest in politics. My grandfather, not surprisingly, had been a staunch Socialist and despised Thatcher while my mother, always trying to be fair and just, felt the Unions were just greedy and lazy and she held a particular dislike, for whatever reason, for teachers' unions, journalists and above all lawyers. Unfortunately much of my thinking was framed by my mother, as she has had such a powerful influence over my upbringing. I felt I had inherited much of her judgmentalism, closed-mindedness and even negativity. I certainly had inherited her thriftiness, which was not a bad thing.

End of first and third year Exams at Oxford were quite an event in themselves. They were held in the grand, historic Exam Schools on the High Street and students were required to wear formal attire, i.e., black suit, white bow tie and cap and gown. It was quite an occasion. Often when walking to or from schools one would be stopped by an eager group of camera wielding Japanese tourists. As is typical of Oxford, which had its own police force termed Bulldogs who were allowed to pursue students into Colleges unlike the regular Police, even the exam process had some strange old rules. The one I found most amazing was if you turned up at Schools in full military regalia, including your sword, you were permitted to request that the invigilator bring you a flagon of ale. I never heard of anyone in living memory who knew of this rule being put into good effect.

That summer was spent in Jersey with a couple of mutual friends of my brother and mine visiting for a couple of weeks. Much of my time was taken up with cricket, still a good outlet for my anger, and at the beach. My mum did have an annoying habit of saying, "Don't you have any College work to do. This time last year your brother was reading such and such a book". I said little but this really grated inside. My Mods results arrived and I had done perfectly well: solidly in the middle of the pack, which I felt was good given that everyone at Oxford was very bright, some exceptionally so.

Soon it would be time to head back to College for the New Year. Michaelmas term began in early October but Duncan and I went up a week early for football and rugby training. That term I would play number 8 for the rugby team and joined Duncan in the 2nd XI football team. Our College was very good at football due to the innovative recruitment campaign of Dr.Tanner as many of our students came from comprehensive schools where football was the main sport as opposed to the "posher" schools where rowing and rugby were stressed.

Along with working hard, as was necessary, and playing sports many a fine evening were spent in the College bar or at the pub. I was having an increasing tendency towards becoming violent when drunk and would even head butt my friends, sometimes sending them reeling to the floor, as a "mark of respect". One particularly angry night saw me in "New Quad," the newest of Hertford's two quadrangles, connected to the "Old Quad" by the famous "Bridge of Sighs". I was angrily picking up large, heavy concrete rubbish bins and smashing them to pieces and then hurling large chunks of concrete in all directions. Luckily nobody was hit as the Quad soon emptied of people. Equally amazingly no windows were broken. Shortly after this a couple of my older friends had a chat with me in an attempt to curb my drinking which led to such violent and destructive outbursts.

Typically all 1st and 3rd years lived in College and all second years spent the year living out but since I had spent last year in a College house I was allocated a room in College along with the new comers (freshers) and the 3rd year students.

As the term drew to a close, I became friendly with a young freshman Geographer from Deal in Kent named Judith. She looked incredibly sweet but was extremely mischievous and was very light hearted and fun, as well as extremely bright. Her parents were both teachers.

That Christmas at home was pretty much the usual disappointment. At least my brother and I were old enough to escape the house as we had access to a car and could spend many an evening with our local ex-school friends.

My dad of course was drinking and he took extreme pleasure in teasing me over a Christmas card that I had received from Judith. He would many times play one of his favourite Jim Reeves albums, especially the track titled "Old Christmas Card". He would also ask ridiculous questions like what was the name of that big lad who played rugby at school and lived in St. John? Knowing full well his name was Kent (Pinglaux), he just wanted to have me say Kent, as that was where Judith was from. This behaviour was quite ridiculous and totally infuriating. I barely knew the girl yet my mother, as was her wont, insisted on asking a hundred different questions about her and of course when she learnt that her parents were teachers she made her disdain for that profession well known. My mother had this annoying habit of asking an enormous number of questions whenever Duncan or I went anywhere: who was there, what did you do, what colour was the carpet and on and on and on. The following Hilary term came and went. We won the 2nd Team football "Cuppers" competition of which we were all rightly proud. At the end of the term all sports Clubs had black tie dinners, usually in the dining Hall of College followed by some serious drinking and singing in the College bar.

"Rugby is a good occasion for keeping 30 bullies far from the centre of the City". Oscar Wilde

We also had a memorable rugby season. While we played League rugby before Christmas the following term was for "Cuppers" and for this each College had the availability of their Blues who prior to Christmas were playing for the University before the annual Varsity match at Twickenham in early December. We had the good fortune to have two of the Blue's back row, Jon Searle an open-side flanker, and Tony Brooks, a towering number 8 who actually also played first class rugby for Rosslyn Park. With Brooks in the team I had the unfortunate necessity of moving to the front row where I played loose head prop. I was not at all keen on this position as I came across some enormous and far more experienced beasts but I generally managed to hold my own and not suffer any serious injury.

We had two superb victories over Wadham and Jesus both of whom had beaten us in the regular League season. The presence of Brooks and Searle had an incredible effect and seemed to lift the level of play and intensity of the rest of the team. Wadham had an extremely fast and gifted full back who gave us all sorts of trouble during the league match the previous term. This time we were ready for him. Tony Brooks said right from the kick off we were to hoist a high ball for him to catch and then the entire pack was to descend upon him, led by Searle and Brooks in all likelihood, and after that he would be very much less inclined to try any of his strong attacking runs. The plan worked to perfection.

In the quarter finals we were to play Keble who were to stacked with a large number of Greyhounds, i.e., members of the University 2nd

29

XV. In an incredibly close fought and bruising encounter we had two clear cut chances to win but both we blew. One blunder was in attack and the other in defence. The latter error was made by our Japanese post graduate full-back, Katsuhiko Oku. A harmless ball drifted behind our try line but as Katsu ambled to touch it down an alert Keble player nipped in and beat him to the ball and touched it down for a try. What a shame. Katsu was a wonderful chap and after College joined the Japanese Diplomatic service. He was tragically killed when his car was blown up in Iraq while there on a diplomatic mission. To this day Hertford plays an annual rugby match against Old Boys in his memory and honour.

At the end of the season Andy Beverly the Captain appointed me the Captain for next year.

During the Easter break at home Duncan and I, along with my best school friend Steven, were presented with our Duke of Edinburgh Gold Awards by Prince Philip himself who was in Jersey to open a new sports complex in the Parish of St. John dedicated to the late Sir Billy Butlin. It was a great honour, of course, to shake hands with the Queen's husband. Robert, Steven's brother decided not to attend the ceremony but instead chose to go to Buckingham Palace to collect his award which sounded grand but he would not receive the Award from the Prince himself or indeed from any dignitary of note. The Awards were presented at a fine lunch and there of course, at the top table, was Jimmy Saville.

Cricket

"I tend to think that cricket is the greatest thing that God ever created on earth - certainly greater than sex, although sex isn't too bad either". Harold Pinter

The summer of Trinity term of your second year was especially enjoyable as you had only half of your regular work load, i.e., one tutorial per week. I had been invited up a week early to train with the "Blue's" cricket team, along with another close friend at Hertford, Roger. I was absolutely thrilled yet extremely nervous as most of the players were from very accomplished cricketing schools and four already had professional contracts with First Class counties. I did not even have my own equipment and typically played in a white Marks and Spencer polo shirt. I managed to make the first team squad which was a great honour and we practised daily at the famous Oxford Parks. The team was student run but that year we had employed an ex-West Indian international cricketer, Vanburn Holder, as coach. Training was great and Vanburn would always lend me his bat to practice with as I did not have one of my own.

Vanburn was indeed a lovely, jovial chap. He had also been in the West Indies Test side touring England in 1976 and captained by his close friend, Clive Lloyd. It was after the final Test of this series that Lloyd announced he and most of his team were joining Kerry Packer's Australian Channel 9 "circus" as it was dubbed in the press. This sent the world game into turmoil for the next 3 years as each Test nation effectively had two teams: one officially recognised by the country and one, arguably the better one, playing in Packer's "circus" complete with night games, for which a white ball was used under flood lights, and coloured uniforms. Ultimately the "circus" arguably helped players by seeing their remuneration substantially increased. Packer eventually achieved his goal of having exclusive rights in Australia to all international cricket on his Channel 9 station. Vanburn explained that as the final Test ended Lloyd went around the dressing room having a quiet word with everyone individually. It was only Vanburn to whom he did not speak. Vanburn was not invited to join the Packer team. He was understandably deeply hurt by this apparent act of betrayal by a man who he considered one of his very best friends. Several years later I would experience such a betrayal.

It was still traditional for Oxford and Cambridge to play first class matches against professional county sides throughout the summer term. Funnily enough since we had no official sponsor and we could not violate the Test and County Cricket Board (TCCB) rules our kit had to be without any logos so I was made to put a small band aid over the Marks and Spencer logo on my shirt. The matches were featured in the national press and arguably a cricket Blue was the 3rd most prestigious Blue you could earn, behind rugby and rowing, which was by far the highest standard of all the University sports. In order to win an elusive Blue you had to represent Oxford in the end of year 3 day Blues match at Lord's, the home of cricket.

We of course were usually totally destroyed by the counties but it was still an incredible experience. To my utter amazement I was selected to play as a bowler in the first match of the season against Lancashire. Lancashire had numerous famous cricketers such as Graham Fowler, Paul Allott, David "Bumble" Lloyd, David Hughes and a very fast South African bowler, Steve Jefferies. Somehow we managed to survive the entire first day without being bowled out with our star opening batsman, Richard Ellis, carrying his bat the entire day. He was earmarked for greatness but unfortunately had a temperament similar to mine when drunk, except permanently. At the start of the second day it fell to me, as the last man in, to join Ellis out at the crease. David Hughes was bowling slow left arm from one end and the South African quickie was on at the other. Now batting was hardly my strong point and furthermore wracked with nerves I was especially vulnerable. David Hughes made a total fool of me with his first few deliveries which I totally misread, but he failed to get me out. I somehow managed to catch a couple of fine edges that flew past the wicket keeper, Watkinson, and made 3 runs in that fashion as Hughes and Watkinson cursed relentlessly at me. Then out of the blue I smacked a Hughes delivery straight back over the bowler's head towards the pavilion for four runs. The crowd, or rather small contingent of keen observers, erupted with applause as Hughes hurled a full volley of expletives at me. One of my three singles actually occurred after the four and I now had to face the fierce pace of Steve Jefferies, hurling his left arm thunderbolts hopefully at the stumps rather than at me. The first couple of balls I barely saw and then a straight one smashed into my wicket and I was out but physically unharmed. There was then to follow a 30 minute change over period and Lancashire would bat.

It was an ominously cloudy day with rain clearly threatening. Our two opening bowlers bowled about 6 overs each without troubling the batsmen, both of whom had played for England at one time or another. The Captain signalled to me and tossed me the ball as my moment of glory had come: I was about to bowl in a first-class cricket match to David Lloyd of Lancashire and England. Having marked out my run up I turned to begin the approach for my first delivery and as I did so a massive thunder clap resounded around the ground and everyone rushed to the pavilion. The rest of the day was rained out as was the 3rd and final following day. My moment of glory would have to wait. That Saturday night there were stories of Ellis getting hammered with the Lancashire boys and they ended up literally wiping the floor with his sorry carcass. In addition to Ellis our team featured Anthony "Dusty" Miller who was at Haileybury with Ellis and also under contract with Middlesex. He had an amazing summer that year with the bat for Middlesex. Similarly contracted was John Carr, son of the Chairman of the TCCB. I believe John, some two plus decades later, after a successful career with Middlesex assumed a senior role in the TCCB. Our fourth professional was Kevin Hayes of Lancashire, playing against his county team mates.

The following week we were set to play Glamorgan and again I was selected. I could not wait. We batted first and had nine wickets down pretty late in the day when I was called to once again accompany Richard Ellis, who had survived all day. I only lasted a few balls before Mike Selvey bowled me with his gentle but accurate medium pace. Unfortunately I lasted a little too long as there was not time for Glamorgan to begin their innings and once again rain denied me my moment in the limelight as the next two days were entirely washed out.

Unfortunately and for whatever reason our next scheduled first class county match was a couple of weeks away. I was even featured in an article, complete with a head shot of me and an embarrassingly awful lopsided haircut, in the local newspaper, the Oxford Press entitled "Have you seen this man?" It struck them as odd that having been selected as a bowler for the first two county games I was not selected for the third. In the meantime I had played a couple of games for the University 2nd XI known as the Authentics.

Mid-term at the Parks we played a couple of non-first class three day games against well-known Club teams. The most prestigious being against the MCC who often fielded a few elder statesmen of the game. I recall facing the great spinner, Fred Titmus and when I had a chance to bowl I had Brian Bolus, once of England, caught smartly in the slips. Admittedly Bolus was about 25 years passed his prime but I was delighted nonetheless.

The other game in which I featured was against the Free Foresters. This game was shortened by rain but on the first evening I had a pretty good, nippy spell and took one wicket, clean bowled.

At this time Oxford and Cambridge still fielded a "Combined Universities" Team against the Professional Counties in the one day Benson and Hedges Cup tournament. On May Day, i.e., May 1, a day the pubs in Oxford stayed open all night, we headed to Cambridge to play them in a one day trial match at Fenner's after which a Combined Team would be selected. I was selected in the starting XI but once again the weather looked ominous. At that time Cambridge featured an all-rounder by the name of Rob Andrew who became better known as fly half for the England Rugby team and is now Overall Head of the England Rugby setup, a position possibly in question after our disappointing World Cup performance. As was now to be expected the game was rained out without a ball being bowled.

Next up on the cricketing calendar of major significance was the Annual Oxford vs "Lord's Taverners" match in the grounds of Blenheim Palace, the childhood home of Winston Churchill. The Taverners were a charity organisation of sporting and entertainment celebrities and usually this game garnered a crowd of some 10,000 or so. It was a superb event. Needless to say on the day of the match we never left Oxford as the rain was incessant and the match cancelled.

> **"I saw Len Hutton in his prime,**
> **Another time,**
> **Another time."**
> **Harold Pinter**

Thus ended my first-class cricketing career. I never actually "turned my arm over" in anger. I took some consolation from the fact that I did actually bat twice and featured in two first class games but I was understandably deeply disappointed. Obviously there was always next year but next summer I would be having to prepare for my Finals and I did not think I would be able to study sufficiently and play cricket seriously which was extremely time consuming. One well known Oxford sportsman a few years older than me famously did earn his cricket Blue and was always to be seen studying away in the pavilion when not in the field where he played as wicket keeper. This was Richard Luddington who was better known for winning five rugby Blues as scrum half.

Luddington was a close friend of Richard Ellis and the summer after Ellis graduated, Luddington served as best man at Ellis's wedding to his long suffering girlfriend, Sarah. Ellis really was an unbelievable talent and it was a tragedy he was not able to put it to better use. If my memory serves me correctly he scored a century in each of the two county games in which I played. That was quite an achievement.

Anyway, at his wedding after Luddington had finished his speech the end of which he spent extolling the virtues of Richard's bride, Sarah, Richard staggered to his feet and prepared to deliver a few choice comments. "Well, I'm glad someone fucking likes her!". The marriage did not last long.

Another consolation for my cricketing efforts was the fact that I was entitled to wear the Oxford University Cricket Club tie as well as to join the ancient and world renowned Oxford sports club, Vincent's.

The Vincent's Club tie rarely goes unnoticed. Even to this day I receive an invitation to the annual Vincent's Dinner, often held at the Cafe Royale on Regents Street but I have yet to attend. I do once recall going into the Cafe Royale and being thrilled to see my cricketing hero, Bob Willis. Willis was a world class fast bowler who I so much wanted to emulate. I even started to listen to Bob Dylan as Willis was a massive Dylan fan and had changed his name to Bob G. Dylan Willis. The Cafe Royale also brings to mind my recent reading of the magnificent autobiography of Robert Graves, "Good Bye to all that". Obviously much of it centred on the horrors of the First World War but I also remember his describing life in London, walking past familiar landmarks and visiting the Cafe Royale, almost a century ago. It also struck me that he knew Thomas Hardy, who first allowed me to enter the realm of reading great literature. I similarly enjoyed Graves' "I, Claudius" and "Claudius the God" which of course were dramatised by the BBC starring Derek Jacobi. I have yet to watch these series but I did in 1986 see Jacobi in a magnificent performance as Alan Turing in "Breaking the Code" which was basically the play version of the movie, "The Imitation Game," made almost 30 years later starring Benedict Cumberbatch.

At the end of the season and culminating in the Blues match at Lord's, for which I was not surprisingly not selected, the Oxford team went on a short tour to play Surrey and Warwickshire. I was selected for the squad to play Surrey and so went down to London where we stayed at the Oxford and Cambridge Club. Interestingly I slept in the "Nevil Shute" room, where he frequently had stayed. Years later I read his novels, "On the Beach" and "A Town called Alice," the latter I found deeply moving and quite affecting.

I was named as 12th man which meant I did not play but simply sat on the balcony watching proceedings and at roughly 3 hour intervals I would carry a tray of refreshing drinks to our players. At least I can say I have carried the drinks on to the Oval. I was also sanctioned for sun bathing on the players' balcony without my shirt on. At that time Surrey fielded a very young Alex Stewart who went on to have an illustrious England career.

Whilst I was concerned with cricketing matters and a minimal amount of work my brother and his friends were consumed with Finals. When these were over it was a massive relief and it was common for the students leaving the Exam schools on the High Street to be met with friends showering them with champagne. This did not do much to ingratiate the students or the University with the regular townsfolk and this year was the last year that this tradition was permitted. After this, such dousing in champagne and general revelry had to be confined to the privacy of the colleges. This was just one example of the friction that occasionally popped up between "Town and Gown".

That summer was again spent in Jersey, playing cricket, on the beach and doing a great deal of weight training as Duncan and I sought to bulk ourselves up for the coming rugby season. As far as cricket went I was never much of a batsmen with very poor technique but a fairly good eye. However, I had practiced so much at Oxford during the preceding term that my eye had improved markedly and I was now often seen to be smacking the local club bowlers all over the field in an otherwise totally unknown fashion. It was great fun and quite amusing.

My brother was inches away form a first class degree which was very difficult to achieve. In fact so close was he that he was called in, after his exams, in front of a panel of splendidly regaled Professors to further explain some of his examination answers in what was known as a "viva voce". Unfortunately he failed to sufficiently impress and ended up with the top second class degree in Physics. He was, however, offered a place to take a doctorate, known at Oxford as a D.Phil, in experimental High Energy Particle Physics which meant he would have another three years at Hertford. Even though a post graduate student he was allowed to play in the College sports teams.

My final year at Hertford found me back in College, working hard and drinking to excess less frequently. The work was becoming more difficult especially my chosen elective of nuclear Physics with which I really struggled. As I ploughed through this and Solid State Physics and some optics, I began to see how all of the various subjects within physics, from electromagnetism to thermodynamics to quantum mechanics, could be seen to be inter-related and to be essentially derivable from the same first principles. This broad realisation was quite satisfying, though for me it lacked the clarity and precision, by degrees of magnitude, of that experienced by those with keener minds.

As Captain of the Rugby Team I was expected to give an inspirational speech at the start of every match, rather like Henry V at Agincourt, but I found this pretty tough going. I stuck to some basic principles: get stuck in, hit them hard, fight for your team mates and the like. As Captain I was faced with one incredibly difficult decision for our Cuppers match versus Teddy Hall: should I pick my brother Duncan as full-back or another guy by the name of Steve Kimpton. I plumped for Kimpton. Duncan of course was deeply disappointed. We were heftily beaten by Teddy Hall as they were well known for their sporting prowess. At that time rugby was still an amateur sport and on that day we faced the Irish International full-back, Hugo McNeil and should have faced the sometimes England fly half, Stuart Barnes, but he arrived back in

Oxford late from his England training camp. Barnes is now perhaps the foremost commentator on UK TV for rugby. He, for sure, downed a few pints with his good mate Ellis in Vincent's. During the match, my opposing prop, bound with one hand clutching my throat. Obviously I took exception to this, and jabbed him, best I could, with my left hand. As the front rows parted, he caught me with a sharp right hand to the chin. I wound up my right hand for a retaliatory hay-maker, only to find my arm grabbed by my fellow prop. I was most disappointed but he probably saved me from being sent off.

It was at the end of Michaelmas term that I reacquainted myself with the young Geographer, Judith. We actually began a somewhat secret relationship. While I lived in a College room, Judith had rented a small house-boat a couple of miles away down the Abingdon Road. She was full of life and very bright and breezy and also quite political. She hated Mrs. Thatcher and took part in Campaign for Nuclear Disarmament (CND) demonstrations at some of the nearby US air bases supposedly housing American nuclear missiles. I of course was pretty much an ignorant fascist and broadly intolerant of other opinions and often a mere echo chamber for my mother's thoughts. My mother's influence remained so powerful on my mind.

This was also the time when a career had to be considered. Some people seemed to know exactly what they wanted to be but I had no idea. I shot off maybe 20 job applications to the likes of Shell, Exxon, Rio Tinto Zinc, Mars Foods, Cargill, Arthur Andersen Consulting, Citibank, Bank of America and even Clarks shoes. Several companies had open nights where you could eat and drink for free while learning a little about what they did, which generally did not mean very much.

The only Company that did not grant me an initial interview was BP, something that years later would be quite ironic. Several of the first interviews were in hotels in Oxford while generally for a second interview I had to head to the companies' main office in London or in the case of Shell, Cheshire. One dreadfully rainy day I set off, without an umbrella, in the rain up Parks Road to the Lincoln Lodge Hotel for my interview with Citibank. My drowned rat appearance did probably not create the greatest of first impressions and neither did the first couple of questions. "What do you think you could do for the bank?" asked the young interviewer. "Well, I was rather hoping you'd tell me what sort of options existed and we could take it from there". He was clearly not impressed with my preparation and abruptly ended the interview. I thought it sensible to cancel my appointment with Bank of America as they were likely equally humourless Americans. Exxon had an especially gruelling second interview in London which involved a form of team game.

Eventually I was offered a job by Arthur Andersen, Exxon, Mobil and Clarks shoes though the kind man at the latter company suggested I could do much better and should go elsewhere. Since I really did not know what I wanted to do with my life I thought the Andersen Consulting route offered the broadest options and exposure to various types of industry. My good friend Andy also chose Andersen. My tutorial partner John was determined to be a stockbroker and had even taken to reading the financial times during our last couple of terms. I always read the paper from the back and only the sports pages. Almost all of my friends were going to end up in London. I accepted the Andersen job at an annual salary of 8,000 pounds which was about average. Exxon actually offered more money and some of my friends received as much as 15,000 from the likes of McKinsey or Schlumberger but I had not applied to these companies.

That Christmas was the usual disappointing affair and my brother and I both returned to Oxford as early as possible. I actually arranged to meet Judith for a couple of days in London before going back to College. I recall she was wearing a rather odd cap as she hated her latest haircut. We had a great couple of days in London including seeing Elaine Paige in the musical Evita.

I think Judith's influence cut down my appetite for drinking, somewhat to the disappointment of my more hedonistic friends. I also realised, with finals in June I had to work hard. My brother at this time also had his first serious girlfriend, a loud, cigarette smoking Jew named Hayley. She seemed to cause him a great deal of grief and he was going through quite a depressive phase with his obsession for New Order and Joy Division Music and Nietzschean Philosophy. One night I noticed he seemed particularly distressed as he left the College bar for the mile or so walk to his house. I decided to follow quickly, but unseen, behind him. Just as I got to his room I found him tying a noose in a thick rope and preparing to throw it over the door or construct some otherwise suitable contraption. Quite how serious he was to do self-harm I do not know but we chatted a while and all was well with the world by the time I left.

On March 5 of that year I turned 21. Instead of the customary ten pints of beer and an incredibly hot curry I decided to take Judith to one of the nicer restaurants in town, Luna Caprese. I had finally found someone to whom not was I only deeply attracted but who I felt really cared for me and wanted to be with me. For the first time in my life I told someone, i.e., Judith, of my dad's drinking problem and how it invariably ruined my Christmas, at the very least. Being with Judith made me happy. We got on incredibly well and laughed at each other's jokes. She considered me an absolute philistine, which was not inaccurate, and when she went to the cinema to see

Roman Polanski's "Tess of the d'Urbervilles" she informed me that I was not invited as it would be totally lost on my uncultured self.

That year, because Easter fell late in the Year we actually had seven weeks off at Easter. I had already decided not to play cricket even though I had a fair chance of winning a Blue. I just did not see how I could cope with the work and cricket and so I opted for work. I basically revised 8 hours a day, seven days a week for eight weeks. It seemed to work as I did pretty well in my Finals achieving a solid and perfectly respectable 2nd Class Honours Batchelor of Arts in Natural Science (Physics).

While I studied extremely hard Judith had the benefit of her second year Trinity term and so was having a very relaxed time. Eventually my finals were over and I celebrated with my friends in the College Old Quad. My time at Oxford had come to an end. I was both sad and excited. I would of course be visiting many times in the future as both Judith and Duncan would still be there.

There was still one major event in the University Calendar: the various grand summer Balls, known as May Balls and confusingly held in June. Every summer at the end of term several colleges would hold extremely grand balls with headline bands, various other types of entertainment and of course masses of food and drink. There was a veritable cottage industry in trying to crash these Balls all of which had heavy security. One Hertford chap had the misfortune of climbing up a drainpipe as he tried to scale the outer walls of Keble Cottage and as the drainpipe parted company with the wall he fell about 20 feet onto the pavement below, shattering a great deal of bones. After a lengthy recuperation he had suffered no permanent damage.

Judith and I went to the Keble Ball where "Squeeze" were the main act. We had a great time though dancing was not one of my strengths and I managed to avoid the need to participate, to any meaningful degree.

Politics and Celebrity
"A celebrity is one who is known to many persons he is glad he does not know".
H.L. Mencken

"The whole aim of politics is to keep the public alarmed (and hence clamorous to be led to safety by menacing it with hobgoblins, all of them imaginary".
H.L. Mencken

"Democracy too is a religion. It is the worship of jackals by jackasses".
H. L. Mencken.

Oxford is of course renowned for producing many of Britain's political ruling class for centuries. In my lifetime alone we have had Margaret Thatcher, Tony Bliar (spelling as intended), and David Cameron as Prime Ministers from Oxford as well as senior politicians such as William Hague, Tony Benn, Benazir Bhutto, Alan Duncan and Jeremy Thorpe. Cambridge appears to have gone in more for the spy game with the Blunt, Burgess and Maclean notorious Russian spy ring coming to mind shortly after the War. Many of the Oxonians mentioned above were Presidents of the world famous Oxford Union. Regrettably I never set foot into that revered and austere institution.

Hertford was a small College not known for attracting the elite of Society but even during my short three years there several of my fellow students were to gain national renown of one form of another. Perhaps most significantly Jacqui Smith, the President of our JCR (Junior Common Room) became Home Secretary in the cabinet of Gordon Brown and Tony Blair. Jacqui was a close friend and tutorial partner of my best mate Dave and frequently over breakfast we would discuss politics. Jacqui was always hard line Labour and was utterly committed to the Party line no matter how ludicrous it may have been. She was a great girl and one of the "boys" when it came to drinking down the college bar. Soon after College she threw herself headlong into the Labour Party and was soon elected to the House of Commons as an MP and was known as one of "Blair's babes". She rose to arguably the fourth most powerful office in the British government and sadly ultimately had to resign over a silly movie rental (admittedly a porn movie) that her husband had allegedly charged to her government expense account. My friend Dave, slowly and steadily, moved his career along culminating in being given the onerous yet prestigious task of being Financial Director for the London 2012 Olympics. This was a massive and prestigious job with responsibility for a budget of some

9 billion pounds, which he managed to just sneak under. It is quite amusing that these two tutorial partners at Hertford would one day be sitting in the Home Office discussing the Olympics as Home Secretary and Olympic Finance Director. Dave had kept touch with his friend Jacqui but when he went to meet her the first time to discuss the Olympics her first comment was "Blimey, Dave, what a job you've got!". Dave replied in a similar fashion. Dave moved on to be Finance Director of London Transport and then to be Director of the development of the massive Olympic Park that had been constructed in East London. This brought him into very frequent and close contact with the London Mayor, Boris Johnson, for whom Dave had a great fondness, though their political views did not always align. Earlier this year Dave and Boris, and another colleague made a trip to Washington DC to negotiate plans for the Smithsonian to open an overseas branch in the Olympic Park. The British Museum has similar plans. (I hope I am not disclosing any national secrets.) Furthermore part of Dave's job was to negotiate with West Ham football Club a long term lease of the main Olympic stadium. This, to put it mildly, was very interesting and challenging. For his noble efforts Dave received the CBE from Prince Charles.

Not that I knew him but in the year above me, and well known to Dave and Jacqui was a thin, quiet pale boy studying PPE named Jeremy. He soon rose to prominence in the Civil Service and became the Private Secretary to our last three Prime Ministers, Blair, Brown and Cameron. Sir Jeremy, as he is now known, is currently, I believe, busy redacting the much awaited Chilcott report on the UK participation in the Iraq War.

Most people will fondly remember the part of the Opening Ceremony when "The Queen" parachuted into the stadium accompanied by "James Bond". Tragically about a year after the games the stunt man who played Bond was killed in a sky diving accident in the Alps. Even during rehearsals security was extremely tight such that no liquids were allowed inside. However, at the end of the day Danny Boyle, the Director, and his associates still managed to enjoy a relaxing glass of wine inside the stadium at the close of another long day. How did the wine escape security? Well, the Bond stuntman would parachute in each day with a bottle of wine tucked inside each sock and up his trouser leg.

As far as celebrities go the best known is Fiona Bruce who has had major rolls on the BBC with shows such as the Antiques Roadshow and various news programs. I once read that at Oxford she was rather in awe of a lot of the people who she deemed extremely posh. To us she was posh and largely unapproachable but that is more a result of my short comings and narrow thinking than hers.

Andy "Teflon" Tighe also became a high profile BBC political correspondent frequently seen on the news. Teflon referred to the fact that he was one of our goalkeepers and his hands seemed non-stick! When I last communicated to Teflon he reminded me that I had always said I wanted to make a significant amount of money and then effectively disappear. I did not recall making this comment but it was indeed true and much to my regret I was unsuccessful. Alternatively, though in no way was I thinking this at the time, perhaps my expressed desire was really just a deep-seated wish to die.

Also on the BBC I frequently hear the China correspondent, Carrie Gracie, who was in the year above me at College.

There were very few Americans at Hertford. I can recall three. However, one of these, Allegra Huston, was the daughter of John Huston, the famous film director, and sister or half-sister of the actress Angelica Huston. She spent much of her time with one of Hertford's few apparent aristocrats, Guy Leaf, who proved himself to be invaluable in our rugby team's second row.

I think I will add to this list someone with whom I have recently communicated after hearing him on the BBC World Service discussing the death of the famous poet, Nicanor Parra. This would be my old rugby team mate, Niall Binns, who is himself an accomplished poet, educator and respected authority on a whole host of poets ranging from Pablo Neruda to Dylan Thomas. Niall was amazed that I had heard him on the radio.

I read in a recent edition of the Hertford magazine about a physicist in the year following me, Salman Ullah. He was a pleasant, happy fellow who I am ashamed to say suffered the indignity of me being unnecessarily rude to him on a couple of occasions. While my life plummeted into the depths of despair he has enjoyed an illustrious career in Silicon Valley highlighted by spearheading the Google purchase of YouTube while in a senior role at Google.

Knowing, as Mark Twain says, "Comparison is the death of joy," I mention the above partly out of interest but more so to juxtapose it with what I consider to be my totally failed life of sadness, regret, despair and squandered opportunities.

Most of that summer would as usual be spent in Jersey but I would have to be in London by early September to start my career with Arthur Andersen. Four of us, my good friend Andy, John, who came from North West London, and Kieran decided to share a dumpy semidetached house John had found for us in Hendon, way up the Northern Line. It was cheap and that was the main thing. Meanwhile Judith and I had planned a three week backpacking trip to Turkey. I had never done anything quite so adventurous but I was so excited. Turkey at that time was only barely on the tourist map for British tourists. We were trailblazers. In Jersey I purchased a tent and my mother made no effort to hide her disdain and disapproval of my planned trip.

We had an absolutely wonderful time exploring the major sites of Western Turkey. We flew from London to Antalya and spent our first night in an extremely cheap hotel. It felt so strange to be in such a faraway unfamiliar place, especially when the myriad minarets of the Mosques made their evening call to prayer. Antalya was on the turquoise coast with its beautiful beaches and the Taurus Mountains as a spectacular backdrop. It was here on the Antalyan beach that Judith persuaded me to read my first serious literary work (my friend Dave had also recommended I give it a whirl): "The Mayor of Casterbridge," by Thomas Hardy. I absolutely devoured its rich, descriptive prose and spellbinding story. I managed to finish the entire book in one day, struggling as the sun slowly fell beneath the horizon. I could not believe what I had been missing all these years. I was soon to voraciously devour his other major works including the widely considered inaccessible, "The Woodlanders," and of course the ultra-depressing "Jude the Obscure". After this epiphany I became a massive fan of quality literary and frankly a bit of a snob. I would never admit to reading a Grisham or a Michael Crichton though I was once stuck on a plane with "Jurassic Park" as my only companion so I did read it and I admit I quite enjoyed it. The only negative I can remember was the night we left Antalya by overnight bus to Denizli from where we would visit the amazing white pools of Pamukkale. For some reason Judith had been telling me about some of her friends at home, one of whom was especially promiscuous. As I pretended to sleep on the bus I was actually awake angrily brooding and seething, quite why I don't know but I felt terrible. I was perhaps experiencing jealousy and anger but with no justification.

The only other negative of an entirely different nature was when our tent was filled with a cloud of mosquitoes as we had foolishly pitched it between a night light and a pool of stagnant water. I spent half the night splattering their blood engorged bodies on the side of the tent with my flip flop. I did not realise it was my blood with which they were engorged. I suffered literally hundreds of bites and about 12 hours later went into paroxysms of itchiness as their effect fully came to the fore. We found a campsite near Ephesus where we lay low for a few days as I recovered and I was particularly put out by the fact that, despite my obvious plight and pained state, another fellow traveler would not share some of his antihistamine cream. I had previously never experienced mosquitoes but fortunately we were both taking the standard malaria pills as a precaution not that they are 100% effective and not that there was actually reported malarial activity in western Turkey. Since then I have been paranoid about mosquitoes which are always strongly attracted to me.

After Turkey we returned to our respective homes for a few weeks before I visited Judith's family for the first time in Deal. They lived in a large four story house in what was a quaint small town near Dover and were very hospitable. Judith's mother was especially gregarious and made me feel right at home. Her father, like her two younger brothers was much quieter but still welcoming. I really liked being at Judith's and still recall the two posters they had hanging in their downstairs TV room (both were in French): "If you don't have what you want, want what you have" and "Flowers of the Mountain, respect them".

I know my mother in particular hated my visiting Judith's family. She made no secret of her disdain for teachers or for the fact that Judith studied Geography which was not a "real" subject like Physics. Physics was by far the best as opposed to wishy washy nonsense like Philosophy, Politics and Economics. My mother was so opinionated and judgmental. However, for me I felt very much at home with Judith's family and I was clearly becoming very attached to Judith, and vice versa. I pretty much chose to study Physics by default as my brother was studying it and because of my mother's strong opinions though I did love the subject and found it fascinating. During my last couple of years at school I had an Oxford Educated English Teacher who suggested I study English as I appeared to be half way decent at writing but there was no way my mother would have allowed me to entertain such frivolity.

Working Life

"Work is the curse of the drinking classes".
Oscar Wilde

"Choose a job you love and you will never have to work a day in your life".   Confucius

Life in London

September arrived and so I made my way to our rented house in North London where my friends had kindly given me the largest downstairs bedroom. For some odd reason my mother insisted on my taking a microwave oven. I had very few possessions: two dark suits, a couple of cheap ties and 5 shirts which I ironed myself every Sunday night before the week began.

The tube ride down to Andersen's office near Temple took about an hour, together with the short walk at either end. Andersen was known for its intensive training so after 3 initial weeks in the London office all the new recruits, of which I was in a group of about ten, were sent off to St. Charles, Illinois, just to the west of Chicago where they had their main training centre. After these three weeks we would be sent home and out on our first job. While I was in Chicago, Judith and I exchanged letters a few times and I was of course thrilled to see her once I had returned to London. Somewhat to my surprise my brother was upset that I had only written one post card to him and our friends. I actually had written a letter but it was greatly delayed in the post, as luck would have it. Typically I would take the train up to Oxford from Paddington station to see her at weekends.

My first job was a tedious data entry affair at a British Telecom office. My paycheque provided enough for food and drink and every Friday I would meet my old College mates in the pub if I was not going up to Oxford. As usual at Christmas I was obliged to go home but this time for a much shorter period. Judith noticed how depressed I sounded on the phone. Our only phone was in the kitchen and it was impossible to have a private conversation. You could take the receiver out of the back door of the kitchen into a freezing rear back entryway, but this felt uncomfortable, so if we spoke on the phone I would wait till my parents were in the front TV room and close the door. Of course they would find a reason to come into the kitchen to eavesdrop and would always kindly turn down the TV so that they, I mean I, could hear more clearly. I could not wait to get back to London and back to Judith. Typically she and I would exchange simple gifts upon my return.

After British Telecom I was given what was considered a pretty plum assignment, working for the Statpipe North Sea gas pipeline project in Haugesund on the West Coast of Norway. This was really exciting and it was on February 18, 1985, that I flew to Stavanger and then on to Haugesund where I would be housed along with some 20-30 other Andersen folks in a hotel. I was one of the lowest ranked Andersen employees and basically was employed as a computer programmer. We worked hard, enjoyed camaraderie but looked forward to our three day weekend off every other weekend. On our off weekends we were permitted to fly home or to fly our significant other out to Norway. Judith came out a few of times and we explored by car the magnificence of Hardanger and Sogne fjords as well as the City of Bergen. We also scaled up to the top of a glacier in the spectacular Hardangervidda National Park. Over Easter we underestimated the fact that the shops were closed from Wednesday lunchtime to the following Tuesday which made for a dull few days.

Shortly after moving to Norway I had a chat with my housemates back in Hendon. They told me how late one night they had all been watching an especially tense World Championship snooker match on the TV when suddenly there was an almighty crash in the downstairs hallway behind them. Not to be distracted from the absorbing snooker they waited until the game was over before venturing into the hallway where they saw the upstairs toilet lying smashed on the floor together with a large gaping hole in the ceiling above. Apparently a couple of weeks earlier they had had a party at the house and too many people had urinated on the floor of the toilet such that the wooden boards rotted and were soon to give out. Quite an evening by all accounts.

Back in Norway, at the end of one particular weekend of exploration I recall returning to Haugesund only to find myself confronted with a massive traffic jam which was quite abnormal. Ignoring the obvious possibility that there was an accident up ahead, I simply decided to zip past the entire line of traffic as my hotel was not too far up the road. Not surprisingly I soon found myself stopped by several angry police officers who suitably ticketed me for my foolishness. However, not for the last time, I would leave the country before the court system caught up with me. The local authorities were actually quite fed up with the number of traffic violations rung up by us Andersen interlopers such that they even threatened to have us all kicked out of the country if our collective behaviour did not improve.

My time in Norway was only three months before Andersen sent me to another programming job at BP, in Broadgate, near the City of London.

This was another pretty tedious job but I realised that Andersen did offer great experience and a path to partner in potentially as little as ten years. However to a 22 year old ten years is an eternity. Several years at Andersen would make you into a very valuable employee for other companies but barely 14 months into the job I was getting itchy feet.

Meanwhile Judith had cruised through her finals and moved to the Far East end of the London Tube line as she had decided to pursue a PhD at Queen Mary College, London. Her subject was the effects of vitamin D deprivation on the Indian and Pakistani population of women in London. She was a good hour plus away from me by tube but of course we could meet in the centre of London.

That summer Judith and I had again ventured abroad, tent and backpack in tow, for an adventurous three weeks travelling around Israel. Israel was enjoying a period of relative calm and so we were able to travel freely and safely from the Sea of Galilee in the North to Eilat in the South. Jerusalem was of course incredible as too were our visits to Bethlehem in the West Bank and the church on the spot where Jesus was assumed to have been born and to Masada. We of course did the obligatory float in the Dead Sea. In Jerusalem we carefully and respectfully ventured into the ultra-orthodox neighbourhood of Mea Shearim. Signs made it clear that visitors were not really welcome and we had quite a start when an arm flashed out of a window and smacked Judith's bare arms. We had thought we were appropriately dressed but apparently not appropriately enough. A few months prior to our visit two stupid young American girls decided to go into Mea Shearim dressed in nothing but bikinis: they were stoned to death which explained the plethora of T-shirts being sold in Jerusalem with the slogan "get stoned in Mea Shearim".

In Eilat, which was then just a small beach resort at the corner of the Red Sea from which one could see into Jordan and Egypt, I took my first and arguably best ever scuba dive. The proliferation of sea life was incredible. I was not certified but the instructor simply tied us together with a loose rope and said, do as I do, as we walked into the teeming water.

As Christmas approached once again I had to prepare for my obligatory trip home. Anything more than two days would make me depressed. Just before Christmas I found an advert in the paper placed by Shell UK Oil looking for recent graduates to join it's trading and marketing teams. Well, it seemed like a good idea and before I knew it I was interviewing with a genial, urbane chap in Shell-Mex House on the Strand with whom I shared a love of cricket. When asked if I preferred trading or marketing I answered trading, not that I really knew what it meant and in a couple of weeks I had an offer of a Junior Trading job for Shell UK in Shell-Mex House. I resigned to the Andersen manager of my job at BP who made a weak effort to persuade me to stay but he realised my mind was made up.

Oil Trading: Shell UK

My new oil trading career began in the middle of January 1986, just as oil was plummeting due to Opec over supply, from $32/bbl to around $9/bbl. I had no idea what trading entailed. I did not know the difference between a trader and a broker. I sat at a square table between the two main traders for Shell UK and for a couple of weeks was meant to just listen to their conversations to try to learn how things worked. I had no idea what was this "market" that they spoke to. I created visions in my head of all the people they spoke to, especially a couple of Swedish brokers Lennart and Johan, neither of whom resembled in real life how I had imagined them.

The other two traders John Irving and Jaap Hoogcarspel, broadly split their responsibilities between physical trading and "paper" trading, not that I knew for several weeks what exactly that meant. I could not grasp the difference between "wet" and "paper" barrels. The former conjured up images of a large tanker loaded with actual physical oil dripping wet. Slowly as time went by I grew to understand the oil market more each day and absolutely loved it as it seemed so exciting and was always in the news and oil was the very lifeblood of our modern way of life.

Jaap was an extremely tall Dutchman with a deep voice who was well respected within the European industry. John, or Dr. John as he liked to be called, was in my view, borderline insane. Perhaps this stemmed from the fact that his Uncle was the notorious Holocaust denying Historian David Irving. John would often proudly mention that a bust of one of his ancestors stood in Trafalgar Square. He loved the attention that he received from all the brokers and other traders as Shell UK at that time was a huge participant in the "15 day Brent market" a "forward, over the counter market" in which cargoes of 600kb +-5% were bought and sold actively every day. Brokers were paid 1ct per barrel on every cargo they put together which amounted to $6,000 so you could see why they were keen to flatter and entertain active traders of which John was one. Our recently installed new boss was a tough old chain-smoking Shell man, named Peter Ward. Peter enjoyed trading himself and would often, as he put it, have a "pre-stats punt" on a Tuesday evening. "Stats" referred to the American Petroleum Institute's (API) weekly inventory figures in the US for crude oil, gasoline and heating (or 2) oil. Peter would almost always have his "punt" through Lennart the Swedish broker at PVM who, in his earlier days, had dated one of the ABBA girls before they became famous.

John would typically spread his business amongst four of five brokers. This way you got more Christmas gifts and more expensive lunches. On my first day he arranged for another Swede,

Johan, to take us to lunch at Ormond's, in Ormond's yard. I immediately took a liking to this tall, suntanned, handsome Swede and we became good friends. Johan mentioned how fortunate I was to have this job at such a young age and I would not too far in the future be a very rich man. He was almost correct but sadly not. I had little to contribute to the conversation at lunch after my attempts to discuss the previous weekend's football matches were met with a cold silence. Dr. John preferred to pontificate about his theories on Opec production and the like as the oil market was actually in the middle of an effective free fall from over $30 to under $10/bbl. Saudi Arabia, I learnt had given up its role as swing producer, rather like they did in November 2014, and decided to compete with other producers for market share.

Shell UK was responsible for providing crude oil to their two UK refineries in Shell Haven in the Thames Estuary and at Stanlow, not far from Liverpool. We had a list of crudes that the refinery liked and that showed the relative economics of each grade within the refinery. Other traders such as Phibro, at that time the largest trader in the world, and Marc Rich would show us their crude oil availabilities from the North Sea, West Africa and the Mediterranean as would other major oil companies like BP, Exxon and Mobil. Shell UK was not really in the business of speculating. The main speculative vehicle would be the 15 day Brent market. Shell, along with Exxon owned one-third of this massive field which loaded at a terminal in Sullom Voe in the Shetland Islands. We would have around 15 cargoes a month that we had to sell, or on occasion, take "home," if it made sense, to one of our two refineries. We also had offshore production to sell such as Fulmar, which loaded in the North Sea at a massive buoy attached to one of the giant North Sea Platforms. Now not only did we wish to achieve the highest price for our oil but we also wanted to pay the least PRT (petroleum revenue tax) to the UK treasury. At that time this rate was around 87.5%. So, we engaged in a lot more activity than simply selling our 15 cargoes and paying the tax on that. If we could make it look like our actual "equity" (i.e., cargoes we owned and produced from the field) were sold at a low price then the tax would be commensurately lower. For this reason we engaged in a great deal of buying and selling, often simultaneously, in a process known as tax spinning. Oftentimes traders for reasons of credit or otherwise could not deal with each other so we would go in between the buyer and seller, for a 2 cts/bbl profit for appearance sake, to allow the trade to go ahead and to place two more trades on our book of business. For example if we had just one equity cargo and we sold it at $30 we would pay 87.5% tax on $30. However if we had a series of buys and sales at a whole host of prices say down to $10, and we had one more sale than purchase then we would tell the Treasury that it was the $10 sale that was our equity sale and thus paid tax on this much lower price. During 1986 Shell UK, via this practice, cut its tax bill by well over 100 million pounds. The Treasury however soon wised up to this game, that the likes of Exxon and BP also played with their equity production whether Brent or in the case of BP mainly Forties. A new Law was enacted that any sale of 15 day Brent that was made had to be declared as equity or non-equity within 48 hours. This greatly complicated the task of effective tax spinning.

On one memorable occasion Peter Ward had to leave the office for the day. Typically he would have to approve any transaction. He gave John and Jaap instructions to go no more than one cargo long or short. And so begun a veritable orgy of trading: John bought and sold about 10 cargoes each but never went more than one cargo long or short! It was on a day such as this, after a good, i.e., boozy lunch, that John decided, instead of writing down his transactions in the customary fashion on a deal sheet to be given to the operations and support staff, he wrote them all on a roll of toilet paper. His memory somewhat impeded by drink, it took the operators quite some time to decipher the day's activity.

As Peter Ward made a point of telling me, other traders and brokers were extremely nice to me not because of me but because of my job as a Shell UK trader. I understood this. There was clearly massive amounts of money made by traders and brokers alike but traders at the likes of Shell and Exxon were paid standard oil company salaries which were orders of magnitude below those of the top private traders and brokers. The industry was also one non-stop entertainment circuit. Working at Shell we were invited to just about every major sporting event in the UK calendar from the British Grand Prix to Wimbledon to the Open. I must confess this new lifestyle was quite amazing and intoxicating and I thoroughly enjoyed it but I still suffered from a certain emptiness inside, the source of which I could not identify.

I began my career at Shell in January 1986 and in mid-February was the annual Institute of Petroleum Week in London during which there were countless black tie dinners, expensive lunches, grand parties and general revelry. Oil company traders and executives from around the world would come to London to meet each other but generally to enjoy the masses of hospitality.

Since we were required to attend a dinner each night Shell allowed us to stay in a nearby hotel to make our lives a little easier without a commute that week. I spent three days in the magnificent Waldorf Astoria on the Aldwych. I could not believe the opulence. Judith joined me for three splendid days of luxury.

I recall one of my first fancy dinners with a couple of brokers who were well known for giving their clients Rolex watches if they did deals through them. At dinner I ordered, totally cluelessly, steak tartare, well done. Fortunately for me the waiter politely and delicately pointed out my error with a few whispered words and I chose something more to my liking.

At another industry dinner I was introduced to the delights of teppanyaki at one of London's finer Japanese restaurants. I was also introduced to sake and unfortunately I consumed a little too much such that I fell asleep on my Tube ride home. I awoke at Wembley Station, two stops passed Dollis Hill, where I lived. I therefore ended up staggering the two plus miles home in a drunken stupor through one of London's less salubrious neighbourhoods. Luckily I made it unscathed.

The oil market was international and was greatly influenced by the US futures market, the New York Mercantile Exchange (or NYMEX), on which were traded US crude oil at Cushing, Oklahoma and US gasoline and 2 oil (heating oil) in New York Harbour. This market opened at 2.45pm London time and did not close till 830pm. At least one of us stayed in the office until the NYMEX or "merc" close. This meant I missed out a lot on meeting my friends for a drink after work as they would be long gone by 830pm and I felt a little lonely.

Obviously at Shell I learnt a great deal and had my first taste of speculative trading. I desperately wanted to be a success and be able to buy and sell cargoes and make a profit on an outright price basis. I felt this was the only way to be a truly successful trader yet the next 30 years would show me that very few people had the capacity to do this and it was absolutely not necessary: there were far less stressful ways to make money. One Tuesday night after the APIs showed a huge build in US crude oil inventory the market immediately fell 50 cts. Jaap and I were in the office. We agreed that this was incredibly bearish information but we failed to extrapolate our thinking to say that that was why the market dropped like a stone 50 cts/bbl. Surely the market must plummet tomorrow. We agreed to short a cargo which we did to a then German refiner URBK. The next morning the market was back to unchanged. The negative APIs had been expected and we had foolishly fallen for them. It really did not matter one iota to Shell UK but personally I was gutted: I felt like a total and utter failure and hated myself for being such an idiot.

At this time my relationship with Judith was a little rocky but it survived. We spent a week in Tangiers which I must confess was pretty grim. Tangiers is a very European City but the minute we set foot outside our hotel we were hounded by incredibly persistent youths constantly repeating "Get high before you die" and "There's no hope without dope". I never stopped to consider that they might have had a point. I was definitely not sorry when that trip was over though a coach ride into the Atlas Mountains was both beautiful and interesting as we visited small local villages where the youths were not constantly trying to peddle dope.

Judith was understandably a little uncertain if she wanted such a serious relationship as she forged a new life for herself doing her PhD at Queen Mary, perhaps not least because I was indeed a pretty closed-minded, judgmental philistine with anger issues. I tried to dispel the philistine thing by taking her to the dreadful musical, "The Bounty," starring David Essex. However, I think our trip to see Ben Kingsley in Othello at the Barbican went down a little better.

Later that summer Judith and I again set off for three weeks but this time nothing quite so daring as normal. We decided to visit Venice, Florence and Rome which were of course magnificent. We both camped and stayed in cheap hotels. I had virtually no knowledge of the arts and unfortunately somewhat scoffed at it. Judith, on the other hand, had quite an appreciation, so she delighted in explaining to me the significance of Brunelleschi's dome and Ghiberti's doors in Florence and many of the amazing sites in Rome. During this trip we discussed the possibility of my leaving Shell UK and joining my friend Johan as a broker at his company, Fearnoil, part of the Fearnley group owned by the massively wealthy Asdrup family. Although brokers made lots of money they were generally looked down upon by traders and often treated very rudely. Judith asked if I was prepared for this. I would no longer be treated like royalty, as I was at Shell, but would suddenly switch to the other end of the spectrum where I would be subjected to verbal abuse at times, and have my success lie largely at the whim of other traders as they decided to transact through me or through someone else. These were very valid points but it was difficult to overlook the fact that my compensation package would be almost 20 times what I was making at Shell. Of course I could wait and other lucrative offers would come along. Dr. John had told me that Shell International (SITCO) who sat on the opposite side of the river to Shell-Mex House had recently lost one of their top prospects, Ian Taylor, to a private trading company, Vitol. A friendly Scot named David Morgan of Britoil had also told me to be prepared to receive financial offers that, "Would make my hair curl". David himself ended up for over two decades at Morgan Stanley with his fellow ex-Britoil Scottish colleague, Colin Bryce, who went on to reach great heights within the bank. Nonetheless I pretty much decided, when I got back to London, that I would accept Johan's offer.

Although summer, the nights around Florence could be cool and one day we set out on a rented Vespa, Judith riding pillion, to the surrounding hill sides where we stumbled across the incredible site of San Gimignano: what an utterly amazing place. As the afternoon drew on we realised it would be dark by the time we returned to Florence and as the sun set I recall us both being freezing on the journey back, but we made it.

"A cynic is someone who knows the price of everything and the value of nothing".   Oscar Wilde

It was during this trip that two events come to mind of which I am deeply ashamed and saddened by. I was still small-minded, overly thrifty and judgmental. I wonder why. Though I loved Judith I twice made her cry. Once she let our camera slip out of the tent and it got very slightly scratched but not damaged. I was furious and yelled at her for not respecting such an expensive piece of property. My reaction was totally out of any reasonable proportion.

In Venice we were strolling the streets, looking for a place to eat. We were not flush with cash but neither were we broke. However, every restaurant Judith stopped at to view the menu would result in me saying what on earth was she thinking? How could we spend the equivalent of say 5 pounds on a plate of pasta when you could buy the same at the supermarket for less than one-tenth of that? This brought her to tears. It could so easily have been my mother talking as she and my dad had on many occasions said similar things when we went to restaurants in England or Jersey.

On returning to London I was set to have a final meeting with Johan to go over the exact specifics of my offer and to ultimately accept it. Johan had wanted his boss, Anders Johannsen, another Swede, to join us but Anders stood me up for lunch with Boris Becker. Anders had been a top Swedish tennis player some years before and, the Swedish tennis circuit being relatively small, knew Bjorn Borg. He had won a tennis scholarship to Rice University in Houston where he supplemented his income by giving tennis lessons. One of his pupils was Lynn Wyatt, wife of the legendary oil man Oscar Wyatt. Through Lynn, Anders met Oscar who soon gave him a job in the trading department of his company, Coastal, in Houston. Anders had then been approached by the Asdrup family to run a 15 day brokerage business which he did with offices in New York and London. Anders was convinced that tennis players made great brokers as they were tough and individualistic so he employed a couple of top young tennis players who were not quite good enough to play on the professional circuit. One was a young German, Peter Vaitl, in London and the other, another Swedish graduate of Rice University, Fred Gradin. Fred was a friend of Matts Wilander and an absolute expert at networking. At Rice his best friend had been Olav Hermes, of the Hermes fashion house. In New York he became friends with George Soros through tennis and also somehow with Prince Rainier of Monaco. He was an impressive guy and an extremely successful broker. A year or so later I had dinner with Fred in New York along with his beautiful Swedish/African American model girlfriend from the Ford agency. I recall pulling up in his Porsche outside the then hottest night club in Manhattan, Nell's, and then walking right past the throng waiting patiently outside, to be allowed straight in with a "Good evening Mr. Gradin". I found this more amusing than impressive but enjoyed it all the same. Another tennis playing Swede in their office was Finn. He started around the same time as me and his claim to fame was that he had once, in his youth, beaten Stefan Edberg: perhaps the fact that he was at least two years his senior had something to do with it.

So the time came for me to resign to my manager at Shell. Peter advised me not to leave as I had barely been there six months and had a great deal more to learn. He also stressed how life as a broker was much tougher than life at Shell UK. I knew this but my mind was made up. Funnily enough he and another colleague, Mark Uffen, shared with me at this point that when I joined Shell I had been viewed as a long term employee who would likely never leave. Richard Gates was disappointed to see me go especially as he had never had the chance to get me to play cricket for the Lensbury (Shell) Club in Teddington. I had, however, turned out for the rugby club once which was not a pleasant experience.

I actually had played in one industry cricket match with a mixture of brokers and traders. Although my fitness had dropped dramatically since my College days only 2 years or so passed I was still able to charge in and hurl the ball down at a fair rate of knots, certainly enough to make the batsmen hop around in fear, which I liked. It was at this cricket match that I first met Ian Taylor, who in typical style turned up late, and bounded onto the field like an over excited school boy sporting his school PE kit, i.e., a white T-shirt and white shorts. He was quite a sight but not a cricketer.

Broking in London

One of the attractions of joining Fearnoil, located in a very nice office on the fashionable Jermyn Street a few short yards from Fortnum and Mason, was that I would be allowed a company car, up to a value of 15k pounds. I immediately headed off to the nearby South Kensington Porsche dealership where it became apparent that my budget would only stretch to a slightly used, low mileage 924s. This was fine. A few nights later Judith and I excitedly picked up the car. I recall the thrill of driving it out of the dealership and, as my headlights popped up and out of the bonnet as they do, I drove onto the streets of South Kensington. There was however one problem. By now I had moved from Hendon to a flat owned by my friend, John, in Dollis Hill, a lot closer in than Hendon but not exactly the fanciest place in London and one where a Porsche would stand out like a sore thumb. So I took to renting a garage where I kept the car stored and only used it at weekends. A couple of times while filling the car with petrol I was approached by police officers and engaged in conversation: they were obviously trying to see if the car was mine or if I had stolen it as may well have been suggested by both my youthful appearance and scruffy attire. I shared the flat with John and our old house mate from Hendon, Kieran. One evening we came home to find that we had been broken in to which was not at all uncommon. Apart from the TV they had taken some of John's football kit and absolutely nothing from my room. I was deeply offended.

With a much improved salary I now decided it was time to jump onto the London Property ladder. Judith and I spent quite a while looking at 2 bedroom flats in Clapham, South Kensington (too expensive) and Blackheath (not convenient for work). We eventually chose a two bed in a high rise development called the Falcons in Battersea that literally overlooked Clapham junction train station. The flats had previously been council flats but a developer had purchased them and refurbished them and sold them off to the likes of myself. The flat was nothing special but Judith and I had decided to move in together and so we set about painting the lounge and two bedrooms ourselves and then buying some furniture which I left up to Judith: she did an excellent job.

Though we were now living together I can honestly say the idea of marriage had never entered my mind, which of course was odd. I simply felt we would always be together and were inseparable: Jonathan and Judith, that was it. I once saw myself as a semi-circle made into a complete circle by Judith. We simply got along so well it was incredible, in spite of my occasional angry outbursts and unreasonable responses to certain expenses. Shortly after finishing College we had attended in Paris the wedding of my old tutorial partner and now stock broker, John Chester. He had always known exactly what he wanted: he was to marry his French girlfriend upon graduation, become a stock broker, have one child and retire early. He executed his plan to perfection unlike me who never really knew what he wanted other than to escape from something and to lose this feeling of emptiness with which I felt cursed.

My mother in particular was obviously appalled at my moving in with Judith but I seldom saw my parents other than during the obligatory trip at Christmas. I phoned them once a week as I had indeed done at College, every Sunday evening after formal hall. My parents did once come up to London for a quick visit and I gave them a whistle stop tour around central London in my new car.

Most weekends Judith and I would drive down to see her family in Deal. She was extremely close to her parents and brothers and I always felt at home there. In some ways I felt a pang of guilt at not seeing my parents as frequently but they were a plane or boat journey away so it was in no way practicable.

Work as a broker was indeed pretty tough. I was given a list of companies to call, as were the other four brokers who sat around a large rectangular table with two phones each (Johan had three). Johan was an absolutely amazing broker and I once saw him close a three way deal using three phones speaking three different languages to the three customers namely English, French and Swedish. Anders would do a little bit of brokerage but in the main he managed the proceedings and coordinated with our four Swedish brokers in New York. Anders was good friends with the head of trading at the Japanese Shosha, Mitsui. This gentleman was named Nobby and he would allow Anders to transact on behalf of Mitsui with an acceptable counterpart, if at least a profit of 2 cts/bbl was achievable. At times the 15 day market could be quite inefficient with buyers bidding above the offer of sellers. In fact one time at Shell UK I recall we could have bought from BP at $9.05, and sold simultaneously to our sister company, Shell International (SITCO), at $9.50. However, at the last minute, Peter Ward decided this was a little too naughty and we allowed SITCO and BP to find each other. A similar situation occurred whilst I was at Fearnoil but with about a 10 cts/bbl margin. Anders simultaneously bought a cargo in the name of Mitsui and sold it to Phibro for a 10 cts/bbl profit. Now Phibro had relatively advanced computer systems for this era and all their deals were time stamped. Barely five minutes after concluding these two deals John Carr called in to speak to Anders. He said he'd noticed that two deals occurred at precisely the same time. We were caught red-handed. Quite how Anders talked his way out of that mess I do not recall but we were not blacklisted by Phibro, thankfully.

Being the newest recruit, along with a young lady named Karen, I was not given the most active companies and had to try to cultivate relationships with companies with which Fearnoil was not particularly successful. In Europe we were not successful with Phibro who operated out of Zug in Switzerland so I was given them as an account. In the US quite the opposite was true: our lead broker Hans, who had a rapid fire voice like a motor racing commentator, had an amazingly good relationship with Andy Hall, the head of Phibro's vaunted trading operation and widely regarded, even to this day, as arguably the best oil trader ever.

I of course had Dr. John Irving as a customer, as I wrongly assumed, he would support his old colleague and protégé. John had finally left Shell and now worked for the oil trading arm of a massive German conglomerate, Metallgesellschaft. I would speak to John and we'd get on fine and then five minutes later I'd discover he'd just closed two or three deals with a rival broker, typically, Lennart at PVM. I was convinced Lennart must have been giving John a kick back but in retrospect I am not sure. Certain brokers did give kickbacks to traders as there was a lot of money flying around and freely available. Every cargo that was transacted earnt the broker $6000 from the seller. Why not guarantee this business by giving the trader involved $1000 or so each time. On the other hand some traders simply had their favourite brokers with whom they had a close personal relationship and chose to use them for most of their business. Fearnoil typically were very fast and had as good a set of numbers as anyone but still there were certain companies we could not break in to in the fast moving 15 day Brent market.

On one occasion I had just spoken to my contact at Phibro, John Carr, an extremely loquacious Irishman, who demanded to know who my buyer was. Now, if I gave the buyer's name that, in theory, ethically bound the trader to only execute through me. A minute later we heard that Phibro had just sold to my buyer. I was confused and annoyed but then John Carr called in. Before I had chance to say anything he said they would cover me on that deal at one half of a cent per barrel, i.e., only $3000. In that way he had forced us to accept the fact that from now on Phibro would only pay half a cent per cargo instead of a full cent. Companies like Phibro spent millions of dollars annually on brokerage so you could understand why they would constantly try to reduce commissions. Brokers of course resisted but in reality there was little brokers could do but take what they were given. Some clients continued to pay 1ct and some even 2, thinking that they would get better service. Of course as a broker we would try to do a deal with a 2 cts paying customer over one who paid half a cent but with the market moving so quickly you generally just closed whatever deal you could. Another conversation with John Carr involved him mentioning to me that they were looking for a new young trader, ideally with some major oil company experience, and did I know of anyone. Obviously he was asking about me but I missed the point entirely and said I would let him know if I could think of anyone.

It was in 1986 that Goldman Sachs, under the name J. Aron, and Morgan Stanley, seriously entered the oil market. Previously Phibro, owned by Salomon Brothers, had been the only bank involved in the business. Aron and Morgan Stanley quickly began to do huge amounts of business which was great for brokers. However, they resented paying millions of dollars in commissions and it was this that led to a costly mistake by J. Aron. At this time most phone lines were not recorded but because of protocol on Wall Street those of J. Aron and Morgan Stanley were. The Aron traders called a bunch of other traders getting them to agree to jointly hit all the brokers with the news that the commission on a 15 day cargo was now only half a cent. One brokerage firm, I never knew which, got wind of this collusion and sued Aron who were caught red handed as a result of their recorded lines. I believe this cost Aron a considerable amount of money and shortly after, I similarly believe their lines were no longer recorded. Now all lines in the industry are recorded but if people want to make a "private" call they obviously just use their cell phone, or use an unregistered line or better still speak face to face.

One thing that struck me as strange at Fearnoil was that although in Europe all the brokers in the fast moving Brent market sat in London, the actual deal confirmations were sent out by a man in Geneva named Torre Toms. We made it appear that he was a very busy man and closed all the transactions himself. This of course would be impossible but it was done so as to avoid paying UK corporation tax. I cannot believe that the UK exchequer was fooled by this but it appeared to work. Now a couple of years later most of the Fearnoil brokers led by Johan in London and Fred in New York left Fearnoil and set up their own brokerage firm named Spectron. In this way of course they kept more of the profits themselves without having to pay the likes of Anders or indeed the Asdrups. A couple of Fearnoil brokers stayed put including Peter Vaitl and the main broker in New York, Hans Bergland, together with a heavy drinking Swede named Mac Barkman, who reminded me of a Swedish Lee Marvin.

Spectron used a similar structure to Fearnoil except in their case they sent deal telexes from Bermuda instead of Geneva, but effectively pulling the same tax ruse. However, for some reason after about ten years in 1998 the tax authorities came down on Spectron. I never understood why, as many companies, both brokers and traders, operated in this way, but Spectron were harshly dealt with. The homes of their brokers in London were raided and Johan was even placed under house arrest. Eventually things were sorted out and I presume the necessary tax was paid but this was the end of Johan as a broker as he returned to his native Sweden.

Johan had told me that previously he had been married to a beautiful Norwegian, the daughter of an immensely wealthy shipping magnate. However, living in Paris at the time, they were divorced. Johan was truly devastated and confided in me that he had contemplated jumping off a bridge in Paris to kill himself. Something inside him, fortunately, prevented his demise. This potentially tragic scene brings to mind my favourite actor, Daniel Auteuil, in the magnificent film, "The Girl on the Bridge". I actually saw M.Auteuil one evening enjoying a quiet dinner in London's Nobu. I desperately wanted to tell him how much I admired his work but in the end chose not to disturb his privacy. As for Johan, somehow he heard about some fellow Swedes working the 15 day market as Fearnoil and he pestered Anders to such a degree that eventually Anders relented and agreed to let Johan try out as an unpaid broker. Quickly Johan became the most prolific producer in the London office. One of his main clients was Statoil - the Norwegian state oil company. He was extremely close friends with their main trader Oystein Berentsen, who did a great deal of business. Through Johan, I too, became friends with Oystein.

I was not really enjoying my life as a broker as I felt totally at the whim of the traders to whom I spoke and I felt unfairly treated by several. However my productivity was acceptable. There were also some very nice fringe benefits. The Asdrups owned a magnificent hunting estate in Scotland and twice an autumn we would invite clients to a weekend of pheasant shooting and grand hospitality at this superb locale. Typically we would fly to Edinburgh and then drive in limousines to the country estate. In prior years helicopters had been used to ferry the hunters from the airport but at half a cent, we had to watch costs. Now traders obviously wanted to be invited on these extravagant outings, so these magnificent trips were an incentive to use us as brokers. On the product side of the business the Asdrups made available their salmon fishing lodge in Norway.

The Scottish estate was absolutely amazing. There were about ten extremely grand bedrooms upstairs and downstairs the halls were decked with original works of art by the likes of Picasso and Francis Bacon.

The shooting itself was an outstanding experience. All equipment was provided unless you chose to bring your own shot gun and each shooter had a man assigned to load their gun after they had discharged both barrels. While we enjoyed a sumptuous lunch at the main house the loaders would clean our guns and prepare for the afternoon hunt. I shot a few birds and was perfectly satisfied. Unfortunately my French customer from Elf shot a white pheasant which was extremely rare and deeply upset the local beaters and loaders.

On the second day of the shoot we would walk the moors and look for hare which were far less abundant than the beaten pheasants on the first day. We would also have an evening duck and goose hunt when we would hide in blinds around small lakes as the birds came in to roost for the night. I only managed to wing one goose, which fell into the pond right next to me and proceeded to use its one good wing to swim around in circles before, exhausted, it finally drowned. That certainly put a stop to my quest for blood that evening.

When we left, those who wanted were given a brace of pheasants, one male and one female to take home. I attempted to take them onto the plane in a plastic bag and put them in the overhead compartment but this was not permitted: they had to be checked. It was quite a site back at Heathrow when the luggage carousel for the flight from Edinburgh was covered in dead pheasants amongst the suitcases. I picked up a brace and headed home, putting the birds in the cold stair well of my block of flats.

I actually left the birds there for a few days not really knowing what to do with them before I heard of a butcher in Sloane Square who would dress them appropriately. I slung them in the back of my car for a few days before heading to the butcher who commented on how perfectly hung they appeared and should be absolutely delicious. The following Sunday we roasted them and they were indeed delicious.

That Christmas I decided to head into work on Christmas Eve. My colleague Hayden and I closed one spread (i.e., a two legged trade involving two cargoes in different months) and thus made $12,000. Not a bad mornings work. Hayden was quite a character and a very productive broker. I recall him once scratching his forehead and exclaiming in pain as he then pulled out a shard of glass: a couple of years prior he had been in a dreadful car accident and gone through the windshield. Hayden had a couple of clients that gave him dreadful verbal abuse, as traders often did to brokers, but after he replied in kind the traders then appeared to respect him and proceeded to give him a great deal of business. He was a man who liked his drink. One evening after taking the train to his Surrey suburb he then hailed a cab but became disorientated and had the cabbie drop him off in the middle of nowhere. He spent the night sleeping in a ditch and had lost his briefcase in which he had $6000 in cash.

It was around this time that my brother finished his thesis and was awarded his doctorate. Though living in Oxford his experiment was located in CERN, Geneva, now home of the Large Hadron Collider. I decided to pay him a surprise visit in Oxford one evening when I knew he was having a small celebration. I made the 50 mile journey in no time as I pushed the Porsche up to 120 mph and somehow got away with it. As my brother's time at Oxford was drawing to a close he mentioned something that Dr. Tanner had recently told him: Jonathan is probably too soft for the business world. Interesting words from one of the most insightful, kind, intelligent and generous people I have had the good fortune to meet.

I was not quite so fortunate perhaps a year later when I was invited by a brokerage company to a splendid weekend at a magnificent old country mansion, turned hotel, in Devon, a few hours drive from London. On the way down I treated the speed limit with gay abandon but eventually saw the ominous blue flashing lights of a police car in my rear view mirror. The officer made me jump into the back of his car while he checked my documents and from the backseat I saw what must have been my speed, 100.1 mph. It was also close to 10pm so I thought about saying to the officer "My goodness. Is that the time?" Wisely I did not.

That relatively minor infraction required me to make another trip in around a month's time to the small village in Devon to appear in court and I received a 30 day driving ban. Fortunately it was not particularly inconvenient as living in London I could simply use the tube to get to work and the court appearance had the added benefit of affording me the chance to visit the wilds of Dartmoor once again, previously the site of two of my Duke of Edinburgh Award expeditions.

Again at Christmas I would go home and Judith would go to her family. It seemed a shame that we never spent Christmas together but that was the way it was. Judith invariably noticed both my tone on the phone and my demeanour upon my return to be depressed. We did of course have New Year's Eve together but I had left it too late to book a decent restaurant so we ended up at an admittedly upscale Indian near Piccadilly. The tube journey home was noteworthy for the fact we got stuck between two tube stations for about an hour in a hot, sweaty carriage full of drunken revellers.

Shortly after Christmas I was sitting at my desk when I suddenly began to feel unwell and I noticed spots appearing on my arms and stomach (when I checked it) literally before my eyes. I had Mobil on the line and their trader Michael Bloch asked me where the market for a specific month was. I quoted him the market as something like $15.10 at $15.20. My colleague, Karen, sitting to my left, had Coastal, with whom we struggled, on the line and they were the buyer at $15.10. Now ordinarily buyers and sellers would negotiate rather than hit the bid or lift the offer but in this case Michael said to me "Ok. Give that guy a firm offer at 15.10". Now contrary to real estate in the oil market an offer always meant sell and a bid meant buy. So, I said to Karen, OK tell Coastal that Mobil are firm to sell to them at $15.10. "Done" she exclaimed and I reiterated to Michael that he had just sold a cargo to Coastal at $15.10. "I'm buying, I'm buying" he screamed in his unmistakable high-pitched voice. I quickly told Karen there had been an error and the deal was broken. Coastal were furious and refused to deal with us after that. I promptly stood up and left the office to find the nearest Accident and Emergency Room. The Doctor on duty immediately diagnosed chicken pox and told me to go home as I would be contagious for maybe three days. Three days later I was back at work and as I travelled on the tube people were staring at my scab covered face.

I was not sure that life as a broker was really going to be for me for the long term and that seed was watered by a conversation with Dr. John who asked me if I'd like to join him as a trader at Metallgesellschaft. I thought trading offered a better long term future and I was tired with being circumvented, or ignored or otherwise treated badly. Judith and I went to visit John at his home in the New Forest. We agreed financial terms which were about only 40% of my broker's compensation but I felt offered much better long term prospects. MG also agreed to buy my car from Fearnoil and let me keep it as my company car. After all, I really liked my car.

Anders was extremely disappointed at my choosing to leave but Johan and the rest of the team understood and wished me luck. Obviously they assumed I would put my business their way. As a broker I sat opposite another Swedish guy named Peter Rage, who happened to be deaf in one ear, quite a handicap for a broker who frequently operated with phones at both years. Somehow he managed to contort himself to use just the one good ear and he was a perfectly good broker. The following year he took me to Wimbledon one evening, scalping some tickets outside the tennis centre.

Peter was an extremely nice, intelligent chap and it is with great sadness that I write, after speaking briefly with him for the first time in over a decade, he was soon to die in the massive South East Asian Tsunami. His English wife and children survived but sadly Peter did not. His family had a horrific time trying to find his body and locate British authorities to bring them home. It is obviously reminiscent of the Ewan McGregor movie "The Impossible".

Broking to Trading

When I left Fearnoil Anders suggested to Johan that they offered me a kickback on any business I did at MG through them (not that we did any business). Johan refused, he later told me, saying," Jonathan would never do that". He also told me that sometimes he would have lunch or dinner with traders at major oil companies, who earnt much less than brokers and private traders, and that they complained about not being paid much, effectively asking for a kick back. I only know for certain of one European who received such a deal from Fearnoil.

The Metallgesellschaft or MG office was just a short walk from Fearnoil at the corner of Albemarle Street and Piccadilly right by Green Park Tube Station. My commute was effectively unchanged as I would take the train from Clapham to Victoria and then just a couple of stops up the Jubilee line to Green Park. I hoped I had made the right choice.

MG had a large office in New York but thus far did very little oil trading. In fact we did virtually nothing. Dr.John was working on all sorts of weird trading theories that made little sense. They also had a small counter-trade department in London who did equally little. The only person in this department was an interesting American named Vladimir Egger. Not surprisingly he spoke Russian. In his mid 40s, he had had quite a varied career, at one time being an NBC reporter when he had interviewed the IRA hunger striker, Bobby Sands, who ultimately died of starvation.

The power within the oil group was in New York where the head of all trading sat, a cold eyed German named Siegfried Hodapp. Hodapp was a personal friend of the Chairman of Metallgesellschaft, Schimmelbusch, back in Frankfurt. Hodapp did not want us to simply speculate but to try to become more of a market maker which was a fine idea but in reality about ten years at least ahead of its time. We employed a physical crude trader in New York called Jane Nagy to join the team and we had many meetings in New York. I would use those meetings to fly economy class instead of business class to New York and spend a few days in the City with Judith. After a short while Hodapp said this was Verboten as it was not the money but the idea of business class was so that we would be ready to work once we had arrived.

The bulk of that year, 1987, was very frustrating in that we essentially did not do anything. Dr. John then had the bright idea that we needed more experience and gravitas in the London office so he approached the Swedish former Head of Scan Oil (a subsidiary of Volvo) Carl Winberg to see if he was interested in joining, effectively as John's boss. Winberg was a heavy drinking Swedish aristocrat, related supposedly to the Swedish Royal family and who talked a good game. He was currently employed at Coastal London with his two friends Nigel Whitely and Phil Stoddard. Winberg knew that the writing was on the wall as far as Coastal in London went and so he sensed a chance not only to jump to MG but also to find a way to bring along his two associates. Of course we did not need two more traders.

In the same vein as my earlier conversation with John Carr while at MG I received a call from my contact at Louis Dreyfus. He said they were looking for a young trader mainly to cover accounts. Again, foolishly, I missed the obvious and said I would let him know if I thought of anyone. I actually thought he was referring to someone with an accounting background! Why I did not realise that accounts referred to a person's contact list I do not know. Clearly I still had a lot to learn.

Winberg quickly set about ingratiating himself with Hodapp or Ziggy as he referred to him and I could see that he could not be trusted. Vladimir had in the meantime been brought on to join me in the crude team so that we could do nothing together.

Somehow Winberg persuaded Hodapp to employ Messrs Whitely and Stoddard to join our motley crew. Dr. John was primarily buried away in the back of the office slowly losing his mind.

Whilst at MG I often joined the rest of the bored traders and support staff in the pub after work. Sometimes the evenings dragged on quite late into the night and we would end up in a Piccadilly night club. An older, bleached blonde, office manager came up to me and asked if she could have a word. "Of course," I said. She went on to explain that although I was living with someone she could tell that there was something between us, some sort of chemistry, which there most definitely was not. My reaction, however, was to go absolutely ballistic and to start yelling and cursing venomously such that she was reduced to tears. My anger was certainly tough to contain.

Perhaps my most exciting time at MG was the massive stock market crash known as "Black Monday". This came the day after the South-East of England, including London, was hammered by a powerful hurricane, uprooting thousands of old trees and depriving many people of power. Amazingly, I slept through the storm only to awaken and look out the window over Clapham Junction, one of London's busiest train stations. Obviously this was usually a hive of activity, but on this occasion I did not see a soul nor a moving train. The odd piece of paper fluttered about in the now gentle breeze, giving the ghostly scene an eerie look as if we had been struck by some kind of apocalypse. Funnily enough, the previous night, the BBC's main weatherman, Michael Fish, had, now famously, taken the time at the end of his broadcast to address an elderly lady who had called in because she was concerned about a possible hurricane. He assured her that there was absolutely no such risk. Michael Fish never lived this down. Luckily in my flat I had a battery powered radio and soon discovered what had happened. Motivated more by my need for coffee than dedication to work, I decided to walk the roughly five miles to the office, happily finding some coffee when I hit the King's Road. It was quite a day.

I of course still had 4 weeks of annual vacation so since there was little if anything to do at work Judith and I headed off for two weeks to Thailand. Again, like Turkey, Thailand was just beginning to become popular with British tourists. We spent three days trekking, partly on the back of elephants, in the jungles in the North near Chaing Mai where we visited villages the occupants of which had rarely seen Western man. In one village the children would rub the legs of a Canadian woman who was wearing nylon stockings as they had never seen or felt anything quite like it. In the same village we saw numerous short but incredibly strong women carrying huge loads up the mountainside to their village. There was no sign of any men. Then as the sun started to go down these painfully thin, sallow and drawn men would emerge from their huts. They simply spent all day smoking opium in their huts and not surprisingly died at a pretty young age. The Thai government had an extremely strong anti-drug policy as many foreigners would find out to their regret, but the indigenous villagers were allowed to grow a certain amount for their own use. The village was also full of small dogs and that night the villagers cooked us up a stew of dog meat which we all politely declined to eat.

We spent a few days in the frenetic city of Bangkok with its famous floating market before heading to the peace and serenity of Phuket, which was to be devastated some 20 years later by the enormous Tsunami that had claimed my colleague Peter's life. Off Phuket we visited Kho Phi Phi which were famous for the birds that nested in the caves there and whose nests were harvested and sent to China and elsewhere in South East Asia to make birds' nest soup.

It was off Phuket that, still uncertified, I took my second scuba dive. This one was a little more daring as it required taking a boat ride out to the ominously named "Shark point". The instructor simply told me to stay close and do what he did. I was pretty much oblivious to the hazards to which I was potentially exposed. The sea life was nowhere near as prolific as in the Red Sea but we did encounter an eight foot leopard shark at which point I made sure there were several divers at all times between me and the shark. We also came across a huge head of coral from which emerged a large spotted moray eel and what seemed like dozens of its babies which swam out amongst us. Judith meanwhile was gamely stuck on the anchored boat above which, of course, was being tossed around and she became sea sick.

Shortly after our return to London my brother was due to receive his Doctorate at Oxford. Now when one earnt a degree at Oxford you did not have to attend a graduation ceremony shortly thereafter or indeed you did not have to attend one at all, instead simply picking up your certificate from an office located on Little Clarendon Street would suffice. If you did wish to attend a ceremony there were several to choose from each year. A very arcane Oxford quirk was that three years after completing your bachelor's degree you automatically received a Master of Arts. This degree was essentially worthless but it did have the advantage of impressing American employers. The timing worked out well: my brother and I both attended a ceremony where I received both my Bachelor's and Master's degrees and my brother his Master's and his Doctorate for which he wore a magnificent scarlet and blue long gown. My parents of course attended but we rejected their offer to have professional photographs taken, deciding instead to make do with their Kodak snaps.

Upon returning to London Hodapp invited me to New York and asked me if I would like to transfer there. The thought was somewhat appealing but the New York office was as inactive as was the London office so I saw it as a potentially futile gesture. I began to sniff around for other possible opportunities and one presented itself in the form of a young American trader who had previously worked for MG but now worked for a small South African based trading company called Tiger Petroleum owned by a South African named Mark Wohlman. We only had preliminary discussions and I questioned whether there was a potential fit but the situation resolved itself very soon when Wohlman was found dead in the bullet ridden trunk of a car on a Durban beach. Apparently some West African cocoa deal had turned a little sour.

Around this time Hodapp had run into a group of traders who hedged 2 oil, primarily for north eastern jobbers and end users, based in Maryland, under a chap named Art Benson. Benson would in about three or four years or so be responsible for the multi-billion dollar fiasco that not only destroyed MG trading but almost bankrupted the almost 100 year old German conglomerate, once Germany's 15th largest corporation, and precipitated one or two murders and suicides in Germany.

Benson essentially took an enormous position on the NYMEX to hedge his sales to North Eastern US end users. The position grew to biblical proportions and every month he would have to roll it to the next month. The entire industry was aware of this so would get out in front of Benson each month and greatly exacerbate his losses. Eventually the whole thing imploded and an ex-Sun employee Nancy Kropp was brought in, at considerable expense, to liquidate the mess.

Long before MG imploded I had been let go as was inevitable. It was now the spring of 1988 and Winberg put the final touches to his plan, firing Vladimir and me so as to make room for Whitely and Stoddard. I was not surprised nor particularly disappointed but of course I would need to find a new job though I did not think this would be especially difficult. MG had paid well considering we did nothing but it had been a boring year. They also paid for our membership at the gym Champneys, a short walk down Piccadilly, in the Meridien Hotel where many celebrities could be seen sweating away in the gym or saunas. In addition they had bought my company car from Fearnoil so I still had the pleasure of driving my Porsche. I was often teased that the 924 merely had a VW engine but I was always quick to point out that the upgraded "S" actually had a Porsche engine.

I once had a shower next to the singer George Michael, who was at the height of his fame. One elder statesman of the oil industry, Marcus Green, who now ran Arcadia, was eating lunch at Champneys when his lunch guest said, "Look, there's George Michael!". "Who does he work for?" responded Mr. Green, dryly.

Arcadia was a small London based firm owned by the Japanese Trading House Mitsui. Marcus had worked previously in Tokyo for BP and Phibro and had won the respect of many of the Japanese traders. Arcadia focused its energies on Nigeria. A young peer of mine Peter Bosworth, with whom I frequently had lunch, had bounced around rather like myself but had landed an interesting job with the Philadelphia based refiner, Sun, who also had quite a large trading presence and activity in Nigeria. He left Sun to join Arcadia where under the tutelage of Marcus he carved out an extremely successful career for himself around Nigerian crude and dated Brent, the benchmark for Nigerian and much of the Western hemisphere's crude oil pricing.

Immediately after getting the boot from MG I went to the gym at Champneys. I had actually attempted, out of pride, to pre-empt Winberg by offering to resign but he explained I was better off being sacked as the 15,000 pounds I was owed would be viewed as a tax free severance payment. At Champneys I happened to bump into a young Norwegian, Stig Willerson who I understood had just left Statoil to join Vitol. I congratulated Stig on his new job and he thanked me but explained that it had not happened. A ha! I thought. I cut short my workout and immediately headed out to place a call to Ian Taylor, the Head of Crude, and President in waiting of Vitol. So was to begin the main chapter in my oil trading career.

During my time at MG most of my weekends were spent visiting Judith's family in Kent. In fact so much time did we spend there that we thought we should look for a small country house in the area.

After a brief search we found a wonderful property in Waldershare Park about half way between Dover and Canterbury. The Grand Main house had been converted into flats and there were seven adjoining Mews Houses. It was an extremely stately property and rightly considered a listed building. I purchased No.1, The Mews, from a very pleasant gentleman named Mr. Bolt who worked for 3M. The house had 3 bedroom upstairs, two bathrooms, and an extremely modern kitchen and a large marbled foyer with a spacious living and dining room. It was beautiful. Judith and I furnished the house very cheaply actually having the three piece suite of two armchairs and a sofa made by a man in the East End of London and we drove it down in a van we had hired for the day. From then on we had a place of our own to stay when visiting Judith's family and we would often invite them over for dinner and invite friends down from London for the weekend.

Sometimes on a Sunday afternoon I would feel for the first time, and for no apparent reason, the pure, hollow, emptiness of what I can only assume was depression. I was able to shake it off by going for a couple of miles jog through and around the grounds. One weekend, however, my symptoms lasted longer and I felt desperately sad. We stayed down at Waldershare for a couple of extra days and I called in to work saying that my grandfather had suddenly passed away and I had to attend his funeral. Somewhat of an extreme excuse, perhaps, and a false one at that.

My parents came to visit us at Waldershare once. My mother of course was still seething at the arrangements and continued to bad mouth teachers and indeed now journalists as Judith had recently abandoned her PhD and taken a job as a writer on GP Magazine, part of a large magazine group owned by the politician (and ex Oxford Union President) Michael Heseltine.

Now Judith's parents were keen hikers and would every weekend go for a hike with a group of friends in the Dover, Canterbury area. It so happened that the weekend my parents were visiting, Judith's parents' walk took them through Waldershare Park, which had beautiful grounds, and not unnaturally Judith's mum, who was very outgoing and bubbly thought it would be nice to pop in and meet my parents for the first time. When she knocked at the front door my mum realised who it was and, I am not sure if they actually faced each other or not as I opened the door, quickly bolted like a startled rabbit to the back of the house into the kitchen. The moment was clearly awkward and after a brief chat and with great understanding Judith's mum strode off to join her fellow hikers. I was appalled and embarrassed my mum's ridiculous behaviour but all the time I'm sure her subliminal messages were making inroads into my brain which was already very much like her own in terms of narrow mindedness, critical judgmentalism, and negativity.

Jonathan Ford

Vitol London

"All Men are Frauds. The only difference between them is some admit it. I, myself, deny it." H.L. Mencken

After leaving Champneys I immediately placed a call to Ian Taylor at Vitol. I explained that I understood that they were looking for a crude oil trader and that I would be interested. Ian suggested I come over to their office at Bowater House, Knightsbridge, the following day at 530pm for an interview.

The next day at 530pm I was there, patiently waiting in the office lobby. At 630pm Ian came bounding out and apologised profusely that he had to run to an appointment and could I come back at the same time tomorrow. I of course agreed. Vitol was primarily a global products trading firm with offices all over the globe including Singapore, Tokyo, Bahrain, Los Angeles, Houston and Connecticut. They had a superb global network of contacts and were experts at intercontinental arbitrage.

The next day I arrived at 530pm and this time Ian was prepared to see me. As we met in the lobby he introduced me to Ton Vonk, the President of Vitol who, putting on his trench coat, was on his way out of the office. Ton, probably at that time in his 50s, was a tall, serious Dutchmen with a lazy eye which made his stare all the more intimidating. Ian explained that I was a candidate for the crude oil position which was greeted with a half grunt by Ton.

Oddly enough the effective second in command of Vitol, Bob Finch, the Head Fuel Oil Trader, also had a lazy eye which could be used to similar effect. Ton was one of the original 6 Dutch partners, and one English, who started the firm in the late 60s in Rotterdam. They had subsequently grown to some 130 employees worldwide. Ian took me into their impressive main trading room. It was filled with large green trading desks arranged in pods and each trader had two phones attached to a dealer board. We sat down for a brief chat during which Ian explained basically what they were looking for and I explained my relatively modest experience and gave him a copy of my CV. He also explained the typical compensation package which would involve me taking a pay cut from my year at MG of about 50%.

Ian was a wiry, bald ball of energy who in the eyes of some cheeky colleagues resembled Gandhi, a comparison he deeply disliked.

Within a week Ian had offered me the job at Vitol and I started in March of 1988. He would later tell various other traders how proud he was that he had found someone willing to take a 50% pay cut to come and work with him.

I was assigned a desk next to Ian, my co-crude trader, on a large green trading pod along with the naphtha/gasoil trader, the two fuel traders and a couple of vessel operators. I felt somewhat overawed as everyone else seemed to know so much more about the business than I did. However, I quickly learnt at the side of Ian for whom I had great respect and admiration. He was clearly earmarked as the next President once Ton retired down the road. My main focus was on the paper markets, i.e., the 15 day Brent and the NYMEX futures market. I also conversed frequently with a long time employee Richard Flyg in Houston. The US operation had recently been split between Stamford, Connecticut and Houston and the board composed of the original partners and Ian and Bob Finch had to decide upon one location. They eventually chose Houston, much to the disgust of many of the New Englanders in Connecticut, but almost every one of any significance went along with the move.

The main physical crude focus at that time was on Iranian crude. The National Iranian Oil Company, NIOC, did a number of large crude for product swaps with traders such as ourselves, Phibro and Marc Rich. Rich of course was the infamous American who had fled the US with Rudy Giuliani hot on his heels to avoid tax evasion charges. Rich settled in the canton of Zug, Switzerland. There actually was an extradition treaty between the US and Switzerland but the Swiss were so angered by an American attempt to kidnap Rich from a Zug restaurant that they subsequently refused to entertain any thoughts of extradition. Rich meanwhile consolidated his position in Zug through his philanthropic efforts. He was of course famously pardoned by the outgoing President Bill Clinton some years later but he never set foot again in the US.

Typically on these crude for product exchanges the profit was made on the products and our job on the crude side was just to dispose of the crude as well as possible. It was seldom an easy task. Ian was responsible for negotiating these deals and could frequently be heard arguing for hours with his Iranian counterpart as they hammered out the deals. The crude we were given was almost always for the West, i.e., north west Europe (NWE) or the Mediterranean. If we went to the Med we would take the VLCC carrying up to 2 million barrels (or 2mmbbls) of Iranian crude and pump it through the Summed (Suez-Med) pipeline that ran from Ain Sukhna at the top of the Red Sea to Sidi Kerir near Alexandria in Egypt where it would be loaded onto smaller 1mmbbls ships and taken to a Mediterranean port. Together with Ian, I had to work out the economics of bringing a full VLCC around the Cape of Good Hope and on into the Med or up to NWE, or to use the Sumed Pipeline. Mostly we would head to the Rotterdam refining centre where many European refiners were keen buyers of Iranian crude, whether Heavy or Light.

Today it would be obvious but back then it was not so clear: I spotted that if we sold a VLCC of Iranian crude that we had just purchased to a Korean refiner, we could increase our profit by well over $1m. The only problem was we were contractually obliged to head to Europe. Cargoes heading to Europe were sold at one price, indexed off Brent, and those heading to Asia were sold by the Iranians at a higher price, indexed off Dubai. Now Vitol, I quickly learnt, were not ones to be put off by mere contract details or even many rules and regulations. The vessel in question carrying 2mmbbls of Iranian crude was the Eastern Power. We quietly sold it to Korea making a handsome profit. There was still the small problem of the Iranians who informed Ian that they wished to send a representative to Rotterdam to witness the discharge of the ship. Somehow Ian and Stuart Whitelock managed to arrange with the authorities at the Port of Rotterdam not to allow the Iranian representative into the terminal so we got away with it.

The crude ships were handled by operators who supervised the loading and discharge of all the vessels. The Iranian business was handled by a large, loud, jovial fellow by the name of Stuart Whitelock. He would also frequently have long heated discussions with his Iranian counterparts as they argued about the schedule for crude loadings or product discharges. Stuart was also a general Mr. Fix-It operationally. He once opened his desk draw and said, "Here look at this". He showed me a host of official stamps that would enable him to produce an official looking bill of lading from just about any major port in the world.

My job was unbelievably interesting and exciting. One minute I would be working an Iranian cargo into NWE, the next I would be bidding on a West African crude oil tender say Kole from the Cameroons. We also often worked cargoes of Angolan crude in conjunction with Richard in Houston into the US Gulf Coast. The profit margins were always thin as it was a competitive business and the Angolan buyers pretty much exactly knew our economics.

Working with Ian was quite an education and even an adventure. We would attend many business lunches together and usually be late such that on many occasions we would literally end up running to the restaurant. Ian would usually order very quickly and immediately ask for the bill before we had even been served.

Vitol at that time had a very sophisticated internal email system run on a Data General system that enabled its offices around the world to communicate instantly. Every lunch time and evening Ian or I would write a "midday" or "overnight" update to be sent to Houston effectively handing the business over to them. However, since the NYMEX was so dominant it was very common for me to stay in the office until 830pm, i.e., the NYMEX close. The product guys operated similarly. Houston would likewise write an overnight report for the benefit of Singapore and Tokyo and then those offices would keep the ball rolling in our direction. The information flow was very impressive. I would usually read the product comments as well as the crude but I was always afraid to show my ignorance. For example the product guys would often write about "Cactus" and "Tulip" and "The Island Exchange". I had no idea what they were talking about but after some time listening carefully and maybe a few discrete questions, which did not result in me making myself look totally stupid, I found out that those three terms respectively meant Iran, South Africa and Cuba, the latter with which we had an exchange whereby we supplied them with fuel oil and if we were lucky the Russians would give us Urals crude oil on behalf of the Cubans. All of these locations were politically sensitive but none of this business was illegal. South Africa, or Tulip, was under sanctions so it would be illegal to deal with them but we did not. They were supplied in the main by Marc Rich and Transworld Oil. Transworld was owned and operated mainly out of Bermuda by a Dutchman with a heavily scarred face as a result of a shotgun accident named John Deuss. In appearance and reputation Deuss resembled a character in a James Bond movie. He had a yacht in Bermuda crewed solely by beautiful women. Apparently he had made his initial fortune by "buying" a cargo of Russian crude oil from the Russians and selling it but forgetting to actually pay for the cargo. Somehow he stayed alive and I believe he ultimately did pay some decades later after a ruling by the appropriate International Court.

When the market was collapsing in early 1986 Deuss, who was very friendly with the Minister of Oman, rather foolishly attempted a Brent squeeze. A squeeze with you ending up with about 40 cargoes of physical Brent to sell in a massively oversupplied market is not a good thing. Transworld lost a few hundred million which actually turned out to be somewhat of a blessing in disguise. To cover their losses they were forced to sell their Philadelphia refinery for about $450m. This was the peak of refining values for quite some time with the refinery probably being worth not much more than $150m for the next ten years. How much, if any, the Omanis helped Deuss with his losses I do not know.

Now Marc Rich traded with everyone. I once saw an interview on TV where he was asked why did he deal with sanctioned countries and those considered pariahs by the international community. "It is simple. We do not discriminate". I loved that answer.

Most people assumed we, Vitol, would deal with South Africa as countries under international sanctions tended to offer the largest profit margins. However, our original "Old Partners" were all Dutch apart from Marian Walecki, a well-spoken Englishman of obvious Polish descent, who lived in Brussels. Four of the Dutch partners lived in Holland. During the apartheid years Shell had an operation in South Africa and the Dutch, obviously being a concerned nation given the status of the Boer, frequently held violent demonstrations outside the offices of Shell. It was for this reason that we did not want to touch South Africa: our Dutch partners did not wish to be attacked or even killed and there may even have been an incident when a fire bomb was thrown at one of our officers in Rotterdam but my memory is not clear on that point. Rest assured we more than made up for that act of "discrimination".

There was absolutely nothing wrong of course for Europeans (or indeed any non-Americans) to deal with Cuba. I presume we used the term "Island exchange" in our overnight commentaries as Americans would read the reports and technically they should not be aware of anything to do with that Island. The US employees were very careful not to get involved in any way with the "Island" business other than helping to push the appropriate Platts quote in an upward direction when we were pricing out a cargo of fuel oil to the Cubans. When board meetings of the Group were held the minutes always stated that the Americans present left the room when Cuba was being discussed. Whether this was indeed the case I do not know.

As for Cactus I saw no problem with Iran. Exxon and others were major buyers of Iranian crude at that time but we used that code name. Ian had actually lived in Tehran during some of his teen years and said it was a magnificent and extremely cultured City.

Each Wednesday lunchtime we would have a traders lunch in the large office dining room. This was an occasion for the various traders to share details of their respective markets and to discuss possible joint strategies.

"The best laid plans of mice and men......" Robert Burns

It was at one of these lunches that the Head of the Gasoline group, Rick Grimm explained that he was extremely bullish on gasoline and that either we should go very long gasoline or the gasoline versus crude spread, i.e., the gas crack. Now we were also quite bullish crude oil but he was correct on both counts: gasoline exploded from here on and the gas crack widened. Unfortunately the conversation did not end there. We began to overcomplicate things. After further thought we collectively decided that it was in fact naphtha, used as reformer feed to make gasoline, was in fact the most undervalued part of the complex so we would probably be better off going long naphtha versus crude but since we were also bullish crude we should just buy naphtha. It was therefore decided that Nigel, the naphtha trader, would buy several European open spec naphtha cargoes for April delivery. Note this is quite different from buying NY harbour gasoline or the gas crack which was the original idea.

After the lunch Nigel bought a few cargoes but naphtha barely budged as gasoline moved significantly higher both outright and relative to crude. So over the next few days several more cargoes were purchased and still naphtha was not moving up, in fact we were down on our position. We then collectively had the bright idea, since we owned so many April cargoes that we should keep buying April and selling May and make a "squeeze" play on April naphtha. Now squeeze is not a word you band about in the trading room and it was with much horror and many glares that David Hughes, The Head LPG trader, was greeted when he ambled into the trading room and announced in his thick Lancashire accent "How's that squeeze going then Nigel?". The market soon picked up that we were extremely long April naphtha and it continued to go nowhere as gasoline continued to rally. Eventually our owning so many April cargoes did cause a modest rally in the April vs May naphtha spread, and we liquidated a couple of cargoes at a decent price, but then April started to tumble. Ultimately, after about a month of arduous work we were forced to abandon the play and once Nigel had liquidated the position we had lost over $5m.

Understandably an inquest was held at a forthcoming Wednesday lunch. Sadly Rick Grimm had been spot on with his gasoline call but we had been too clever for our own good. Nigel explained that we certainly learnt a lot to which Ton, in full lazy-eyed stare mode quipped dryly, "Well that's great. We could've bought a "fucking" University for the amount we lost". That was one of Ton's truly great lines.

My commute to work was a pleasure as all traders had the right to park in the parking garage of the Sheraton Park Tower. Therefore I no longer had to put up with the always crowded and overheated trains and tube. This was a major positive in my view. For most of my life I have always believed that if I did not have bad luck I would not have any at all. As can be seen that is not always the case. One morning, I was driving around Sloane Square about to turn up Sloane Street when the dreadful news that the Piper Alpha platform in the North Sea had exploded killing over 160 people. Obviously this was horrific but at least our small crude group was long crude oil so we would profit from this. It is obviously in a way terrible to profit from the deaths of others but such was the nature of our business. Somewhat similarly the following March Judith and I had taken a long weekend to Dublin. It was March 24 but Dublin airport was hit by an odd late-season snow storm and we were stranded overnight. I called Richard Flyg from the airport. He seemed to doubt my story about the snow but he told me of the Exxon Valdez disaster and how the oil market was beginning to react. Again, purely out of luck, as a company we generally benefitted from this tragic environmental disaster.

As a crude oil group we tried not to speculate long or short too much as this was very difficult and the absolute price of oil was governed by a variety of technical factors often in contradiction to the signals we were receiving in trying to say sell a VLCC of Iranian. Oftentimes the NYMEX in New York, the main global benchmark along with Brent would rally when we were totally unable to find a buyer for a cargo of Iranian. Obviously the market was a futures market and forward looking and did not care one iota about our problems with a single physical cargo. It was thus mentally difficult to compartmentalise your mind to think about how the overall market might react whilst struggling with your own physical barrels.

Occasionally, whilst sitting alone in the office until 830pm at night I would be unable to resist making an outright trade. One night I remember selling 100kb of WTI at $12/bbl to Drexel whose London trader always stayed late and would constantly be probing for business. The market promptly rallied and I took my loss at $12.40. I was gutted. I took matters such as this as a massive personal failing and was so angry and down on myself.

Around this time China was just beginning to open up and the state oil trading company Sinochem began to trade Brent and the similar Dubai forward market that traded 500kb cargoes of Dubai. One particular day the Sinochem trader, presumably working in the middle of the night, called us up and wanted to buy a cargo of Brent and a cargo of Dubai. We sold one of each and the market promptly rallied such that by the end of the day we were down $1m. Once again I was gutted. I left the office feeling worthless and headed on the tube to the Strand where I was to meet a few old College mates for a pint. I managed to shake off this feeling of failure, this time but another time I had lost money on a speculative trade and I headed home and locked myself in the bedroom for the rest of the evening crying all night. At that point Judith and I had her best friend, Jo, living with us and they had a few friends over. I never knew who was there as I never left my room.

Speaking of Drexel Burnham Lambert, the Wall Street bank, with whom Richard Flyg in Houston did quite a lot of business, they were soon to run into financial trouble and eventually take bankruptcy. We were owed $30m by them and that was a significant amount of money at that time for Vitol. Flyg was understandably under a great deal of pressure as he was responsible for 99% of the business but he apparently, I was told by the Manager of the Geneva office, tried to pin most, if not all of the blame, for the Drexel business firmly on my shoulders. Of course no-one believed him and fortunately, through a great deal of effort, we were able to receive the full amount we were owed by

Drexel. It is amazing to think, but not entirely unique, that Flyg was a self-declared genius and God-fearing church goer. Such individuals I am sad to say, exist in abundance in the US.

Ian encouraged me to focus on the physical business and the hedging thereof. He also preferred time spreads to outright long or short trades. We actually needed to do a number of Brent trades in both Europe and Houston to allow us to optimise our company tax exposure. I recall selling a Brent cargo, at a pretty weak price of $13.20 as I sensed the market was about to dip and a decent profit was to be had. Of course all the brokers were all over me calling incessantly and I set a target to cover at $12.90. One broker, PVM, who are still active, brought me a firm offer at $12.92. I stuck at $12.90 and the market swiftly turned around and the following morning I was forced to cover at $13.50. Why did I do this to myself? Bob Finch asked me what was up and I said I'd just had a total disaster. "Hardly a disaster" he commented but to me it was a total and utter failure.

All of us traders in Europe sat in London with the exception of two or three Dutch guys in Rotterdam who traded the Rotterdam and Rhine barge market. We did a huge amount of business in London but operated under a system similar to that used by Spectron and Fearnoil. All of our transactions in London were done in the name of Vitol S.A., Geneva. Confirming telexes were sent by a very busy man named Walter Kuser in Geneva who was our senior contract and credit man. The Brent operations were also carried out in Geneva though all the trades were executed by myself or Ian in London. When we did a trade we would send an email to Geneva "suggesting" they try to sell or buy such and such a cargo with such and such a company. Clearly this was an impossible way to transact business in a fast moving market but once again we seemed to get away with it, at the expense of the UK tax man. I believe we had some sort of deal with the UK exchequer where we paid tax on a cost plus basis but how they could accept this charade was beyond me. Still it worked.

Shortly after I joined Ian decided to employ another crude trader named Simon Boddy who was a very wiry, jolly fellow with a great sense of humour and a very well-spoken deep voice. He had attended Harrow school but only because his parents taught there, not because his family was wealthy. Like Ian and me he was also an Oxford graduate. Simon and I would often at lunchtime go, in his case, for a run, and in my case, for a plod, around the Serpentine. Simon would do two laps to my one which typically left me with a few minutes to relax, prone on the grass, as he finished. It was seven years since I had sat at that Serpentine Cafe dreading my first term at College.

Simon knew a great deal about the business and all sorts of arcane facts about rare and special grades of crude oil. He enjoyed speaking to many of the continental Europeans and had traded a great deal of Russian crude (Urals) at his previous employers. He was however, not a money maker but he fulfilled a function by covering the market from an information perspective and Ian liked him. Bob Finch on the other hand, who was arguably our most successful trader, wanted to fire Simon every year but Ian would always give him a stay of execution. Simon and I got on exceptionally well. He was far more upbeat and easy going than me when it came to trading and did not take losses to heart whether his or the team's. He was however, an absolute tyrant behind the wheel of a car which always amazed me. I made the fatal mistake for any trader of internalising every single deal and letting any loss pretty much internally destroy me. Judith would have to emotionally pick me up many an evening.

One evening I had to sell a Brent cargo late in the London day, i.e., around 9pm and decided to go home and make the call from there. When I spoke to the broker in Connecticut the market was at a great level for us and I was just about to sell the cargo when my home line went dead. I could not believe my luck. I ran out of the flats and to the nearby phone box from where I called the broker. In the intervening ten minutes or so the market had fallen about 20 cts/bbl and I had to sell the cargo for $120,000 less than had my phone not gone dead. I cursed my luck thinking something like that would only happen to me. I even wrote to British Telecom complaining that they had cost my company $120,000 but they did not respond.

On a positive note I introduced Ian to my friend Oystein at Statoil. Statoil generally only sold their crude directly to refiners but because Oystein and I were friends he struck a 12 month term deal with us for one cargo a month each of Oseberg and Statfjord. This was a huge feather in our caps and made many other traders jealous. The deal turned out to be pretty profitable to boot.

We also traded the odd Australian cargo, Malaysian cargo, we had one cargo a month of Nigerian crude oil obtained via the Jamaican government and we would sometimes pick up a North African cargo from Algeria or Libya. Ian purchased a Saharan Blend cargo from Algeria as we often traded cargoes for small margins just to have a presence in the market. The obvious buyer was Texaco who was one of my accounts. I negotiated with Texaco and we were literally 1 ct/bbl or $6000 apart when they backed off and did something else. Ian for the first time blew his top at me but later that night called me to apologise knowing how badly I felt. We ultimately sold the cargo for about a $50k loss. This Saharan cargo had actually been purchased from a Lebanese businessman Mr. Ghattas, and his notorious trading firm, Gatoil, that somehow was still in existence. During the price collapse of 1986 Gatoil had been massively long and were financially destroyed. At that time had they been unable to perform on all of their myriad purchases and sales the entire 15 day Brent market would fall into a complete mess of default and effectively collapse. The main equity holders, especially Shell UK, worked tirelessly for this not to happen and an arrangement was reached whereby Shell would help Gatoil trade out of their position and somehow survive. Obviously nobody would trade with Gatoil given their perilous financial state but during my time at Shell UK many of the Brent trades we executed were on behalf of Gatoil.

Now, in 1989, Gatoil was still alive and kicking in the physical markets of the Med especially but there was no way they could operate in the 15 day Brent market as nobody would touch them. Ghattas cleverly befriended the right people at the large German conglomerate, Kloeckner, and persuaded them to set up a trading company that would effectively be a front for Gatoil. Kloeckner did massive amounts of business so the brokers, especially Stardust in Monaco and United in Connecticut loved them as Kloeckner used these two exclusively. There were rumours that Ghattas was behind their activity but it took a while for that to be widely accepted. Meanwhile Ghattas managed to get himself very long in a falling market and Kloeckner, for perhaps the next two years, would roll their massive length, at great pleasure to the brokers, and at exceedingly enticing prices relative to the market. They would insist on rolling at prices far above the prevailing market price and, in return for doing this they would give their trading counterpart the benefit of about 10-20 cts/bbl on the spread transacted. The Brent market was unregulated so "off market" trading while technically unethical did not breach any actual rules or laws. We would deal cautiously with them trying to manage our overall exposure very carefully but it was a tricky process as inevitably after a year or two they blew up and were heard of no more, Kloeckner taking the bulk of the losses.

This above market rolling of positions was also effected by the US Pipeline and Trading Company, InterNorth, who ultimately blew up to the tune of over $100m. They were run by none other than Ken Lay of Enron fame and they were eventually absorbed into Enron, under Lay. While on the subject of dubious trading companies that bit the dust around this time there is also the case of Arochem, based in Connecticut and with a small refinery in Puerto Rico. Arochem was run by a tall, gangly, Chevy Chase type character who was extremely bright and had cut his teeth alongside Andy Hall at Phibro. However, he wanted to go it alone and soon began to trade up a storm in the Brent market with his small team of Connecticut based traders. As he lost money he would let the banks use as collateral his large storage tank farm full of crude in Puerto Rico. However, there was no such farm so the banks partly got what they deserved through their negligence when Arochem went belly up. Various banks and some traders took a hit and Will Harris, for his pains, was prosecuted, somewhat heavily one could argue, under the RICO statutes. He was the first white collar criminal to have such a privilege. At his trial he chose to defend himself, and offered none. He received around 10-15 years of extremely unpleasant hard labour. He survived but second and third hand I have heard that he had an absolutely horrendous experience, at least at first.

With the growing importance of the New York futures market, and indeed the London gasoil futures market, one of my opportunities was to bring an element of technical analysis (or price charts) to the trading room so we would at least have some in-house appreciation of this "art".

I had learnt enough to be dangerous from old Dr. John at my previous job though I seldom if ever put it to good use. "What are you staring at?" asked our main shipping guy late one evening as I was pouring over some charts on my computer, "You know," I said, "I think the crude market is about to go up $1/bbl in the next day or two". The next day it duly popped a $1. I had not bought anything. Missing something like this was almost more painful than losing money. Either way it just exemplified my sense of failure: even when I was right I was wrong. This would be a theme with me in the ensuing years.

Summer as usual brought the usual invitations to worthy sporting events such as The Queen's Club tennis and Wimbledon. It was at Queen's Club that I first had the misfortune to meet Paul Greenslade, Shell International's main Nigerian crude oil trader. He oozed smarminess and arrogance and as I would later regrettably learn these were probably two of his better qualities.

Judith and I decided this year to ditch the tent and head to Sardinia for a couple of weeks: a week at the beach and a week in the mountains. Lying at the beach I watched a large fat, bee-like insect land on my left calf, then slowly extend its long, nasty looking proboscis and plunge it into my skin. Ouch. Within a couple of hours I was receiving an injection at a local clinic as my calf had swollen to at least twice its original size.

The trip all told was terrific but it contained one embarrassing outburst of uncontrolled anger. I happened to notice Boris Becker playing in Wimbledon on the TV as we stepped out of the hotel to find our small rental car had a flat tyre. I decided to change it myself, which I had done before. However, the jack and tools would not seem to work and I had an explosive fit of anger cursing and throwing tools left, right and centre. Eventually I calmed down and we had a local mechanic take care of things. However, that fierce outburst still disturbingly stands out in my mind to this day.

Dated Brent

It was in 1988 or 89 that a new trading instrument was introduced by Shell named the "contract for difference" or CFD. It basically represented the difference in price between a typical physical or wet Brent cargo, due to load say 8-14 days in advance, compared to the most prompt 15 day Brent price, both prices as assessed by Platts.

Platts, owned by McGraw Hill, was the worldwide publisher of all quotes oil related from just about every traded crude oil to every traded product at every trading Hub in the world ranging from NWE, the Med, the Persian Gulf (or AG), Singapore, Tokyo, Los Angeles, the USGC and New York Harbour and Boston. Most physical contracts of crude or product were traded off a Platts quote which was decided by Platts journalists who would monitor their respective markets and, using ever evolving methodologies for fairness and accuracy, would publish the prices of their products and or crudes in their particular geographic region at or towards the end of that day's trading activity. Of course hundreds of millions of dollars depended on these quotes so traders were always working on ever more devious ways to influence the quotes. These methods ranged from outright lying: Platts typically caught on to this very quickly and would ask for both parties to a deal to confirm it. To combat this traders would agree with their opposite numbers in other companies to agree to off priced deals (often with a hidden second deal behind the first to offset any financial discrepancy). Platts over time would weed out such deals as pairs of companies, such as Vitol and Arcadia on Brent and Vitol and Elf on Mediterranean products would be viewed as suspicious and therefore deals between them ignored or at least given lesser consideration in terms of their contribution to the actual day's quote. The Platts quote was typically a range and products in particular would often price off the low, high or mean of the quote. Crude would almost always just price off the mean. Although Platts would publish quotes for almost all grades of crude including the various North Sea and Nigerian grades most of these grades traded at a differential off dated Brent and thus the importance of dated Brent was massive with millions of barrels of crude oil trading off this one daily number. A huge amount of pressure in opposite directions was put upon the Platts journalist responsible for this quote.

The main reason Shell International came up with this ingenious CFD was the fact that prior to this, physical cargoes were often traded relative to the front 15 day Brent cargo price. Now the 15 day market being a paper forward market and having an operational tolerance of +/5% at the buyer's option had the tendency to be distorted or even "squeezed" by certain players and thus a refiner who was buying a physical cargo tracking the price of the prompt Brent price might find himself in a situation where he was paying $1/bbl more than he should by virtue of the front month Brent being squeezed. If there was a physical or dated Brent price quote against which physical cargoes would price then this should result in a truer reflection of the price of the physical cargoes. For a few years this theory worked quite well in practise but traders, being as they are, devised ways to abuse this system over the years.

Initially, and in fact for almost two years, many traders were confused by this CFD concept. Fortunately Ian and I grasped it quickly as did our favourite CFD broker Kevin Kitson-Jones. Kevin would quickly bring to me deals he could see were slam dunks and I of course would close them and proceeded to make a considerable amount of money off CFDs for the next two to three years. My only real competitor was my longtime friend and future colleague Mike Loya at Transworld Oil. He understood things as clearly as did I and it was often a race between Kevin and his colleague Sandra, who serviced Mike, as to who could get the lucrative deal done first. It was amazing how slow people were to fully understand this instrument but it was great for us. Basically once a cargo turned wet (at 5pm 15 days before the first day of its three day loading window at Sullom Voe) it would no longer be able to be traded or passed down a 15 day chain. Now if 15 day was being squeezed, the value of the dated Brent could plummet relative to the paper, and this indeed was the case. The poor trader who was caught at 5 o'clock with a 15 day nomination that suddenly turned "wet" was now essentially short a 15 day cargo for which he would have to pay dearly, perhaps over $1/bbl, as a result of the squeeze. At this time Phibro were often suspected of squeezing both WTI and Brent and once every couple of years the somewhat mysterious Japanese Shosha, Kanematsu, would squeeze Brent, purely for operational tolerance reasons which I shall explain shortly. The year before I arrived at Vitol, Ian had tried a joint venture Brent squeeze with his friends at Nova (a Greek owned trader) and Arcadia but nothing really came of it. No harm no foul. Nova's main trader was Mike Watson who was great friends with Bob Finch with whom he owned a race horse suitably named "Arbitrage".

Absent a squeeze, in a backwardated market, early dated cargoes in a month would have a small but decent premium to the 15 day of say 25 cts/bbl. Thus if you were lucky enough to receive a nomination of a cargo early in the month you could "Take it wet," i.e. out of the chain, cover your short relative to the next month and then sell the wet cargo thus taken to an eager buyer at a premium. Crucially the buyer had the right to load between 570 and 630kb. This was termed "operational tolerance" supposedly to accommodate the needs of various sizes of ship and conditions at the various discharge ports. However it had massive commercial implications. If for example you had bought a cargo at $20/bbl and the market was now $10/bbl you would want to take that cargo wet and load only 570kb thus saving $10/bbl on 30kb or $300k. This was a huge focus of all Brent traders and it lead to squeezes and all sorts of shenanigans. Shell as the Brent operator and largest equity holder with Exxon always tried to minimise the shenanigans, like squeezes, but there was a limit to what they could do. If a squeeze of say $1/bbl was in play Shell could pull a few strings, or more accurately turn a few valves, and send one of its offshore loading Brent Spar cargoes to Sullom Voe and thus in effect create a new 15 day cargo which was worth $1/bbl extra. Squeezes were not easy to pull off as the squeezer would end up with a lot of physical Brent cargoes that he would often have to sell at a deep discount. This however could be mitigated by operational tolerance considerations, as was usually the case with a Kanematsu play, or by forward selling in advance many of the physical cargoes to ready buyers, or best of all a combination of both, as was the case with the famous Arcadia Brent squeeze in 1998. This Arcadia squeeze resulted from them taking every cargo in one month having secretly cut a deal with the South African Strategic Reserve to buy all of the crude. Many companies were quite badly hurt and one US refiner, Tosco, run by Tom O' Malley, took legal action against Arcadia which I believe was partly successful. The CFD market actually gave the squeezer a new advantage. Knowing he would have maybe 20-40 physical Brent cargoes to sell during a 2-4 week period he would set up a huge short CFD position perhaps via actual CFDs or more secretly through buying other crudes such as Nigerian at that time and then using the wet Brent cargoes to effectively sell "worst" recouping more on his greater volume of short dated Brent positions than he lost on the actual cargoes. Traders termed this "leverage". The Arcadia squeeze was slightly different in that having already placed all the cargoes into South Africa they were actually long dated Brent via CFDs knowing they could bid up the price of dated cargoes as much as they dared given nobody else had one to sell. It took a little while for the market to evolve to this degree but these tactics were used to great effect by several trading companies including Vitol, Glencore and Arcadia, as well as Sempra, over the next couple of decades.

Back to CFDS: I, along with Loya, appeared to understand the natural flow and inherent pattern of how dated Brent should relate to 15 day Brent throughout the month. Obviously mid month around the 15th or 16th the front 15 day month would move forward a month, i.e., on April 15 the next 15 day month would be May as this cargo would require nominating on April 16. This week was traditionally referred to as the transition week and was often where the greatest opportunity lay. Many traders would assume a straight line decline of dated to 15 day over the month but they would totally miss the fact that at the transition point dated would plunge relative to the next month. It was no longer an April dated cargo trading relative to an April 15 day cargo but it was now trading relative to May 15 day. Overall market structure would also come in to play also, of course.

Much to Loya's annoyance, I once just managed to beat him and close a 1million barrel transition week roll, with a trader locking in his 20 cts or so Nigerian cargo profit, that resulted in exactly $1m for us. I would often chat about the market to Mike and his colleague, Jane, who invariably would make fun of my tendency to speak far too rapidly: doubtless early signs of my ever increasing anxiety.

"A true friend stabs you in the front" Oscar Wilde

Even traders like Cargill in Geneva were slow to understand this new CFD market. You could understand a US refiner being somewhat slow to the party but you would think the private and bank traders would be extremely quick to pick up the niceties and exact working of this contract. Perhaps a year or two later the main Brent trader at Cargill, Paul Butcher, not the sharpest tool in the shed, called me up directly to transact a CFD. I almost felt bad taking the free $100k he had given me but what was I to do. As I shall discuss we were briefly on friendly terms and enjoyed the odd game of chess and squash together. However, he would ultimately become a colleague of mine and gain his revenge by stabbing me firmly in the back as one would expect from a character of limited intellect with a chip on each shoulder. He also eventually became a very successful dated Brent trader, not however through understanding and guile, but by the "brute force and ignorance method" as I termed it. This method came to the fore in the mid 90s and has persisted for the next decade or two. Traders would use it to grossly manipulate the value of dated Brent to influence the price of massive quantities of CFDs that they had so positioned during a certain week, whether by trading actual CFDs or by gaining the requisite dated Brent trading exposure from their purchases and sales of Nigerian, Russian, North Sea, Iraqi or North African grades. It was inelegant but highly profitable and aided, along with a variety of other factors, in the effective pillaging of the oil revenues of various countries especially Nigeria. Not to mention simply ripping off unsuspecting refiners but such is the cost of doing business in the unregulated physical crude market: much more of that later.

During this period of my career say early 1989, to perhaps 1993 I really enjoyed trading CFDs as I enjoyed great success. To me it was not speculative but formulaic and it was a great relief from the more speculative aspects of the business which I still pursued and which I literally agonised over on an almost permanent basis.

As I have mentioned products quotes were also, and still to this day along with crude, gratuitously manipulated by traders. I would hear traders chatting in the office about how we had to hold a certain Platts quote for a couple of days and then let it fall and push it in the other direction. It seemed so easy, and many times it was. I must say given that such mass manipulation, and collusion, has been going on for decades in the oil markets that the LIBOR traders, recently prosecuted, must have been pretty stupid to have been caught. Admittedly some Natural Gas traders over the years have been caught on taped lines but generally the oil industry has the common sense to arrange collusive manipulation on untaped lines or face to face. Hardly rocket science.

As 1988 drew to a close I would say that on balance I enjoyed my extremely interesting and varied and exciting work and was, as much as I have ever been, content though still prone to periods of emptiness and sadness. Also around this time I sensed the London property market was about to lose steam so we sold our flat for a quick 30% profit and rented in the same building. This was a stroke of luck, but sadly one of my last.

London Life

Over New Year Judith and I decided to take another adventure, this time to Venezuela. We flew directly to Caracas from London in an incredibly old and shaky Viasa DC-10 that I feared would fall out of the sky at any moment. At the airport, nothing like last minute, we decided to plan our itinerary. We decided we wanted to see Caracas then visit Merida in the mountains, Canaima in the Jungle, the setting for Sir Arthur Conan Doyle's "Lost World," and then perhaps the offshore National Park of Los Roques, a small group of largely unspoilt coral islands. Despite most things being booked up during that time of year we managed to fulfil our objectives. In Merida we stumbled across some local festival where hordes of young boys with blackened faces and wearing red capes ran through the streets shooting what appeared to be small single bore shot guns into the air. We never did quite know what this festival was but it was quite a spectacle. In Canaima we stayed at the famous Jungle Rudy lodge. Flying in, the pilot of our jet gave us a fly past of the world's highest water fall, the Angel Falls, which was of course very high but just a bit of a dribble as we had arrived in the dry season. Nonetheless Canaima was terrific. By now we always took with us a number of carefully chosen books. After Judith had finished I read Isabel Allende's "House of the Spirits" which I loved. I then read John Fowles' "Magus" which Judith had chosen for me. This book was incredible and mysterious and for quite some time after it still occupied my thoughts. I came to realise that many men had a similar experience after reading this deeply affecting book. It was in Canaima that I again performed a pathetic act of meanness of which I am rightly ashamed. Judith wanted to buy a cheap local souvenir for her mother such as a wooden toucan or something similar. At this I erupted into a fury. Why be so stupid? Why do we have to buy gifts? What a waste of money? It was my mother talking once again. Why I had to spoil this time, I don't know.

Before heading home we spent a couple of days at the Tamanaco Hilton in Caracas. From there we explored the City notably the Plaza Bolivar where to our amazement the trees were full of extremely slowly moving sloths. That was quite something.

One of my greatest regrets from this period stems from the Monaco Grand Prix and every year that race triggers a great sense of sadness. Bob Finch and his wife had been invited, together with another couple from Vitol, to attend the race by a very well connected broker in Monaco. We were to fly to Nice, helicopter to Monaco and then enjoy superb balcony seats right over the track. Judith and I were absolutely thrilled to attend and just as we were literally closing the door of our flat to head off to Heathrow the phone inside rang. I decided to go inside to answer it and it was Bob: his pregnant wife was experiencing some symptoms that made travelling not such a good idea. He quickly, however, stressed that Christian, our prospective host, very much wanted us to go. Foolishly I said we would not. I am disgusted still at myself for passing up such a golden opportunity to experience one of the world's greatest sporting events and in such style. However, despite my apparent superficial success I clearly suffered from a certain shyness and sense of unworthiness.

"80 minutes of agony for an eternity of pleasure".
Piet Greyling

Shortly, however, another exiting trip was to pop up for oddly similar reasons but this time I went. Ian was due to accompany Marian Walecki on a trip to visit some of our old contacts in South Africa just to say we were still around and please don't forget us if and when the apartheid regime is over. Ian had not yet arrived at the office and called me from home saying I would need to take his place as it looked like his wife might be about to have a miscarriage. He told me very little other than to get to Heathrow, his secretary would give me the tickets, and once I arrive in Johannesburg to clear immigration and customs and look for a sign that would either have my name on it or the name of our rather under utilised South African agent, Piet Greyling, who, Ian added, anyone would know.

With great excitement I rushed home, partly on the way to Heathrow and packed a bag sufficient for my two night trip. Soon I was soaring at 30,000 feet in the luxurious First Class Compartment of a South African Airways 747. In those days the flight was longer than necessary as you had to fly around the coast of West Africa as those West African nations could potentially be hostile to a South African jet, whether filled with civilians or not. I still have the beautiful little crystal elephant given as a gift to First Class passengers on that flight. I had plenty of time to contemplate exactly what I was up to and the fact that at that time Britain still had trade sanctions with South Africa but I was not sure if that mattered. Surely it was not illegal just to visit and discuss business you would never do?

On arriving at Johannesburg airport I was met by a tall, strapping Boer with a beaming smile and firm handshake. It was Piet Greyling. I had time for a shower and Piet explained we were to go into the City, meet Marian who was already there, and then head over to our first meeting at the offices of the SFF, the South African Strategic Petroleum reserve. As I have mentioned at that time South Africa did import some crude literally under the cover of darkness with the name of the discharging vessel blacked out but it also obtained probably the bulk of its fuel from three massive plants run by Sasol, who, like the Germans in World War 2, used the Lurgi process to convert coal to petroleum products. This was of course very expensive.

Before the meeting we had time for lunch. Piet was an extremely charming and gracious host and asked me quite a bit about my past. I explained I had played a little cricket for Oxford and that I had captained my College at Rugby. To reciprocate I asked Piet, "Did you ever play rugby?" "Yes," he calmly replied, "I captained the Springboks!" Feeling about 2 inches tall I picked my jaw up from the table.

This was why Ian had earlier told me everyone would know Piet. I apologised but Piet just laughed. This would be the equivalent of a college quarter-back in the US casually asking Joe Montana if he had ever played football.

He then proceeded to tell us many fascinating Rugby stories. Throughout his career, South Africa was excluded from major sporting events and operated in isolation. Piet had been a part of the Springboks that toured Britain in 1973 in direct violation of sanctions. Piet said the tour was great fun and as a flanker had several encounters with the great Gareth Edwards with whom he remained friends. On one occasion they had played a game in the West Country and were enjoying a pint or six in a local pub that had been closed to the public. Nonetheless, there was a large contingent of anti-apartheid protesters making a great racket outside the pub. The Springboks had become a bit sick of all the verbal abuse they had been taking, so they decided to open the pub door and let in the protesters who were summarily subjected to a thorough battering.

The afternoon meeting at the SFF was quite embarrassing and a bit of a waste of time. Understandably they asked us why we would not help supply them with crude. Marian waffled through a highly unconvincing answer and soon we were thankfully on our way to Cape Town where we were to meet Texaco and BP. Cape Town, of course dominated by Table Mountain and with its spectacular Dutch colonial architecture, was beautiful. I could really live here I thought. Our meetings were brief, pointless, but pleasant and the Texaco trader treated us to a tasty lunch. Whilst in South Africa we failed to hear the news that one of the 3 giant Sassy plants had gone down thus increasing the need for imported crude or products, not that we would supply any, but it would impact the regional supply demand balance. When I returned to the office the following Monday Ton was pretty annoyed that we had not informed London of this. I just sheepishly stood as he gave me that intimidating, lazy-eyed stare. In Cape Town, unfortunately the world famous Cape Nelson Hotel was fully occupied so we stayed elsewhere. Piet kindly took us to his house that afternoon where we relaxed with drinks around the pool. The next day I was heading back to London but this time had to rough it in Business Class.

On arriving at Heathrow the immigration officer asked me why I had made such a quick trip to South Africa. Again I was a little nervous given sanctions and all. "For a wedding," I replied trying to be nonchalant. "It's a bloody long way for a wedding," he answered, to which I replied "It's all relative". I was allowed through without further ado.

My lack of confidence once again came to the fore that summer. Our London office was going to play their annual cricket match against our main legal representatives, Ince and Co., who had a pretty large staff. I was asked to play and agreed. After much probing my colleagues eventually got me to disclose that I had actually bowled for the Oxford 1st XI. They could not believe my reticence. During the game I opened the bowling. I was pretty rusty but bowled pretty sharpish. Even Bob Finch commented "You are pretty good at this," which was considerable praise coming from him.

Geneva

"In this world nothing can be said to be certain, except death and taxes".
Benjamin Franklin

In the late summer of 1989 our corporate tax specialist, Erik Von Monsjou, explained to us that the UK authorities were beginning to question our status. You don't say I thought to myself. To make our situation appear a little more believable it had been decided that we would move one actual trader to Geneva, where we had our main financial and contractual staff, who would still perform his usual trading duties but in particular be responsible for executing all, or as many as practicable, of the futures that London traded. It was apparently the futures that the UK Exchequer had a particular problem with as it was highly improbable that we could possibly in reality be executing all these through Walter Kuser who was already busy doing a myriad of physical cargoes.

So it was proposed that I move to Geneva. I was not against the idea. It sounded interesting and would certainly be an experience. Of course I would miss my friends in London and I was aware that the NYMEX in Geneva closed at 930pm making for potentially very long days. There were already a couple of trading companies based there notably Elf and Cargill.

After a quick trip with Judith to find accommodation I, for whatever reason, chose a large three bedroom, ultra-modern, brand new house in the suburb of Veyrier. It was only about a 10 to 15 minute drive to the office. In hindsight, a small apartment in the middle of the admittedly very quiet town centre may have been more appropriate, but I liked the house. As part of my compensation deal, the rent was paid and I was allowed a reasonable company car. Finally after several years I had to part with my beloved red Porsche 924s which one of the support staff in London purchased. In Geneva I chose a black Saab 900 convertible.

I moved to Geneva in November when it was particularly grey and cloudy. For whatever reason my relationship with Judith was again a little rocky probably because of my still recurrent periods of sadness and emptiness: I wrongly, I believe, assumed it was my relationship that caused this as what else could it be. For the time I was in Geneva we rented the Waldershare house to a very nice British couple who were coming back to England for a few years from their adopted home of Vancouver. The house was in very good hands which pleased me.

The office had been set up so I had a direct line to the crude traders in London, namely Ian and Simon. I would continue to trade as per usual but would execute most if not all of our crude futures.

Any that Simon or Ian executed were documented as if they had been concluded by me.

It was a little odd sitting in a very quiet administrative office that emptied at around 6pm and I would sit there alone until 930pm most nights by which time most restaurants in the area were shut for the night. One of the contractual operators, a young Swiss French man, named Samir Zreikat was assigned as my assistant. He would maintain what would become a critical spread sheet of all our dated Brent exposure. He would enter into this spread sheet all our dated related physical cargoes as well as our CFDs. In addition he would have the spreadsheet calculate how many net barrels we were buying or selling each night so that we could hedge that volume appropriately during the Platts "window". This window was the 30 minutes from 4-430pm NY time during which all transactions were taken into account to determine the Platts quote for that day, at the day's close, for the absolute price of 15 day Brent and indeed cash WTI. For the next couple of decades plus, this "window" would, of course, be the subject of much aggressive manipulation by traders. Other products in other markets such as Singapore gasoil had a similar 30 minute window.

Samir was a great, upbeat and hardworking colleague. He was of German and Jordanian decent. Interestingly his mother had once, as a baby, been kissed by Hitler and on his dad's side, his great grandfather had sold camels to Lawrence of Arabia.

Unfortunately I think the physical isolation from the other traders had a very negative effect on me. I would almost always be in a foul mood, cursing at the screen and being very curt and unpleasant to Samir who was doing his best to work with his moody colleague. Nonetheless we became friends. I would literally stare at this screen for hours, especially late in the day cursing and swearing and grinding my teeth. I would break pencils and bang on the desk out of despair and frustration. I also had a habit of buying a whole chicken for lunch and devouring it at my desk. After many such feasts there was quite a grease stain beneath my chair. I did at least two or three times a week go to a nearby gym at lunchtime to exercise. I also on the odd occasion played squash with my then friend Paul Butcher of Cargill. Several of the Vitol office workers enjoyed tennis so some lunchtimes I would join them for a quick hit around. However, the old demons returned. I would curse and swear and yell wildly at every mistake I made. My head was simply full of the same old fury from when I played tennis with my family. After a few attempts we decided tennis was best left alone.

Before moving to Geneva my final few weeks in London were spent living with my colleague Simon and his wife in their Islington town house. One Saturday afternoon, hampered by crowds of football fans and police from getting home, Simon enquired of a policeman what was going on, such was his oblivion to the nearby existence of Arsenal's home ground, Highbury. Judith had moved in to a tiny room without windows in the area near her office towards the north-west corner of Hyde Park. That Christmas I worked in the London office for a couple of weeks and again stayed with Simon. I only now realised that the original or "Old" Partners had been working with the new Senior people such as Ian and Bob to arrange a transfer of ownership or management buyout. Under the new structure I believe the Old Partners were still to own one-third of the company for a period of time. Vitol had an incredibly complex corporate structure mainly I think for tax reasons. London was I believe a branch office of Geneva as was Houston. Singapore was a different entity, Vitol PTE. Above this was a Dutch entity and I think then a Luxembourg entity and maybe one in the Antilles. I never fully understood the structure. Nonetheless the start of 1990 would be a momentous occasion as the Old Partners effectively gave up control and ownership. Prior to this long serving senior members such as Bob and Ian and several in Singapore and Houston were so called "shareholders" or "partners" in the firm such that they received a share of the annual profits but under the new structure many newer employees such as myself were to be given a small percentage of "ownership" or profit share. Except it appeared I wasn't. Ian told me that since I was young and not married, an odd combination of reasons, I would not be made a shareholder. I was deeply disappointed.

Now right about that time I went out for dinner at a great Chinese restaurant near the office called the Noble House. In attendance were a couple of the younger gasoline traders and the Head of the Gasoline group, an American by the name of Rick Grimm. After some fine food and a good few bottles of Chablis we walked back towards the tube station at Knightsbridge, effectively above which sat our office. Rick asked me if I was to be included in the new partnership arrangement. I said apparently not for the reasons Ian had stated. Rick was amazed and said that was utterly ridiculous and would have a word on my behalf to Ian and Bob. I also made a point of mentioning my conversation with Rick to Ian but he appeared unmoved. Rick had made sure his "boys" were very well taken care of such that their share of profits would also grossly exceed their contribution to the bottom line. Were I to be so lucky.

A couple of days later was the London office Christmas dinner to which of course spouses and significant others were invited. I sat at a table with Bob and towards the end of the evening he nonchalantly mentioned to me that I was to be included in the new "shareholder" arrangement. I was shocked and delighted such that a tear, quickly wiped away and unnoticed, came to my eye. I was so proud and grateful. Unfortunately, I was only given half a per cent whereas the likes of Grimm's "boys" had three times that and in the next couple of years that was to make quite a difference. Still, I had been included; I was one of the team, young and unmarried as I was. I was absolutely thrilled.

Rick Grimm was indeed an absolute expert on all things gasoline and after a successful spell at Vitol he ran his own Monaco based gasoline trader/blender, "Blue Ocean". In the early 90s he had a stress related condition that required him to miss work for what I think was a few months. I recall having a conversation with one of our founders, Jaques Dettiger, a charming elder Dutchman, on this subject. Jaques commented that it was a shame and concerning how "modern day" traders seemed to operate under so much more stress than when he was active, some two decades prior. These words, of course, struck a chord with me and have stayed with me to this day.

Returning to Geneva after Christmas meant we were now in the height of the skiing season. My old friends at Spectron would come out to Verbier almost every weekend so I would typically join them, often with Judith, who like me had never skied. My first attempt at skiing was a nightmare as I tried to join a group of non-beginners and as we got off the cable car at the top it was apparent that I was clueless. Furthermore I had left one of my gloves on the cable car so I spent the rest of the morning chasing that down. Finally, with two gloves and a beginners' instructor I took to the slopes in the afternoon. After a couple of weekends I could basically navigate blues and greens but was never particularly bothered about attacking blacks and certainly not the knee shattering moguls. Johan of course was an expert skier. However, his friend Oystein, who frequently came to Verbier, was not much better than me so things worked out well. Judith too, slowly became proficient and I really took a liking to the sunshine in the mountains and absolutely loved our skiing weekends. Unfortunately, however, that season was one of the worst in recent memory with regard to snowfall and at the annual combined London and Geneva office ski weekend in Courmayeur, Italy, the pistes were equal parts snow, sheet ice and exposed grass or rock. Those were the toughest two days skiing of my life (other than a pathetic attempt I had made in Norway a few years earlier while working for Andersen). It was also warm so I was sweating like the proverbial pig. As the season wore on I became ever more competent and by the end of April I would even venture up to Verbier on my own and ski alone.

It was during a similar industry ski event in Meribel that I recall seeing the famous golfer, Nick Faldo, striding manfully to his point of rendezvous near the ticket booths. I assumed he was about to be whisked away in a helicopter for a spot of daring off-piste skiing in a hidden spot in the valley known only to a select few. However, a couple of hours later I saw him, knees trembling, in the snow plough position, on the beginners' slopes! Not what I had expected. Through my old friend Roger from College I discovered that a good friend of his and fellow football Blue, Ned Metaxa, worked for Cargill. For the rest of my time in Switzerland we were good friends but regrettably I lost touch with him after leaving. Ned was both an expert skier and fluent in French and was committed to his girlfriend in Australia who of course he barely ever saw. He once confided in me that he had met a very attractive English girl working in the Body Shop in Geneva and was feeling torn. Without any feelings for Judith, he tried to set me up with this girl, Rebecca, but I naturally refused. Several years later Ned and Rebecca (code name peppermint foot lotion, as we referred to her) were married.

Work, because of my attitude, was still massively stressful. I internalised and agonised over every single gyration of the market. At times, and throughout my entire career, it felt like my brain was being squeezed in a vice or wrung out like a wet cloth such was the twisted pain and torment that I suffered. Samir, despite my moodiness and brooding anger, tried to keep my spirits up. He was living with a young financial worker, Georgia, who he was later to marry and shortly thereafter divorce when she ran off with the French, office computer guy. Soon followed one of the most emotionally scarring and significant events of my life. One that I have reflected upon, from both angles for much of the last 25 years.

Samir and Georgia invited me to their house for dinner. We had a few glasses of wine but I felt able to drive and the roads at that time of night were virtually empty. Nevertheless the sneaky Swiss had cameras strategically placed around Geneva and the surrounding area and if you were snapped speeding you would be sent a fine in the mail. The boss of the office, Jaap Nobel, brother of one of the founding partners, Hans, always found it amusing when one of these fines landed on his desk as the car was registered to the Company.

As I drove off, an enormous owl swooped in front of the car. A portent of doom, perhaps? I cranked up my stereo, and soon had the Jesus and Mary Chain blaring as I sped home through country roads. As I listened to my favourite track, "Between Planets," I noticed the speedometer passing through the 80 mph mark. Suddenly there was a bump and a whoosh as the windscreen shattered: "Oops, I've done it now," I thought.

The next thing I knew I woke up, with the car on its side. I had no idea how long I had been unconscious. Frantically, I tried to pull out the car keys which were between the two front seats but to no avail. Then I recalled that you had to depress the clutch to remove the keys which I duly did. I crawled out of the ripped roof and decided to run home. However, I ran in totally the wrong direction and found myself near Ned's apartment building. I entered the building, took the lift up to his floor and rang the doorbell. "Oh my God" he exclaimed. I was wearing a white cricket sweater which, I had failed to notice, was covered with blood gushing from a large gash on the right side of my head. Sitting me down, Ned took out his Cargill manual on what to do in the event of an accident in Geneva. He called the police on my behalf and did his best to describe where the accident had occurred. I could just remember that it was near some tennis courts I think near Veyrier. Ned then took me to hospital where they promptly put a dozen stitches in my head, without asking any awkward questions, and we were back on our way. We decided to go and look for my car. We drove back and forth several times passed the tennis courts but no car was apparent. Then, we noticed a dark shadow of a car lying on its side maybe 100 yards from the road. As we walked over to the car we passed all sorts of detritus that had been flung from the vehicle. I attempted to push the car back over but Ned said there was no point as there was no way it would be drivable. Choosing not to argue, I asked him to drive me home, which he did.

The next day I awoke, aching all over, my body was as stiff as a plank but I was ok. I called a cab to the office and sat down at my desk as if nothing had happened. When Jaap came in he gave me a quizzical look and called me to his office. He explained the police had called him and found my car in the middle of a field, totally written-off and had then gone to my house that morning, after I had left, where they found drops of blood. The police told Jaap that I must have been going well over 80 mph when I flew off the road but the odd thing was, there were no signs of my attempting to swerve or brake. The car had hit a bank which flipped it 90 degrees so that I had somehow miraculously sailed sideways between two large, concrete pillars which, had I hit them, would surely have killed me. It then appeared that the car had somersaulted several times and in different planes, as every part of the car, the bonnet, the boot, the roof and the sides, were all smashed in. Apparently, the sturdy windshield frame which acts as a roll-bar, had effectively saved my life. It was quite an accident.

"What's past is prologue". Shakespeare's "The Tempest"

For years I have reflected upon this accident and thought that there must have been a positive reason for my surviving it. However, for the last few years I have cursed my luck wishing that I had indeed hit those pillars and thereby avoided the brain crushing and heart wrenching life that I have led these last 25 years. Of course, there have been moments of pleasure and joy this past quarter century, but I would gladly have given them up to have avoided all else that I have endured during that time and the incredible depression and mental torment with which I have been afflicted.

The next weekend Judith and I went to see the car and it was incredible how badly damaged it was and how anyone could possibly have survived a crash of that magnitude. Fortunately the office had a VW Golf as an office car and Jaap allowed me to use that henceforth.

Although the subject of many a joke, I think Ian felt that I was losing my marbles in the isolation of Geneva. Coincidentally, Richard Flyg, the long serving crude trader in Houston has decided to retire at the end of 1990. Ian therefore suggested that in August I transfer to Houston to have 5 months with Flyg and then take over his responsibilities. It seemed to make sense to me. We employed a pure futures trader to take my place in Geneva as the token trader.

Shortly before I left Geneva the police decided to prosecute me with dangerous driving and damage to public property. However, I soon skipped the country and never had to face the charges: neither did it have any effect when I entered Switzerland a couple of times in subsequent years.

I was in Geneva to enjoy England's 1990 World Cup campaign, most of which I watched with Ned. It was probably our best chance to win the Cup in our lifetime and still, like all true England supporters, I am gutted by the loss to Germany on penalties, especially after Chris Waddle hit the post in extra time. The night of that loss, not surprisingly, Geneva was full of celebrating Germans and Swiss-Germans.

My last week in Geneva was actually quite eventful in terms of the oil market. Saddam Hussein had just written an article published in the major papers, ahead of the coming Opec meeting, that the Kuwaitis were responsible for the declining price of oil and that Iraq would soon "pluck out the eyeballs" of those who sought to hurt his country. I had met the Kuwait minister that week ahead of the Opec meeting and tried to imagine him with his eyes plucked out. Not a pleasant image.

That weekend, the first in August, I spent in the beautiful Hotel des Armures in the Old Town Centre. I awoke on the Monday morning to hear that the oil market had gone crazy as Iraq had invaded

Kuwait. Typically times of such strife in the oil markets are when traders made most of their money so there were certainly exciting times ahead. I was due to fly to London for one night before heading to Chicago to visit my brother for a week, and then down to Houston to take up my new position.

I kept to that schedule, having dinner with Judith in London that night before agreeing we would meet again at Thanksgiving after which time, she would stay with me in Houston. She would obviously be giving up her journalistic job late in November.

After a week in Chicago, or rather the western suburbs near Fermi Lab where my brother worked on a Particle Physics experiment, I flew down to Houston, which at that time of year was not the ideal spot by any stretch of the imagination.

It was a Sunday and I drove downtown to my hotel, the Lancaster, which was across the street from our office on the 74th floor of the Texas Commerce Tower, then the tallest building west of the Mississippi. Downtown Houston was like a ghost town at that time as few people lived there. Rubbish blew in the warm breeze and homeless people strolled aimlessly around. It was once again a different world, one I would live in for the best part of 18 years and one that I would forever try to escape.

"What is called a reason for living is also an excellent reason for dying".
Albert Camus

During my time in London and Geneva I estimate that I was depressed around 20% of the time. During the last 25 years that number has switched to at least 80% depressed and over the last couple of agonising years been over 90%. In many moments of despair or reflection I wonder why and how I have lived so long. The answer, I am certain, is my children, of which I have four, two from each of my two marriages. Obviously I deeply love my children as would any father but what keeps me going as much as anything is that they deeply love me, enjoy spending time with me and apparently need me. Over the last couple of years I have come to terms with the religious aspects of suicide: I believe Christ forgives all our sins including that of taking one's own life. However, the thought of inflicting severe emotional damage to my children by killing myself is in effect more intolerable than the misery of my existence. Most people would consider laying down one's life for another as the ultimate sacrifice: I consider it to be living.

"We're born alone, we live alone, we die alone. Only through our love and friendship can we create the illusion for the moment that we're not alone".   Orson Welles

Sadly for most of the last quarter century I have suffered from a deep and aching loneliness. As Jung states, this loneliness comes not from having no people around me, but from being unable to communicate the things that seem important to me, or from holding views that others find inadmissible. This feeling was oftentimes accompanied by a chronic sadness that welled up behind my eyes. The sadness enveloped me like a damp blanket and was and is very hard to shake. At times, when alone in the car, I would let it take over and profusely weep which would perhaps relieve the feeling for a while. With my heightened anxiety this was an insidious combination of feelings that had me living for so much of my life on the edge of an emotional precipice which I would all too often tumble over into a dark abyss.

To America
"America: stifles life and kills dreams".
John Steinbeck in East of Eden

"The reason they call it the American Dream is that you have
to be asleep to believe it". George Carlin.

And so with the oil market in turmoil after Saddam sauntered into Kuwait I made my way through the thick, Houston air across one road and into the lobby of the Texas Commerce Tower form where I took the elevator to the top, i.e., 74th floor.

"Democracy is the theory that the common people know what
they want and
deserve to get it good and hard"
H.L. Mencken

"Democracy is the pathetic belief in the collective wisdom of
individual ignorance"
H.L. Mencken

Downtown Houston was certainly more alive on a Monday morning than it had been on that dreary hot Sunday afternoon prior. To combat the heat, downtown had an extensive network of underground tunnels that connected all the major buildings and in which there was just about every type of store and a multitude of restaurants. Houston reminded me of Blade Runner, without the androids, though with time that view grew to change a little. Those fortunate enough to have a decent job would leave their air-conditioned residence, jump into their air-conditioned car and drive to their air-conditioned offices, leading a comfortable and sanitised life. Meanwhile those less fortunate, such as the many homeless, lived outside in what I termed the primeval soup of Houston's thick, humid, smog infested air, where they could die obviously from the heat or even from the annual outbreak of West Nile virus that in fairness, like Marc Rich, did not discriminate amongst its victims in terms of class.

I would soon realise that while Americans thought we Brits were stuck in a class system America had one all the more rigid and insidious: the populace were basically brain-washed to believe that anyone could become anything through hard work. With this falsehood firmly installed in their naive and optimistic minds the bulk of the lower classes of America could easily be fooled and manipulated and indeed abused by the ruling classes. De Toqueville's "Tyranny of the masses" was alive and well. Over the next 25 years more and more enlightened commentators would expose how the supposed upward mobility in America was actually just about the worst of any nation in the developed world. Anybody could indeed become anything as long as they were born into a family who could afford to pay for good health-care and a good education. America was very much controlled by the military-industrial complex as forewarned by Truman almost 50 years earlier and as was about to be demonstrated in the next few months and at regular intervals over the next 25 years.

"I like your Christ but I do not like your Christians. They are so unlike your Christ."   attributed to Mahatma Gandhi.

As you see since my simplistic, "Fascist" days I have developed somewhat more of a political awareness. I am still relatively right wing by British standards but can sympathise with much of the British left wing (absent Tony Blair). However, in America I discovered that they had a different spectrum of politics: the left was basically in the centre and the further right you went you effectively fell off the political spectrum and entered a dystopian world occupied by stupidity, ignorance, hate and fear. Oddly this frightening realm was occupied by the self-styled "religious right" who were clearly neither. I was convinced that, were Jesus to return to the United States, he would be condemned as a subversive Communist and likely killed by the so-called Evangelicals. I would eventually believe that androids did exist in the form of the fanatical right-wing, cultist Tea Party.

On entering the very impressive Vitol trading office, with it's amazing views of downtown Houston, I was immediately greeted warmly by one of the two resident board members, Gary McCarthy. I was introduced to most of the office workers and soon shown to my desk on a large trading pod next to my colleague Richard Flyg. Given the chaos in the oil market everyone was already very busy. The Houston office was however, on the surface at least, much more casual than that in London and in the background music from one of the local radio stations played. Over the next few weeks I would soon grow to be sick of the sound of Bonny Raitt and Wilson Phillips.

I picked up my trading responsibilities which were similar to those I had had in Europe immediately. I continued to successfully trade CFDs and the company, including the crude group, was clearly making a good deal of money as we profited from the bullish market. Our term contract with Statoil also made considerable money. We still bought one cargo per month of Oseberg and Statfjord from them. One month we had over $1m of profit in our end month Statfjord cargo. However, purely within the letter, if not the spirit, of the contract, Statoil let our cargo slip into the next month and our $1m profit vaporised. I was mortified and took this as a personal affront from my friend Oystein. I do not use the term "friend" lightly. At that time I felt I had maybe five people in the industry I considered friends: Oystein, Ian, Simon and the brokers Kevin and Johan. Oystein, however, had the decency to call me and explained he had no choice: he had to do what was in the best interests of his company and was sorry that it caused me so much distress. This phone call had the effect of removing any ill-feeling I may have had and increased my respect for Oystein who had shown great honesty and integrity.

Flyg would introduce me over the phone to his many contacts in the US market as I was soon to be their principal contact. One thing Flyg managed with great care and privacy was our relationship with the Jamaican Government Oil Company, Petrojam, His contact was actually an English gentleman by the name of John Dobson. At that time the Nigerians were willing to sell their crude on a netback basis ,i.e., on a formula based on the price of a basket of products less a certain discount. Generally such deals were very profitable. It was obviously one of Flyg's duties to explain how those deals worked to me but I was shocked when I asked for an explanation that he responded "why would I do that". So, I simply worked it out myself. Richard Flyg has always reminded me of Ken Starr, absent the "peeping Tom" glasses.

The Houston office was run by two board members, Neil Kelley and Gary, both ex-Mobil as were several of the other traders. I knew the American fuel oil trader, Mike Metz, well, as he had worked in London during my time there. However, after many years abroad, he had decided to return to the homeland. Mike and I were viewed, I began to realise, with a little bit of suspicion by Neil and Gary because of our close ties to London. Mike was especially close to Bob Finch and likewise I was close to Ian. There was clearly some friction between the two offices which basically came down to money. Neil and Gary would like at the end of the year to have as much profit as possible on the Houston books so they could argue for the best bonus possible for themselves, and supposedly their Houston colleagues. However, it was not in the interests of the Company as a whole to show much profit in Houston as it was taxed at around 30% higher than the rate paid by Geneva.

Houston was a branch office of Geneva and as such any deals between the two offices was transacted at cost, regardless of the market. In a bullish market this meant that many cheap cargoes of primarily straight run fuel oil and Algerian condensate were purchased by Geneva and sold below market to Houston who would show a handsome profit. It was for this reason that we traded 15 day Brent both in Geneva (i.e., London) and Houston. 15 day Brent had the benefit of being a forward market and transfers of such cargoes did not occur between Houston and Geneva often long after the cargoes had actually been bought and sold and thus their contractual price was often far from the prevailing market price. I learnt from Ian and Ton that the Brent operators, in Geneva, were instructed to attempt to move profits from Houston to Geneva or losses from Geneva to Houston by carefully matching up the appropriate buys and sells in the right manner. In this way we could greatly reduce the profit shown in Houston and thus reduce the overall tax paid by the overall "group" and commensurately increase the Group's profit. I could soon tell that Neil and Gary and even Flyg did not particularly like this as it went against their desire to show maximum profit in Houston. However, it was how the rules were set up, i.e., transfer at cost between branch offices, so I could not see why anybody would stand in the way of what was the greater good of the Group.

Now our Singapore office operated as a separate company, Vitol PTE, Singapore and transactions between different companies such as PTE and Geneva or Vitol S.A., Inc, in Houston and PTE were transacted at "arm's length," i.e. a price that reflected the prevailing market when the transfer took place.

I was not the only person to recently move to Houston as the Connecticut office had only recently been closed so many people were in the midst of transferring. Equally we had several new employees such as Antonio Maarraoui who we had just employed from Maraven in Venezuela. We also had two young Harvard educated analysts, Rick Tibbetts and Will Trout who along with Antonio and I all lived temporarily in the same short term apartment complex about 20 minutes' drive away on Voss. Fortunately we had parking either in the office building itself or in the adjacent parking structure. I became pretty friendly with Rick and Will who were not that much younger than myself.

Obviously my relationship with Judith was now on the telephone only. We had agreed that we would take a trip to the Galapagos Islands and Ecuador at Thanksgiving and then she would move with me to Houston.

The Houston office was pretty social and many nights were spent together over dinner or drinks. We also had a small Los Angeles office to cover the US West Coast and each year the two offices would get together for team building and to discuss business. This year we were to go to a magnificent resort called the Boulders just outside Phoenix Arizona. Here I played my first ever, and what turned out to be my best ever, round of golf.

My Houston compensation, as in London and Geneva, included a company car up to a value of $30k. Clearly at this stage I did not wish I was dead as I decided to purchase another Saab 900 convertible after one had saved my life in Geneva. Now $30,000 was barely enough for such a car but the dealer downtown, Bland, explained that they had received a car to sell that someone had won in a lottery and wanted to sell instead of keep and that I could have it for $30,000. When I went to the dealership, with $30,000 check in hand, I was angered to discover that the price quoted did not include sales tax. So incensed was I that I threatened to sue the dealer saying that we had agreed to a price of $30,000 on the phone and that in my business an agreement on the phone is legally binding. Frankly, my behaviour was embarrassing and I am now thoroughly ashamed of it. However, the salesperson calmed me down and I eventually paid the $30k plus tax.

After a few short weeks I found myself a two bedroom apartment about ten minutes from the office in a newly built mid-rise complex on Buffalo Speedway. Work was going pretty well and on the whole I felt pretty good. Houston was a dreadfully humid, mosquito infested armpit of a City with little or no natural beauty for several hundred miles yet it appeared to be an easy and convenient place in which to live and work. In some ways I regretted not being in New York or London as I considered those two cities to be the global centres of commerce and I felt Houston was somewhat of a backwater. I had to get used to the often overly friendly tone of the local Texans who would almost always great you when you entered a store with the all too familiar "Have a nice day". That contrasted greatly with London where you barely spoke or knew your neighbour and people generally rushed about their business without making eye contact.

Once as the elevator doors in our building opened I immediately stepped forward straight into the back of the tall gentleman standing in front of me. I did not realise that it was expected to wait until the women on the elevator had exited it first. This nicety certainly did not exist in London and was actually quite ironic as Texans were notoriously sexist. In fact Houston was famous for its many top-less dancing clubs where many a corporate expense account was put to excessive use.

Soon after my arrival Richard Flyg suggested that I take his invitation to the annual Conoco industry get together at the Purple Sage Ranch, near Bandera in the Texas Hill Country: it would be a great chance for me to meet a lot of the US market participants. It was a very casual affair with many traders bringing their spouses. We spent hours by the pool, skeet shooting and generally relaxing and chatting. Being from Europe I of course wore my usual "speedo" style swimming trunks and did not think once about it. However, a couple of weeks later a young trader from Phibro confided in me that me and my speedos had been the subject of much amusing discussion at the ranch. Oops. Fortunately, I was at least in better shape then than I am now.

It was not until October that there was any real let up in the intense Houston heat which made me wince when I stepped outside. I learnt that not long ago Houston was considered a hard-ship posting by the British Foreign office and I could see why. The evenings were becoming bearable but the mosquitoes never failed to seek me out. I developed a friendship with the two young analysts, Rick and Will. Will, I could tell, was showing signs of stress and acted very nervously. I became concerned for his wellbeing and would frequently check on him in the evening and often go out with him for dinner. I sensed he was depressed. One cloudy weekend he and I drove the 40-50 miles down to the beach at Galveston. Perhaps it was the weather, but the grey sky, grey water, dotted with the odd oil rig and the grey sand made it the ugliest beach I had ever seen. It was enough to depress anyone and I vowed never to go back though I did break that vow in a couple of years.

Will clearly was not well and after a few weeks he went back to Boston to visit his family. His family immediately noticed what I had seen and had him treated for depression. He was briefly put into a hospital and would never return to Vitol in Houston. His parents called to thank me for trying to take care of him which was in total contrast to the cruel comments I often heard to my disgust about him coming from the likes of Gary.

Rick on the other hand was extremely out going and high spirited. He took to learning to fly and to do aerobatics. He even took me up for a spin one weekend but after one manoeuvre, that I am not even sure of what it was, I quickly told him to take us down.

Rick got on very well with the likes of Neil and Gary and the idea was that he would learn the ropes and eventually become a trader. However, I had the distinct impression that they were more or less stringing him along and that he would never progress to the role of trader though he did progress to the role of ship operator. My suspicions were correct.

Thanksgiving soon approached as did my scheduled two week trip to Ecuador. Leaving the country, I would also have to take care of some visa issues at the US Consulate in Quito.

Judith duly arrived and we set off to Quito via Miami. After a couple of days in the high altitude capital, during which time we took the cable car up nearby Cotopaxi at the summit of which it was literally freezing and about 14,000ft, we rented a car and drove to the spa town of Banos. Soon we were on our way to Guayaquil from where we would fly to the Galapagos. We spent seven nights on a small boat with about six other guests exploring the Islands with the aid of a very knowledgeable guide, Orlando. It was while on the boat among these remote islands that we heard the news of Margaret Thatcher's political demise: it felt so distant. The Galapagos were truly amazing and it was a magnificent trip. In Quito, where I only got to the US consulate with about 5 minutes to spare to have my H-1B visa correctly issued, Judith decided that she would spend a couple of a weeks in the nearby market town of Otavalo, where she would enrol in a Spanish language course.

I set off back to Houston on my own with an overnight stop in Miami where I had dinner with Ian as by chance our travelling plans overlapped. It was at this dinner, if my memory serves me correctly, that Ian told me he had recently had talks with Yasser Arafat, or at least his representatives, about building a terminal in the Gaza strip. Perhaps just as well nothing ever came of that.

Once back in Houston I soon reentered the intensity of the oil market. By this time President George H.W. Bush had assembled a coalition, including Britain, who were committed to removing Saddam Hussein from Kuwait by force, if necessary. There had been a massive build up of coalition forces all around Iraq and Kuwait and tensions were extremely high. The oil price climbed well into the $30+ range/bbl. In the Houston office every time President Bush made a press conference on TV we would play on the stereo, "I won't back down" by Tom Petty, and when Saddam Hussein or the eloquent Tariq Aziz made a similar appearance we would play "Free fallin'". This brought some levity to an otherwise intense office.

Christmas would soon be upon us and as much out of obligation as anything I invited my parents over for about three weeks. My brother would also come down from Chicago. My parents had done very little travelling over the years apart from trips to England and Scotland and short trips to nearby France or one of the neighbouring Channel Islands. With Judith living with me I was prepared for a tense and stressful Christmas which indeed it was.

My parents had been with me for about a week when Judith was due back from Ecuador. My mother clearly had her heart set on making a big push at splitting us up. On the day of Judith's arrival she commented how inconvenient it was of Judith to expect me to drive to Intercontinental airport, some 35 miles to the North. Surely she could just take the bus into the nearby Greenway Plaza. Against my feelings and better judgement, I did as my mother suggested which, frankly, was quite appalling.

Inside the flat the atmosphere was pretty tense. Houston was cold at this time but my parents, who loved walking, would often walk from my apartment to the Galleria where they would stroll around the vast shopping complex in amazement. One evening after dinner my mother cleared the table of the dirty dishes but very rudely did not touch Judith's. The symbolism was ugly and all too clear. Generally in the evenings if we did not go out Judith would spend her time in our bedroom working on her computer or reading. I could not believe that my usually timid mother could be so rude but subliminally her methods were clearly having an effect on me. When it came to Christmas Day itself and the exchanging of gifts I gave Judith nothing but a bottle of perfume and a small stuffed penguin, reminiscent of the Galapagos penguins, amongst which we had recently had the thrill of snorkelling. One such penguin had even cheekily pecked my mask. Judith had wanted a nice camera but the presence of my mother influenced my decision to curb my generosity. Judith of course felt insulted.

One evening Judith and I went to meet some colleagues of mine at a nearby pub, the Ale House. Though 26 she looked quite young and was refused entrance as she did not carry an ID. For some inexplicable reason I was angry with her rather than the doorman.

Finally the time came for my parents to leave and I was both relieved but wracked with guilt as was typical whenever my parents left as we had undoubtedly been arguing for several days as was our wont. Again out of a combination of guilt and obligation I would invite my parents over to the US for Christmas every single year I lived in the US and they would duly arrive, with perhaps one exception. Since my dad passed away at the end of 2007 my mum has made the annual trip on her own.

As the new year progressed things were still very intense at work but we as a company had clearly had a great 1990. It was around this time that a friend of Judith's from London informed us that a friend of hers from Cambridge, Martin Hunt, had recently arrived in Houston and Martin and I would become very close friends to this day.

Judith and I began to take weekend trips to Santa Fe, via Albuquerque, where we would ski for a couple of days and then return to Houston. On several of these trips we were joined by a couple or two of friends from the office. I was clearly still angry at something; I don't know what, but I recall having another unforgivable outburst at Judith when she had brought home deboned chicken breasts instead of the slightly cheaper variety with bones. How on earth could I be so small-minded and tight? The thought of this still embarrasses me.

Things inside me still did not feel quite right: I had seemingly escaped much of my past life but sadly I assigned my troubling feelings to the wrong origins, namely my relationship with Judith. This was basically my only connection to my past that still existed so surely it must be the case, I thought to myself. In reality I greatly missed my old friends and my old life in London but I was confused. Partly because she could not work, as she did not have a suitable visa, and partly to lay a marker down on our relationship, Judith informed me that she planned to visit Singapore at the end of March and spend some time exploring South East Asia. I did not dissuade her.

On February the 28th, 1991, as we sat in the office winding up another long and stressful day, the televisions in the office announced that the spectacular US led invasion of Kuwait and Iraq had begun. Our immediate plan was to sell into the expected oil price rally. Crude briefly approached $40 and as the only crude trader in the office it was my job to sell as much as I could both for the crude group and on behalf of the gasoline group to hedge their gasoline length. Phibro for a brief moment were the only buyer and I foolishly countered their Brent bids in the high $30s only to miss several golden opportunities to sell at a handsome profit. I sold only about 600,000 bbls which was far less than we had planned. After Phibro disappeared there were basically no buyers and all sellers. Everyone, of course, in the market had been long for months in anticipation of the commencement of hostilities. The news showed that Iraq was powerless to retaliate and that there was absolutely no threat to oil production other than that already ceased in Iraq and Kuwait. For the next two hours, keeping Judith waiting for me in the lobby downstairs, I watched in hopeless disbelief as the market fell towards $22/bbl by which time I left the office, utterly despondent at yet another massive failure on my part. Why was I always wrong? Why did I never do the right thing? I hated myself.

Judith could see that I was seriously dismayed and we headed home. I had a long chat with Ian in the middle of his night that evening and we agreed that any decent rally was to be sold. But none came. I was mortified.

The next day we were all in the office early and engaged in intense conversations with London. As a company we had lost something over $20m which was not a disaster but still a lot of money. I felt responsible though nobody in the slightest blamed me. We had the good fortune of our fuel group having sold 80,000 tonnes of fuel oil the previous night into a Taiwan (CPC) tender at a huge price. Trying to shake off the gloom and doom of my failure I looked for an opportunity and found one staring me in the face. With the Brent market having just fallen from around $38/bbl to around $20 the +/- 5% operational tolerance would come into effect in a massive way. A cargo owned at $38 could be loaded and minimised and sold at $20 saving $18/bbl on 25kb or $450,000 which was 75 cts/bbl on a cargo of 600kb. Arguably the correct way of looking at this was to say minimising a cargo saved you twice that amount as somebody else could maximise it and you would effectively lose $18/bbl on the extra 30kb loaded.

Prior to the US led attack the market had been heavily backwardated with April/May for example being around $1/bbl. As the market collapsed so did the backwardation and April/May was roughly flat. I realised that this was mispriced. Due to the tolerance issue it should still be at the very least 75 cts/bbl if not more. I discussed this with Simon in London and he agreed. For a couple of hours before the rest of the market woke up to this opportunity I could have purchased numerous spreads at arguably $1/bbl under their true value. I failed to act and when the rest of the market shared my realisation it was too late. Once again I fell into deep self-loathing and incredibly self-critical internal dialogue. What an utterly worthless idiot I was. Why I did not act I do not know. Was I afraid of success? I really do not know the answer but I was deeply distressed inside. Somehow I always kept an intense demeanour in the office and as far as I know nobody ever suspected the agonising internal torture to which I subjected myself.

That March, come bonus time towards the 20th, the spirits in the company were generally very high as we had had a terrific 1990 and were actually off to a storming start in 1991 despite the beating we took on February 28. Neil and Gary made a big deal of privately telling everyone their bonus, accompanied by a glass of champagne. I received $650,000 which of course was a significant sum of money and I felt a small sense of pride and recognition. I had no idea what anyone else received. This sum was far more, even after tax, than I had ever previously handled. For several months I had five cheques for $70k each, sitting in my bedside table draw such that Keith Swaby, our CFO, jokingly asked me if he could have them back since I was not using them. I eventually deposited each in a separate bank, so as to be covered by the FDIC (government) insurance, which came in handy when one of my chosen banks went belly up.

The company had made close to $200m so my 1/2% of the profits was worth $1m. This of course would be paid out at some later debt at the company's discretion and when finances permitted it. I was understandably a little jealous of those in the company who owned 2% and especially of Rick Grimm's boys who owned 1.5%, i.e., 3 times what I owned. One of his "boys" David Fransen was actually temporarily working in Houston to establish a gasoline blending operation in St. Eustatius in the Caribbean which eventually he would run from Bermuda. Ironically the gasoline group made virtually nothing in 1990 and indeed in 91 but Grimm's boys in terms of "shareholding" made millions more than I, something that I felt was grossly unfair.

My life was soon to take a dramatic turn from which I feel it has never recovered and after which I have struggled with all-consuming depression and anxiety for the rest of my life.

Betrayal
"I can resist anything but temptation". Oscar Wilde

"A temptation resisted is a true measure of character".
Dustin Hoffman's character, Dega, in "Papillon"

A couple of days before Judith was set to fly to Singapore, now with the camera she wanted, one of our operators, Cecilia had a small party at her nearby apartment in the Four Leaf Towers, one of the few high rise apartment buildings in the City at that time. Judith did not wish to go as she had work she wanted to complete. She was still writing the odd article for her prior employee and had to have it finished before she left for the Orient.

As I entered Cecilia's apartment I was met by someone I had previously barely noticed, but dressed as she was tonight, I was taken aback at the site of Janet Davis, looking extremely attractive in a small white dress that accentuated the sparkling tan of her arms and legs. Clearly she was interested in me and for reasons of pure physical attraction I decided that I would ask her out once Judith had left. This was a selfish act of pure betrayal for which I would pay deeply for the rest of my life.

> "I know the place.
> It is true.
> Everything we do
> Corrects the space
> Between Death and me
> and you."
> Harold Pinter

As I returned home that night I was already contemplating the weekend when Judith would have gone. Judith left for Singapore on that Thursday. As we parted company at Intercontinental airport that would be the last time we would see each other. She had been my uplifting partner for some seven years and was the only person to ever really understand me yet I stood on the cusp of betraying her and throwing away all that we had.

Janet and I went out that Friday night with a few friends and again the following Saturday. I learnt that she was from Lafayette, Louisiana and was actually going through an as yet uncompleted divorce. She had only been married 6 months when she separated and filed for divorce. I did not really pay much heed to that for whatever reason and whether I should have or not I do not know. Within the week Janet and I were in a close physical relationship but one which we sought to keep hidden from the office. Janet explained to me that her mother had been an extreme alcoholic who had twice attempted suicide and on both failed occasions blamed Janet for her actions. She had a deep sadness about her. Her apartment was pleasantly furnished in another high rise building, 3525 Sage. She cooked me a couple of extremely nice meals. I did not know what I was doing and why I was doing it but we spent most nights together either at her apartment or at mine and would drive to work together though walk in to the office separately.

Judith called the office shortly after arriving from Singapore. She was devastated by what I had to say to her and rightly furious. About a week later she called me at home again from Singapore, almost in tears, explaining that she had no money. I quickly pondered the situation and told her to contact my Singapore colleague, Kho Hui Meng, who I was sure would lend her some money on my behalf. This he indeed did. She also asked me what on earth was I doing and why was I doing it? Could anybody else live with my depression like she did? These words struck a chord but I did not know what to do and I continued my relationship with Janet.

It was obvious that Janet and I were not suited and had virtually nothing in common other than an alcoholic parent. We did not even have that much to talk about and I was beginning to deeply regret what I had done. Often when driving to work I was lost in thought about what the heck I was doing and she would enquire as to what I was thinking. "Oh, just thinking about the market," I would falsely reply.

Prior to the Galapagos trip I had taken a scuba diving course in Houston and become certified though as it turned out I did not dive in the Galapagos as our boat was not suitably equipped and besides the sea life was so utterly prolific, that snorkelling was a perfectly good alternative.

One lunchtime I left the office in deep distress. I called Judith in Singapore from my cell phone in tears. I explained I wanted to take everything back and I was profoundly sorry. She calmed me down and told me to go scuba diving in Mexico for a few weekends and we would talk about things some more. I also received a letter from her in which she rightly vented her indignation and disappointment and one from her mother who explained that things like this happened but that Judith and I had too much together to throw it away. I wrote back to her mother saying that I agreed.

After work Janet and I would often go for a jog around Memorial Park which was an extremely popular pastime, in spite of the heat which had not yet descended in full force upon Houston as it was only May. One day I felt a strange pain in my groin and thought I must have a hernia so I went the next day to see a Doctor. The Doctor immediately diagnosed me with genital herpes. I was dumbstruck, shattered. I barely knew what to say or do. Ordinarily I think I should have been furious at Janet who admitted to me that she had it but had tried to be careful so as not to give it to me as she had not given it to her previous husband. She was sorry. I was mortified and disgusted with myself. Rather than being angry at Janet I simply hated myself for being dirty and unworthy. There was now no going back. How could I ever explain this to Judith, let alone live with it? Furthermore, how could I ever go back to London, where of course they had herpes, but such was my distorted thinking. I was so utterly distraught, it was a struggle to keep it together at work and indeed when with Janet. My self-loathing was intense but somehow I remained effective at work and kept up a semblance of normalcy. However, in my soul, something was incessantly rising up, something that would not quiet down: it was as though I had a crime on my conscience.

By now Judith had moved on to Laos where she was working in some capacity for UNESCO. I had a contact number for her so I parked my car in the middle of River Oaks one night and called her from the car phone. All I did was basically cry. It was a horrible experience and I did not know what to say other than sorry. It was the last time we were to speak.

Little did I know that things were about to get even worse and my self-loathing and depression were to reach further heights.

As the sole crude trader in Houston I was required, with the help of two Venezuelans, Antonio and an elder gentleman, Enrique, to cover the South American continent. We had never done much crude business down there but it was important for the people in those countries to know us and know with whom they would potentially do business. We always participated in the monthly Uruguayan (ANCAP) and Chilean (ENAP) tenders so Enrique suggested that we take a trip to introduce me to them. We also decided to visit our agents in Buenos Aires and Rio de Janeiro. It was an exhausting trip, so much so that Enrique actually had pneumonia upon our return, but I made sure to send a postcard from each location back to my grandfather in Wallsend, something I had done whenever I went on a trip. He treasured those cards.

Our last port of call was Rio where we would actually have a day to relax before heading back to Houston. Our agent, Getulio, acted as our host and explained that after such exhausting travels we should have a massage so took us to a massage parlour. This however, was a parlour that offered a little more than a simple massage and I am ashamed to say that I succumbed again to weakness and went with one of the young ladies working, taking pains of course to use a condom. I was deeply appalled at myself afterwards and would tell no one what I had done.

When I returned to the office the following week Antonio remarked to me that he understood I had had an especially good time in Rio. The agent must have told him. I asked him please to keep it a secret.

I was now in deep mental distress and had no idea what I was doing and how I had arrived at where I was. I wrote a letter at this time to Judith saying that she must consider me as dead as truly I felt that the original me, as troubled as he could be, was dead. I had now escaped everything but myself and found demons yet worse.

> **"Yet each man kills the thing he loves**
> **By each let this be heard**
> **Some do it with a bitter look**
> **Some with a flattering word**
> **The coward does it with a kiss**
> **The brave man with a sword"**
> **The Ballad of Reading Gaol, Oscar Wilde**

Janet had a Doctor's appointment and came home and told me that the Doctor had said she had genital warts. I nearly died. I fell on to the floor of the apartment and began wailing incomprehensibly. What had I done? How could I do such a horrible thing? I told Janet of what I am deeply ashamed happened in Rio and apologised through heavy tears, profusely. My self-flagellation went on and on until Janet could take it no more. She then confided in me that she was sure that she had picked up the virus herself a few weeks before becoming involved with me. Since I had used a condom it was almost impossible that I could have picked it up and given it to her and besides I had no symptoms. This added to my confused state of mind. What were we to do? Who had given this horrible thing to her? She told me she had met someone on a flight to Colorado for a ski trip and had then spent a couple of weekends with him in Miami where he lived. I was suddenly gripped with an utter hatred for this guy and indeed for the whole City of Miami. Irrationally, I wanted Miami to be wiped off the face of the earth by a nuclear explosion.

My misery was almost unbearable. I utterly hated myself. Somehow I still functioned well at work, however. My personal situation and disgust with myself seemed to obscure any angst or anxiety I had over my trading, at least for the time being.

I was invited to a large industry golf gathering at the Mansion on Turtle Creek, just outside Dallas. I accepted the invitation and flew up to Dallas the evening before the scheduled golf for the large group dinner. Janet also had an appointment with her gynaecologist that day. My mind was in a haze and on arriving at DFW I told the cab driver that I needed to go to the Dallas

Doubletree. "Which one," he remarked, "there are several?". I had no idea. We drove towards Dallas. I happened to have my phone book with me and found the home number of another trader who I was sure was going to be attending the function. I called the home number and fortunately his wife answered the phone and she explained that yes indeed her husband had gone up to Dallas for the function at the Mansion on Turtle Creek.

Eventually, and still in a daze not knowing where or what I was really doing, I arrived at the Mansion only to discover that all the golfers had already left for their dinner at some restaurant nearby. In no way did I feel like going.

At the bar I recognised a lone drinker: the Swedish Lee Marvin, or Mac Barkman, the Fearnoil broker, enjoying his usual Black Label. I joined him for a short while and had a couple of drinks and a friendly chat. I then went up to my room to call Janet but was totally unprepared for what was to follow. Already I was beside myself with grief, sorrow, and self-hatred and goodness knows what else but when I got Janet on the phone she unleashed upon me a vicious verbal barrage the likes of which I had never experienced. "How dare I go to Dallas when I knew she needed me in Houston!" I did? I managed to have her explain what was wrong and she told me in her fury that she was at that moment taking a very painful cyst bath as she had just that afternoon had her warts burnt off by her doctor. Again I was dumbstruck. What was this parallel universe into which I had been spun? Where was my old life? Why was everything so utterly horrid and full of anger? I apologised the best I could and said I would skip the golf the next day and head straight back to Houston which I duly did. After the phone call I lay on the bed and cried and cried until I could cry no more. Eventually I fell asleep.

Returning to Houston to see Janet I did not know what to expect. Obviously she was in great pain but apparently, for what little it was worth, it was not my fault. I was aware that I would have to wait for warts to appear on me and I checked frantically every day until of course they did. I felt ghastly. My inner world was in utter turmoil and I no longer was whoever I had been. I still wanted desperately to get away from this new persona, if only I could.

I went in for surgery to have them removed by laser and happened to meet a broker I knew who was also in for some sort of procedure of which I knew nothing. Both in our hospital gowns, lying on beds, I was so embarrassed. I asked him to promise he would not tell anyone that he had seen me there.

As the summer progressed, I screamed a soundless interior scream of utter and soul-scolded woe. I wanted everything to stop. This was not me nor my life yet it was painfully obvious that it was. The warts came back along with a greater sense of self-loathing.

The doctor burnt them off in his office and told me not to be paranoid as the odd one might reappear for a short time but would likely just as quickly disappear. To say I felt unclean was an understatement. I could never imagine being with anybody else. I was given some cream to apply nightly that was meant to prevent a reoccurrence. Diligently I applied the cream.

That summer Janet and I took a short trip to Belize. I remember sitting on the beach, quietly crying, unnoticed, behind my sunglasses. I was mourning my own death.

Marriage
"Marriage is a great institution. But who wants to live in an institution".
H.L. Mencken

"A Man doesn't know what happiness is until he's married. By then it's too late".
Frank Sinatra

Now I assume Janet had decided that she wanted to marry me, as apart from my desperately unstable mental health which most people were not aware of, I was arguably a good catch. Our relationship became common knowledge in the office. Although we did not work directly together, Janet being a gulf coast product scheduler, the management decided that it was not appropriate for us to work in the same office so she was let go. After this she suggested it was pointless paying for two apartments so gave up her lease and moved into my apartment. She made a point of packing up all of Judith's belongings and mailing them to her parents address in the UK. She also sold all of my furniture which Judith had bought in London and which I had moved once to Geneva and then to Houston. I just let it all happen, not knowing what else I could do.

The summer of 1991 was Vitol's 25th anniversary as a company and as usual every five years Vitol would go to great lengths to get every single employee together for a grand celebration. This involved flying people from all over the world to one location and the markets still had to be covered and ships kept in contact with. However, somehow this major logistical feat was accomplished as we all headed for the Forte Village in Sardinia. I had already arranged with Ian to put Janet and me in the same villa, which of course he did. From Houston we had to fly to London and then on a charter flight down to Sardinia. It was an exhausting trip and we would spend barely 48 hours on the Island before heading for the marathon journey home. The first morning I was up bright and early ready to explore and I expected Janet would want to do the same as she had never travelled to Europe and we only had two days. Much to my amazement she insisted on sending me off to find a hair dryer to borrow: I could not believe this, but I complied.

We were not getting on that well, engaging in frequent arguments after which we would make up and then repeat the same sorry, predictable routine, over and over again. Even though we had only known each other for less than six months and were clearly unsuited she had taken me on a couple of occasions to meet her parents in Lafayette. They were a pleasant simple, couple, the father running his own successful "Landman" company in the

Louisiana oil fields. At night I would sleep alone in their spare bedroom where I would always cry heavily before going to sleep. How I wanted to be in the house of Judith's parents. How thoroughly lost and alone I felt. I was in despair.

Around October Janet told me that we needed to go to the Camberg jewellery store and look at engagement rings. Could I have been any weaker? This we did and chose one to her liking which we had shipped to her parents' house to avoid the sales tax and they duly shipped it back to me. It sat under my desk at work for the next month or so.

We decided that Thanksgiving to go to Disney World in Florida. I assumed I was meant to take the ring. One evening, sitting in the garden of the English section, I proposed to her and gave her the ring: hardly any surprise but she was overjoyed. The next day I called my parents to tell them the news. They were surprised but seemed pretty happy. On one level I think I felt I would at least escape the influence of my mother as there was no way she could understand, and therefore criticise, an American woman, I thought. That would sadly prove to be wrong, much later. What did I know or care? My life was over.

The wedding was set for the end of the following March, less than eleven months after we had first met. Janet had finally managed to get her first marriage annulled by the Catholic Church but in any event we chose to get married in a very English looking Church, appropriately named, St. Paul's in the Museum District. It was a Methodist Church. Before the wedding the Minister sat us down and made sure we knew what we were doing. I had no idea.

That November Vitol held a party for the industry at the Majestic Metro Theatre in downtown, near the office, featuring some old country star I had never heard of named Jerry Jeff Walker. The party was extremely well attended with people coming down from the US North East to attend. By any standard measure it was a great success. Janet was in attendance and I recall driving home getting into a blazing argument about something during which we were both screaming at each other and hammering on the dashboard. What a perfectly suited couple. This was pretty much my last major outburst of anger. From now on my anger would be directed inwards at myself in a far more insidious and destructive manner. How terribly this anger would later manifest itself, in terms of acute personality disorders, has only recently come to light. Sadly this realisation was too late.

Most people at work were surprised to hear of our engagement. Janet had not been the most popular girl amongst the female contingent. We invited a number of friends and her relatives and most but not all of the people in my office. One afternoon a Puerto Rican colleague, Hector Ramirez, asked me where our wedding list was registered. "Dillards," I said quickly and then proceeded to spell it out, "D I L L A R D S". I know how to spell it he quipped. I could hardly bare talking about it.

Shortly before we were married Janet decided she wanted to trade in her Mazda RX7 for something more practical like a Honda Accord. We went to visit the local Honda dealer. The terms of the proposed exchange were not to my liking so we left the dealer in the Mazda. However, Janet was not happy and started yelling at me for not buying her the car she wanted. With my usual lack of fortitude we turned around and were soon heading home in the Accord that she wanted.

A few nights before the wedding several of the younger guys decided to give me what was obviously a standard Houston stag do: a trip to one of the famous strip joints. When I got home Janet of course went ballistic.

I invited to the wedding a handful of my closest friends from London namely Dave and Jenny, Roger, John and Andy as well as Samir from Geneva. I had invited Ian Taylor but he was unable to make it but nonetheless sent his gift with Samir. It was a painting that he and I had seen at the Francis Kyle Gallery in central London by the acclaimed artist Jake Sutton. I had gone overboard a bit on Sutton and now owned seven of his works. He actually has one or two pieces on show in the Victoria and Albert Museum and was commissioned by the Royal Mail to design a set of stamps. I had bought my first work by him from a small gallery in Canterbury with Judith. I introduced Ian to Francis Kyle and over the years I believe Ian spent a fair bit of money in his gallery: he carried some pretty well known and highly regarded artists.

The evening before the wedding we of course had a rehearsal dinner. This was to be held at Brennan's at the bottom end of downtown Houston. I had to make a speech: I prepared two. The first was of the traditional variety and the second was slightly different: I was to thank everyone for coming and then announce that the wedding was off. I of course chickened out and delivered the first version. I did warn my British friends to be careful if they were to have a little too much to drink and find themselves lost whilst in Houston. I told them not to run through neighbourhoods and knock on doors asking for directions as a young Scottish man had recently done just that and been shot dead by an overzealous home owner.

"The only really happy folk are married women and single men". H.L. Mencken

My brother was my best man, down from Chicago, and of course my parents were in attendance. As my brother and I waited in the side of the church I thought I could still walk out: but I did not. We were married and had a reception at the Ritz Carlton on San Felipe. My mother mentioned to me in passing. " I think you have a lovely new wife". This meant little to me but clearly in her mind she had won. The following morning we had breakfast with our families and then headed to Hawaii for our honeymoon. It was all like a dream but all too real. Barely 18 months ago I was in Geneva, still visiting my friends in London and skiing with them on the odd weekend and now I was married to someone who I knew was far from a perfect match and furthermore I was utterly and forever unclean. I wanted to die.

Our honeymoon was to be two weeks split between Maui, Kauai and the Big Island of Hawaii. I have subsequently visited Hawaii many times and it is a favourite destination of mine. Obviously I enjoyed the magnificence of the three different islands and was aware that they were basically the North American equivalent, geographically, of the Galapagos Islands though far more under the influence of man.

Neil and Gary had kindly given us as a wedding present a helicopter tour of the Big Island which included flying over the bubbling Kilauea crater and seeing the lava flow spectacularly into the sea. During the flight all I could think of was my disgusting disease ridden body and how the heck was I going to survive the rest of my life.

On returning to Houston we set about looking for a house and we chose a small, wood-sided, two bedroomed house in the popular West University neighbourhood. Back, long ago in a previous life in England I had eagerly painted both the flat in London and the Mews House in Waldershare, but that was not going to happen here.

Barely 14 months ago Judith and I had laughed at an invitation we received from my colleague Mike Metz and his new wife Clare in that it was headlined: "Etienne Skrabo invites you to an open house at the home of Michael and Clare". Etienne was a young decorator from San Francisco and Judith and I simply found it hilarious and pretentious in equal measure. Etienne was actually a very nice, interesting chap. Now it was my turn.

"One life is all we have and we live it as we believe in living it. But to sacrifice what you are and to live without belief, that is a fate more terrible than dying". Joan of Arc

Instead of setting about furnishing the house ourselves and getting on with things Janet said she needed a "budget" for decorating. A budget, I thought? What the heck? Why don't we just buy some things we like and put it together ourselves? "Oh no," she said," we must have a budget as we are going to use Etienne to decorate the house". I was totally in disbelief but gave in easily, abandoning any and all values I had previously held. After all that person, with all his faults, was long since dead. We agreed on about $20,000 and ended up having wood floor put in the large living and dining room, installing a couple of pillars and buying some French antique arm chairs and an antique looking sofa that was dreadfully uncomfortable to sit on.

I had just received my bonus which was not as good as the preceding year's but still pretty decent. By my old standards it would have been a small fortune but I now lived in a different and very strange, lonely world. I must confess at this time the thought of getting a divorce did occur to me and I would often fixate on the idea as I drove in to work, sometimes actually thinking I might do it. However, of course I never had the courage. Janet was unemployed and took art classes and did some volunteer work to occupy her time.

I desperately wanted out of Houston, so much so that I contacted our man in Moscow, Gavin De Sallis, another close friend of Ian's, and said could I possibly be of use there on the crude side, as Russia was slowly opening up and there appeared to be massive potential opportunities. Gavin was all for it. Even Janet was in agreement, though somewhat hesitantly, and perhaps more importantly so was Ian. I was planning a trip to Moscow to look for a place to live when Ton Vonk intervened. He suggested I probably did not know what I was letting myself in for and would be better served staying where I was. After a brief collective reflection the status quo prevailed. In the early 90s I was not overly familiar with our activities in Russia but we did have two employees, the Kulik brothers, killed. The word was it was nothing to do with our business but some Chechen issue, but I have no idea. Also our intrepid Mr. De Sallis was arrested on a trip to Kazakhstan for alleged tax evasion. It was a pretty big deal locally but our brave American accountant, Charlie Parker, volunteered to go to there to secure his release. He was successful.

However, by this time the young analyst Rick Tibbetts, was sick of promises that one day he would be a trader that he took it upon himself to intensively learn Russian and then approach Ton Vonk directly with the idea of his moving to Russia. This infuriated Neil and Gary whose heads Rick had completely flown over without a second thought. Gavin and Ton both thought it made sense given Rick's operational experience and the fact he spoke Russian. Rick was an extremely adventuresome character. He had soon purchased for himself an ex-Russian military Jeep, complete with night vision goggles. When Bob Finch came to visit the office Rick took him for a night drive around Moscow then switched off the vehicle lights, had them both put on the night vision goggles and proceeded to drive across Red Square. Not surprisingly they were soon intercepted by Armed Guards who let them go with a stern warning which was very fortunate.

Rick soon got frustrated with the slow pace of our business in Moscow and jumped ship to partner up with an old Harvard friend of his and started to renovate central Moscow apartments and rent them out at huge rates to American firms just beginning to get a footing in Russia. Rick would approach Russian families who lived in a small but well located central Moscow apartment and offer them the chance to move out a few miles to a much larger apartment and he would then renovate and rent out the central one. One day, some rather threatening Russian mafia types paid Rick a visit and suggested he stop doing what he was doing, which of course he did. He and his friend high tailed it to St. Petersburg where they started an English language newspaper.

It was around this time that our product traders secured two incredibly lucrative large pieces of business in Asia, both involving a fair deal of skullduggery. One was the sale of a huge amount of fuel oil into PEDCO, the Korean power affiliate. We had, allegedly, a "mutually beneficial relationship" with the main PEDCO trader, and therefore were all but guaranteed the business. Unfortunately, we got a little nervous before the tender deadline and unnecessarily increased our offer by quite a bit which left money on the table. Other fuel oil traders became aware of our "arrangement" and complained to the Korean government but nothing came of their complaints.

The other piece of business was the sale of a huge number of gasoil cargoes into Pakistan, where Benazir Bhutto was President. At Oxford, years before, the Tory Minister, Alan Duncan had become close friends with Benazir, they were after all, consecutive Presidents of the Union and he actually managed her campaign to become President. Duncan used this friendship with Benazir to allegedly arrange a great deal of highly profitable business with her husband on behalf of Marc Rich. Her husband had acquired the sobriquet "Mr. Ten Per Cent". Now Ian was also a friend of Duncan's at Oxford, and later at Shell, and after Duncan left Marc Rich he was free to use his contacts as he pleased. He, allegedly, arranged on our behalf with Mr. Ten Per Cent, to dramatically, at the last minute, change the terms of their huge gasoil tender such that we won easily and made a very significant profit. Of course all the other traders were outraged but we won the day.

We also had a special relationship with the main crude buyer for the Korean Strategic Petroleum reserve. This relationship derived from an East London inspector that we knew well and we successfully placed a VLCC of Oman quietly into the reserve at a reasonable profit.

On the subject of senior politicians or more specifically their offspring, we once had Margaret's Thatcher's son, Mark, pay a visit to the Kuwaitis with us as he was supposedly able to open some doors for us. I think he may have opened the exit door as our representatives left the building, somewhat embarrassed. Perhaps we should have asked him to help us organise a coup as coincidentally our man in attendance, Ian, also had the surname Mann, but was no relation to Simon "big splodge of wonga" Mann, the well-known mercenary, who supposedly was involved in a plot to attempt a coup in Equatorial Guinea, with the alleged support of Mark Thatcher.

I believe around this time Ian Mann, based in Bahrain, had been involved in our attempting to move Iranian crude via train through the north of the country. This was highly unusual and our efforts came to an end when one train load of crude oil was intercepted and stolen by armed bandits on horseback.

It was also around this time, a couple of years perhaps after Saddam's ejection from Kuwait, that we came across the opportunity to purchase so called "weathered crude oil" from Kuwait. This was oil that had been scooped up from the desert after Saddam had set fire to the Kuwait oil fields. This crude was obviously dreadfully contaminated with sand and goodness knows what else but it was, rightly, dirt cheap. Our London office sold at least two cargoes, one to Zambia and one to Brazil. The receiving refineries basically shut down suffering serious unit damage as a result of the high sand content. Ian Taylor had to visit Zambia and Brazil personally to apologise and to pay considerable reparations. We also sold 280,000 tonnes to Pakistan to be burnt for power generation. However, the high salt and sand content caused around 100 million pounds worth of damage to the power plants. An inquiry was opened but with Benazir Bhutto still in power and with our friend Alan Duncan on hand when needed the inquiry was soon dropped.

Depression Diagnosed

I was so completely and utterly depressed that it took all my mental strength to hide it from those I worked with. I used to think that every trade I did would go wrong and if one went right I wanted it to be my last as it could never happen again. I felt my company, Vitol, would be better off paying me not to work as all I did was lose money, but this was actually not the case though it was how I felt. However, at home, I let my guard down and Janet caught on to the fact that something was wrong. Also recently while visiting her parents, her dad had seen me staring blankly into the swimming pool and he commented to Janet that there appeared to be something amiss. Janet would frequently argue with her mother such that these trips were generally pretty unpleasant and I asked Janet if she could not try to get along a little better with her mother if for no other reason than it would make my life a little better.

"Pure and Complete sorrow is as impossible as pure and complete joy".   Tolstoy

Janet spoke to one of her old College friends about me. He was a Doctor and he told her that clearly I was suffering from depression. Janet mentioned this to me asking if I knew what could be the cause. "Here's my chance," I thought to myself, I just have to be honest and say clearly we should never have been married and I would be, to a degree, free yet still an unclean, loathsome creature. Of course I chose a different tack and said I was depressed due to the stress of trading, which was not entirely untrue.

Soon I found myself doing what I never in my wildest dreams in my previous life could have imagined, I visited a therapist. It was actually a lady that Janet had gone to herself for some time to work on issues related to her mother which indeed were very deep and raw. Interestingly the therapist suggested that we do some couples therapy as our relationship clearly needed some work but Janet refused the invitation. The therapist recommended that I see a psychiatrist, Dr. Susan Bakes, with whom she worked, and this I did.

Dr. Bakes prescribed Prozac for my depression. She explained that it was relatively new and had been known to have amazingly positive results for many severely depressed people. She also suggested an anti-anxiety medication may be useful to help me cope with the stress of trading as I continued at work to stress over every single tick in the market and its effect on my trades. I declined the anxiety medication.

To further lift my mood Janet decided to buy a golden labrador puppy, which we named Rufus. Sadly, after a few weeks young

Rufus died of parvo and Janet was very upset. Undeterred she then purchased from a vet who bred labradors a black labrador puppy that we named Winston, after Churchill, of course. As all puppies do, Winston tore up our shoes and various other household items and was a general handful but he stayed with us for over a decade during which time he cost us a fortune in medical bills.

That Christmas when my parents visited Winston had torn into my their suitcase and devoured all the Cadbury's chocolate, wrappers and all, that they would always bring over for me. Winston came up to me and was whimpering and his stomach was starting to distend. Realising that something was obviously wrong we put him in the car and raced down to the vet in Stafford from where he had been purchased. The vet performed emergency surgery to clean out his stomach of all the chocolate and paper and foil but also to fix the fact that his stomach had literally twisted as a result of the irritation and had he not done so Winston would very soon have died an agonising death. Winston would, at an older age, develop tumours on his paws that had to be surgically removed. His anal glands became infected and he would constantly lick them so that his tonsils became badly infected. He then had to have the glands and the tonsils removed surgically. In later years he had a tooth removed after chewing rocks, and, in middle age he developed epilepsy such that I had to give him a large dose of phenobarbital twice a day. Even then I would say he suffered an epileptic seizure at least once a week.

After just a couple of days the Prozac seemed to have a positive effect on my mood which I found quite astonishing. Janet, Winston and I went down to the beach at Galveston, breaking my earlier vow, and I pondered seriously the state of my mind. I envisioned my mood as a ball floating in a pool of water and when it went under the water I would be depressed. However, try as I might, under the influence of prozac, I was not able to push the ball under the surface. This I found very interesting to say the least. I still wondered what on earth I was doing with this woman I hardly knew living in Houston but I also asked myself if I could not assume the mantle of this strange new life and survive all the same. I was not sure.

The following spring I received a call from the Mr. Bolt from whom I had purchased the Mews House. Our tenant had recently moved out and he assumed that I would want to sell the house, which was correct. He said a very nice old lady who lived in a flat in the main house wanted to move into one of the Mews houses and I should call her to arrange the transaction. He said bearing in mind the price I had paid, 83,000 pounds, he was sure I would receive over 100,000 from the old lady which was a nice profit for me and it would be nice to keep the house in the community, as it were. I called the old lady, Mrs. Longstreth-Thompson, and after a brief chat about Mr. Bolt's call I said that I wanted 110,000 pounds for the house. She said that that seemed like a reasonable price but due to a recent financial hiccup involving Lloyds of London, she could only pay 105,000. In reality this was perfectly fair but I refused to budge. She was very upset at not being able to buy the house but I acted in a very selfish and greedy fashion and would not agree to her price despite the intervention of Mr. Bolt and the fact the lady so dearly wanted to live in the Mews. This, together with my behaviour at the Saab dealer, were two incidents of which I am not proud and I appeared to be turning, on one hand, into a nasty selfish individual while on the other hand I was a weak self-loathing coward. Anyway, the UK market took a turn for the worse soon after and I sold the house to a Doctor for 78,000 pounds. I guess I got what I deserved.

"Start every day off with a smile and get it over with".
WC Fields

In the office I was generally very intense and focused on my job, such that I would spend almost every waking hour thinking of the oil market. I had recently swapped my Saab for a BMW 525i and one evening, as I pulled out of the office parking garage, my mind pondering the complexities of the Brent-Dubai crude spread, I sailed through a red light and T-boned another vehicle. Fortunately nobody was hurt but both cars were totalled. When I told Ian about this a day or so later he actually confessed that he had done something similar and driven into a ditch with his mind focused on some aspect of the oil market.

It was around this time that management, essentially in London, decided that Ian should move to head up our Singapore office and spearhead a major push into Asia. If anyone could do it he was the man with his engaging personality and boundless energy. From Singapore he would still call me almost every day and I mentioned that his role reminded me of the book I was currently reading "Gai-Jin" and Vitol was "The Noble House". He probably thought I was nuts. Anyway, moving to Singapore would leave a gaping hole on the London crude bench as well as in the London office in general. Ian had for a long time and for whatever reason admired Shell International's main Nigerian trader, Paul Greenslade, who I have mentioned earlier. Greenslade was employed as a trader in London, not to head up the group, but to be nonetheless a senior trader. Ian after all would still be heavily involved in crude even though he was very much out in left, or maybe right, field, so to speak in Singapore. London and Geneva however, were the nerve centre of our crude business. The fact that Greenslade was joining gave me a bad feeling, based both on my earlier meeting with him at Queen's Club and the fact that he immediately set about telling the industry that he was the new crude head of Vitol which was not strictly true. I would have to speak to him several times daily and coordinate our strategies: he was pleasant, knowledgeable and easy to talk to but his sense of arrogance and importance was always apparent. In fact it took very little time for him to be known in the London office as "The Chairman" due to his massively over blown sense of importance but the irony seemed lost on him.

In early 1993 the Houston office was visited by two Americans who were supporters and close advisors of the populist Nigerian Presidential candidate, Moshood Abiola. They asked for our support in return for which we would be given some concessions vis a vis NNPC contracts when their man became President. Abiola indeed had a huge ground swell of popular support. Now these two guys were in close contact with Abiola supporters on the ground in Nigeria and who would engage in the odd act of sabotage on oil facilities in Nigeria in order to unsettle the ruling military government. One night we were told there would be an explosion at the Forcados loading facility. We took on some length in advance of this as it ought to cause the market to pop. When the news hit, the explosion was minor and did very little damage. The market rallied a tiny bit, very briefly as clearly, it turned out, we were not the only company these two guys were talking to. Abiola went on to supposedly win the election but the sitting President, General Babangida, declared the results fraudulent and threw Abiola into jail where he died five years later.

Upon selling the house in England, I would have to empty it of all its furniture. I therefore arranged to fly to London and to meet my parents who would rent a van and take the furniture back to Jersey with them to use or to sell.

When I arrived at Waldershare I was consumed with sadness. I simply could not believe what I had done. Judith actually owned the house jointly with me so that we could get a double mortgage deduction but she did not make an ounce of a fuss and willingly signed away her rights to me. Admittedly I had paid for the house but given the way I had treated her I would have deserved any difficulties she could have caused. That night I slept for the last time in my old bedroom in the little house that I really loved. Once again I cried and cried and cried. The next day we loaded all the furniture into the van and my parents and I were off to our respective homes.

The next spring of 1993 Janet and I flew to Paris for a few days and stayed in a very modest hotel recommended by my friend Dave. From there we took the train to Meribel in the Trois Vallees ski area where we were to meet Dave and Jenny, who was pregnant and could not ski, and my other good friend from College, Andy with his fiancée, Amanda. Dave and Andy had kindly given the "Americans" the largest room with its own private bathroom. The chalet was actually very nice and included a cooked breakfast and dinner which was always superb, and plentiful.

As we skied Janet would complain of being "nauseous" and frequently needed to stop. I was somewhat angered by this as ever since I had known her she tended to complain of being "nauseated". Perhaps if she ate a little more than a sparrow she might not feel so bad. However, on this occasion I was wrong and unfair as when we got back to Houston we discovered that she was about two months pregnant. Janet was delighted and I was stunned into silence not knowing where this weird journey I was on was going or if and when it would ever end.

With a stressful job, a pregnant wife and a generally befuddled mind the positive effects of the Prozac seemed to weaken. Dr.Bakes said this "poop out" after a time was common and she switched me to a different medication but it did not work as well as the Prozac had initially. A few months later I would be back on Prozac.

Janet of course set about decorating the nursery. We had found out that we were to have a boy. She carefully monitored her diet and as the delivery approached she even had me attend some Lamaze classes which I found thoroughly dreadful. Janet's parents already had a granddaughter from her brother and were thrilled at the prospect of having a grandson. I am not sure exactly what my parents thought but they did come over of course the Christmas after the birth.

My son was born on November, 19th, 1993 and tipped the scales at a strapping 9 lbs 3 oz of which I felt justly proud. We decided to call him John. As we were not Scottish and I had never forgiven Dennis Law for stating he wanted England to lose the World Cup Final in 1966, I could not call him Ian. We chose John as the English equivalent. Whether this was directly in the honour of my boss/friend I am not quite certain but it did have an influence on the choice of name. His middle name would be Philip which was my middle name and also that of my father.

I obviously loved the little cone-headed fellow immediately but I had no idea how our lives would now develop. John was an unbelievably fussy eater and would cry for hours before going to sleep. I would spend hours on end walking around the house with him on my shoulder, gently patting his back.

Right around this time we decided, because of a tiny infant, that we needed a bigger house so we moved into a brand new, 4 bed, 4400 square foot house on Westchester, still in West University. Our little house on Marlowe proved to be problematic to sell but we rented it for a few months to a new trader from Connecticut, David Murphy who had just joined us to trade primarily gasoline and heating oil. He was extremely highly thought of within the industry and had spent time with Andy Hall at Phibro.

Boston

A few months later, in early 1994, Vitol purchased 51% of a small Natural Gas trading company based in Boston named Catex. Catex was owned by a chap called Mike Kutsch who had the vision, along with several others in the industry, to see that Natural Gas would soon be a massively traded commodity with huge potential for profit. Catex also had a small Houston office but their main trading and marketing office was in Boston. Neil Kelley was the driving force behind the modest purchase of Catex but it was an astute move. It gave Vitol an entree into the world of natural gas at a reasonable price and their main trader, Mike White, was utterly brilliant and made a great deal of money. Now Vitol wanted, as majority owner, to put one of its own employees in the Boston office. Ian suggested that I express interest, which I did, along with two other Houston employees. The three of us flew to Boston to meet Mike Kutsch. With my interest clear and Kutsch thinking I would be a good fit it was agreed that I should leave the crude oil team and explore the world of natural gas. Of course I would need to be replaced on crude oil in Houston and for this reason I approached and soon employed a Houston based trader from Chevron named Mickey Barrett. Mickey, unlike me, was very positive and upbeat and an excellent addition to the team.

Our new house in Houston sold very quickly to the friend of a friend without an agent and the small profit earnt almost offset the loss we took on selling our first smaller house.

Once Mickey had learnt the ropes of our crude trading activities and how we coordinated with other offices around the globe I was free to transfer to natural gas. At first I worked with the two Houston based traders making bi-weekly trips up to Boston but it was agreed that the family would move to Boston on a permanent basis. I was pleased to be leaving Houston as it was the place where the "old me" died but Janet was sad as she had a number of friends and of course her family were only 3 and a half hours drive away in Lafayette.

Ian was barely 4 months old when we found an ideal property to buy on Chestnut Circle in Brookline and so we moved to Boston. The packing and unpacking was all arranged by the Company but even so it was quite stressful especially with a young baby. For me, though somewhat chaotic, our frequent moves served as a distraction and to a degree kept the demons of depression slightly at bay. Catex was thriving both on the marketing side and on the trading side, led dynamically by Mike White. I was both learning the business and also trading natural gas futures in Mike's shadow but 100% for Vitol's account. I managed to make a few million dollars but it was dwarfed by Mike's trading profits. Although both Janet and I liked Boston as a City, I was still consumed by a general unease, that never really went away. It struck me that Catex did not really need me as it ran perfectly well by itself and it was not that they were hiding anything from us. One afternoon I drove out to the Harbour in my car and called Neil Kelley in Houston: I wanted to come back to Houston. Neil understood my reasoning and agreed that I rejoin the crude bench back in Houston. Although we had literally been in Boston only three months and just bought a house Janet was quite happy to move back though she had made one good English friend with a son the same age as John and had found a very nice grandmotherly type babysitter. We stayed in Boston just long enough for my parents to pay us a visit while Janet and I took a few days off at the Cambridge Beaches Resort in Bermuda, totally unaware of what was soon to become.

During my natural gas phase I attended a conference in London with Kutsch while Mike White was back at HQ managing quite a large speculative position that he and I were jointly responsible for. We were short and the market ticked up sharply and Mike was forced to cover and take quite a nasty loss. In London I commented oddly to Kutsch that Mike White was probably pleased by the loss as we deserved it. Kutsch looked at me like I had two heads and could not understand the logic of my statement. Clearly not everyone shared my twisted view of trading or indeed my twisted view of many things.

Back to Houston

By now we were pretty expert at moving, even with an infant, and we again bought a house in Houston this time in Royden Oaks, adjacent to River Oaks in the Centre of the City. The Boston house had sold immediately for what we had paid for it. I was actually glad to be back on the familiar territory of the crude bench and worked together with Mickey and of course the guys in London, Simon and Paul. The London team had been further bolstered by the addition of Mike Loya, formerly of Transworld but who had spent a brief period trading with Hess, as indeed had David Murphy. Mike and I, as well as being CFD adversaries, were also pretty good friends from my days in London when we would often play squash at the RAC Club. Mike was a large, well-built fellow who had a fearsome "coming around" forehand that scared the living daylights out of me should my service be poorly placed.

For a team building exercise, and essentially a bloody good time, Ian, Paul, Mike and I headed to Chamonix for a few days skiing. Paul was very accomplished having been an instructor in his younger days; Ian was, as you would expect, very determined and fearless though not in possession of the best technique while Mike and I were fairly accomplished but enjoyed a good lunch more than fighting the blizzard on the mountain. I recall having to share a bed with Ian that night. He must have just recently moved to Singapore as he received a call from his rather alarmed wife who informed him that there was a spitting cobra in the back garden of their house. I think it was on this trip that Ian confided in me that if he could have been anyone he would have chosen to have been Prince: he always did enjoy the limelight and was never one to shuffle quietly on the dance floor.

Soon after this trip Ian asked me to approach Enron, in particular a very senior woman named Rebecca Mark who was spearheading a recently announced massive new project to build a power plant in India. The plant would also include LPG facilities and Ian wanted me to see if there was any way we could get involved in this deal, especially the LPG side. When I called her office to arrange a meeting I was put in touch with one of her direct reports and so over I went to the Enron building to meet this chap. He explained that the Indian project was very much still on the drawing board stage but they did have a couple of power plants in the Caribbean for which they regularly tendered to buy 2 oil and that we should become involved. He told me to have our distillate trader, at that time David Gould, contact the person responsible for procuring fuel for these plants, a man by the name of John Barnes.

A tender for 2 oil was soon forthcoming and Gould contacted Barnes to make sure we could make them an offer that would be competitive. On the morning of the tender Barnes called Gould and told him he urgently needed to meet him in a nearby coffee shop. Gould went to the meeting and then recounted his story to Neil Kelley. Barnes had told Gould not to bid and he would make it worth his while not to do so. Clearly Barnes was in the pocket of someone and since Marc Rich was the supplier of fuel to these plants it had to be Marc Rich. Indeed this side of the business was handled by Marc's trusted lieutenant in the US Clyde Melzer who had taken the rap for Rich when he fled the US all those years before. Melzer avoided jail time but had to do community service which he apparently did with great gusto and served probation. Barnes was fired.

Some ten years later the Barnes-Melzer partnership was to re-emerge when John Barnes turned up and was working at Lyondell as a freight charterer. It turned out that Lyondell were grossly overpaying for the freight on their crude cargoes from Venezuela. There were huge kickbacks involved to the benefit of Barnes and Melzer but eventually the scheme was discovered in 2009 and in 2011 both Barnes and Melzer were sent to jail. Melzer, despite his perhaps dubious career operations, had always been highly regarded as a generous gentleman and now a grandfather within the industry.

Now since 1992 Vitol had been processing crude oil at the Come-by-Chance refinery in Newfoundland. This deal was run by Gary McCarthy in Houston and was of course supported by the crude and respective product teams. However, its profitability was always hard to ascertain with any degree of certainty and the refinery had already seen two previous owners go bankrupt. It was about the time that I moved back onto the crude bench that, led by Neil Kelley, a major push was made to buy the refinery. This would be a massive step for the company, one that was unanimously opposed by all the old partners. Neil actually employed one of his brothers as our "investment banker" on the project and the decision to buy it or not was put to a vote amongst the shareholders. Whether a decision had already been made to buy it and the vote was just for appearances sake I do not know. I was afraid of buying it thinking we would have no clue how to run such a complex industrial plant but, rather like the Democrats voting to give Dubya authority to invade Iraq, I felt it was a done deal and so I sheepishly (in feeling) responded to the vote email from Bob Finch with the words "I support". To which he light-heartedly responded, "Who Chelsea?".

As an aside, Bob was a fanatical Chelsea fan. He was a close friend of the late Matthew Harding, the young chairman who tragically died in a helicopter accident in 1996. I have also always strongly suspected, but never actually asked Bob, that he introduced Roman Abramovich to Chelsea which led to his subsequently buying the Club. My suspicion is based on the fact that Bob was tight with the Chelsea board and during the 90s we had a joint venture with Abramovich's company in Russia, Sibneft, called Sibvit. I am almost sure Bob must have dealt with young Roman and one thing could well have led to another.

Perhaps most alarmingly Gary McCarthy who had been running the processing deal was not only against buying the refinery but when the decision to do so was made he resigned! This was a huge shock as he was effectively one of the top four people in the Company together with Neil and both a fair distance behind Ian and Bob.

If we were going to convert the processing deal into an ownership deal we would need someone who at least had a fair bit of refining and processing knowledge and this person happened to be Jeff Hepper who had a year or two before relocated with his family from Los Angeles to Houston after it was decided we could cover the West Coast adequately from Houston. Jeff was a very decent and knowledgable Californian whose prodigious ability to perspire was almost as preternatural as my own.

Many decisions had to be taken quickly. A team of traders dedicated to the refinery led by Jeff would have to be assembled. It was also decided, somewhat naively, that since the refinery would make so much money it would be best operated out of the tax free jurisdiction of Bermuda where we already had a small office with two operators and one or two gasoline blenders to operate the blending operation in St. Eustatius. As previously mentioned David Fransen was sent to Bermuda to run this operation but it was quickly realised that we needed more than one man so one of Grimm's "boys" Richard Black, who we had let go for whatever reason in London, was hastily reemployed and sent to Bermuda.

It was already decided that Jeff Hepper and Simon Boddy from London would move to Bermuda in the spring of 1995 but they required someone with more paper trading expertise. And so it was that Neil and Jeff sat me down and said they would like me to go to Bermuda to work with Jeff and Simon. Personally I loved the idea as it meant I would be working in a tax free environment which was hugely beneficial to a British National. It also meant in all probability that one day I would head back to London which maybe, with the passage of time, I could face. Before moving to Bermuda we of course had to run and manage the refinery from Houston and I was charged with the hedging responsibilities which I immediately screwed up. The main risk factors for the refinery on the product side were the gasoline crack and the heating oil crack. Both can move independently so it is best when hedging to sell equal parts of both at an acceptable average. Foolishly as the gasoline crack rallied and heating oil failed to follow I hedged all of our gasoline production for a couple of months and none of our heating oil production. Both markets then moved against us. Jeff was rightly furious with me as was I with myself. I was once again deep in self-hatred mode and felt thoroughly wretched. Shortly thereafter, I did lead our group to the conclusion that one of the main enemies of a refinery was a backwardated crude market, i.e., prices today were higher than down the road. For this reason I instigated a 3mmbls 12 month front to back spread that did save the refinery some $7m.

Bermuda

Janet absolutely did not want to go to the point of crying. However, I explained to her the financial benefits and, to me, the attraction of living on an Island Paradise. She reluctantly agreed and we made a three day trip to find a house. Housing was, and I am sure still is, very tight in Bermuda and very expensive. You also had to jump through a series of hoops to obtain the required work visa but this really just meant you had to advertise the job in the local paper and make sure that it was impossible for any local to meet your job requirements.

Not only was housing expensive but there was not a great deal to choose from since a large hedge fund manager, Wolfgang Flotl, had just moved a number of people to the Island. This both limited supply and drove up the price of rent. There was one beautiful house in Fairylands right on the water, extremely modern and with air conditioning, which I desperately wanted to take. Unfortunately, Jeff Hepper's wife had deemed the proximity of the water to be a danger to her children and Janet felt likewise, so we did not take it. Instead we chose a huge old classic Bermuda home, very near Hamilton called Birdsaye. It had a beautiful garden, complete with an enormous grapefruit tree, and for a 3 year lease at $9,000 per month the owner, Shorty Trimingham, agreed to build a large swimming pool. The problem was the house was not air conditioned.

Our John was now 15 months old when we moved, once again, to Bermuda. All this moving would be enough to drive anyone crazy but like I said earlier, our peripatetic lifestyle served somewhat as a distraction to me. Janet was literally in tears when we left Houston, having just sold our house that we had bought barely 9 months prior. It took a while for all our furniture to arrive in Bermuda but once it did we had the house set up nicely. However, it was February and already the humidity was intense. We put window air conditioners in a couple of bedrooms and the kitchen to make those rooms bearable.

Simon was already in Bermuda when I arrived and shortly thereafter came Jeff and our Chief Accountant from Houston, Charlie Parker. Also joining our merry band of Islanders were Ian Mann and his wife Mel. He had come to administer the Cuban business. Previously being in Bahrain for about 18 years Ian missed the day to day activity and found the Cuban administration little more than secretarial work which it was. Ian retired a year or so later allowing canny David Fransen to become the very well paid Cuban administrative secretary.

Fransen was a pale, weak-chinned, political weasel and he knew how to play the system and the politics within Vitol. He was not really a trader and neither did he want to be as it involved trying to make money which was not easy. I suspect he could actually have managed the St. Eustatius blending operation quite adequately but he decided he could earn just as much if not more by effectively becoming a glorified secretary. He already had about $8m in "shareholder" equity which he promptly in Bermuda "bed and breakfasted" so that the $8m or so would be tax free when ultimately received. I am only aware of this cozy arrangement, which is perfectly legitimate, as the banker involved was the brother of a good friend of mine from college. He quite cannily suggested to Ian and Bob, to whom he was the ultimate yes man, that the Cuban business, because of time zone, would be better administered out of Bermuda than London or Geneva. In this way he was rather cleverly wriggling free of any decision making commercial responsibilities and instead assuming the role of Cuban administrator. As time went on should any other branch of the Vitol group require a Bermuda Company he would set it up and administer it. Of course to make it look like this was all extremely hard and taxing work he would oftentimes pop into the office late at night and fire off an email to London to make it look like he was beavering away late into the night.

One Saturday morning at home I received a phone call from Paul Greenslade. He informed me that Ian had decided to move Mike Loya over to Euromin, a disastrous aluminium venture we had entered on the sales pitch of some ex-Marc Rich people. It was another disaster and Ian felt Mike would be the best man to sort it out for us, which was probably true. We essentially owned a massive amount of aluminium metal that was now worth about $100m less than we had paid for it. What with this, the refinery and the fact the Cuban business was turning sour in that we were no longer being paid in oil but rather sugar which was very depressed, we were in a fine mess. To replace Mike, Greenslade said we had employed Paul Butcher from J. Aron which seemed reasonable enough.

Immediately the refinery appeared to be losing money and coupled with Janet's incessant complaining about one thing or another I felt my life to be utterly wretched. I would typically get up early in the morning and play with John before taking the short Vespa ride to the office. Upon my return home I was in charge of John until his bedtime. Oftentimes we would go for a jog up into the Fairylands area.

The refinery clearly had problems, not just bad economics. It was decided to replace the catalyst in the hydro-cracker, the most profitable unit in the refinery. Unfortunately we attempted to do this on the cheap by spending around $10m on catalyst rather than buying the actual UOP recommended catalyst for $16m or so. After several months of seriously sub-optimal cracker performance, which obviously cost a great deal of money, we bit the bullet and forked out the cash for the correct catalyst. I was also trying to make money trading natural gas but this was not working and I ended up losing about $1m. I was as usual beside myself with self-loathing and worthlessness. I would continue a habit I had started years ago in Geneva by writing, "FUCK" all over my notebook and etching it deeply into the paper. I would go around and around it in a rectangle ultimately covering whole pages in this sorry way. Simon would laugh his characteristically deep chortle and suggest we have it analysed by a psychiatrist. Many a true word are spoken in jest.

At lunchtime I would often take a break and walk into the nearby park where I would find a quiet spot and, with my head in my hands, openly weep for maybe ten minutes. I had no idea how I was going to survive. Janet was obsessed with the tiles on our kitchen floor and wanted them replaced. Quite why I don't know and the landlord would hear none of it. Our relationship of course was strained by Janet's unhappiness being on the Island, my ongoing despair and then the extra stress of caring for a toddler. In a sense it was business as usual for me in my new purgatory of a life.

At this opportune moment in the depths of my misery I received a call from my friend Steve Hendel at J. Aron in New York who, I had first met whilst at Shell in 1986. Together with his fellow partner Steve Semlitz, Hendel ran the very successful oil division of J. Aron. He asked if I would like to come and work for them in New York. Once again the prospect of a change beckoned and the chance of some short term relief. I went over for an interview and was offered the job coincidentally on the same day Ian Taylor was joining us in Bermuda for dinner, a dinner I made straight from the airport.

With Janet so unhappy and me in despair as usual I called Ian the day he returned to London to tell him of my decision. He was deeply disappointed and suggested I come to London to discuss it: he really saw me as part of the long term future of the company in which I had invested seven years of my life. He of course had no idea how much torment I had suffered during those years but that in no way was the fault of his or the company's. Bob Finch called me similarly and it was arranged the next day for me to fly to London and stay with Bob for a couple of days during which I could have some long discussions with him and Ian about my future. Ian had explained that he had even found a way around the relatively high UK income tax rate: by this I later realised that he was referring to their offshore Trust scheme in Jersey. Ian's suggestion was that I move back to London, something that I did find appealing. Financially, of course I should have stayed in Bermuda at least a year to pull the "bed and breakfast" stunt like Fransen, but I could barely see beyond one day to the next. Ian also told me that the refinery would be OK and that he was working on options already to sell it. One avenue he had explored was selling it to the Chinese arms manufacturer and trader Norinco who could use it to dispose of the Iranian crude they received from Iran in return for arms. The refinery configuration was actually well suited to run Iranian Light and Heavy. This avenue came to nothing but it did earn Ian a visit from MI5 who wondered why we were talking to a Chinese arms dealer. Bob asked me if money was the issue and probably foolishly I said it was not: I just wanted to be treated fairly like everyone else. We agreed that as soon as possible I would move to London. I called Janet, who at the time was in Houston, and flew myself to Houston as Bermuda was under hurricane watch from Hurricane Gilbert, which scored a direct hit. Upon arriving in Houston Ian called me and said upon reflection, it would in all probability be better if I moved back to Houston. He was concerned that Janet would not adjust to London just as she had failed to adjust to Bermuda. Either way I was OK. I now of course had to call Steve Hendel and tell him that the job offer I was 99% ready to accept was being rejected and I was choosing to stay with Vitol. Steve was disappointed, naturally, and tried to persuade me to reconsider but I had made up my mind. He tried to stress that I was much more of an Aron type of person than a Vitol person, whatever that was supposed to mean. However, I stuck by my decision. I believe the main reason for my considering moving to Aron was simply that it would involve a change, as changes, as mentioned, tended to provide a brief distraction from my mental torment. I have no doubt that I would have found the Aron job unbearably stressful.

It was a few more days before I could return to Bermuda to make the arrangements for my move back to Houston as Gilbert had decided to turn around and hit the Island for a second time. Fortunately, houses in Bermuda, painted in their attractive pastel shades, are very well built so there was little if any damage. My colleagues were mostly without water at their homes so would shower for a few days in the office. All the cars parked at the airport at the far eastern tip of the island were totalled, including mine. This saved me the need to sell it. I spent my last night in Bermuda in my large empty house, the furniture already on its way back to Houston, curled up on the hard wood floor with my dog Winston, after a heavy night's drinking with my friend Charlie Parker - the accountant, not the saxophonist

"Why I didn't leave Goldman Sachs"

The answer to the above is fairly obvious as I never joined, despite receiving a very nice offer of $500,000 for my first year. As well as Hendel and Semlitz, I knew their crude traders and at least one of their product traders, John Bertuzzi, who traded fuel oil incredibly profitably. I had first met John years earlier when he worked at MG, New York. At that time he was an accountant. The unsubstantiated rumour was that he had found some irregularities in the accounting of MG, New York, and so had been rewarded with a job as a distillates trader.

During the interview process I was interviewed via teleconference with Gary Cohn, in London. Gary is now second in command at Goldman and interestingly enough, I believe, a good friend of Ian Taylor's. Even at that time the profit objectives for each Aron trader were substantial. Hendel told me that they considered a seat at the desk to be immediately worth $5m to any trader occupying said seat. I presumed much of this $5m was deemed to come from "over the counter" customer business of which Goldman had, and would continue to have, a great deal. Goldman Sachs traded as a principal in the oil markets, as mentioned earlier, under the name J.Aron. They also had a large retail brokerage business as Goldman Sachs whereby they executed and cleared futures business on the NYMEX for a whole host of customers. Obviously there was a potentially massive conflict of interest here as the Aron traders would have dearly loved to know the futures positions of their competitors. Goldman Sachs assured all concerned that a very strong "Chinese Wall" existed between these two businesses and no information was ever shared. In 1990 a Senior Goldman broker, Leo Havilland, sued both Goldman and Aron, claiming that he had been pressured by Aron to reveal customer positions to the Aron traders. Aron and Goldman obviously contested this and I believe the case was resolved in arbitration.

Back to Houston
"Bachelors know more about women than married men; if they didn't they'd be married too". H.L. Mencken

In Houston I rejoined Mickey on the crude bench and Janet and I set about looking for another house. We found a good deal on an older home in River Oaks that needed a little work so we bought it and after about 3 weeks we were in. I was right back to square one. Except of course Janet was now pregnant for a second time and the baby was due in December. This was another reason for her wanting to leave Bermuda as she was not convinced the hospital was up to snuff, which of course it was. We also had to buy two new cars: I bought a year old Porsche 911 which I loved and Janet a BMW 530i station wagon, new. However, after barely a week Janet decided she did not want a station wagon but rather a 530i sedan so off to the dealership we trotted. Though merely a week old it was explained that the station wagon was now registered and thus was less valuable as it would have to be sold as used. So we promptly lost about $5,000. Then about ten days later Janet changed her mind again and decided she wanted an SUV, ideally a Land Rover Discovery. With my usual weakness I agreed and so another $5,000 was lost.

During my marriage to Janet she would always expect an expensive piece of jewellery for Christmas, Valentine's Day and our Anniversary. I ended up reluctantly spending a fortune at Tiffany in the galleria. I simply did so out of weakness to "keep the peace". Some peace: Chamberlain would have been proud.

Our marriage was extremely strained and as such lacked almost any intimacy. My amorous advances were rebuffed on so many occasions that I decided to give up on that department and mentally forced myself to dismiss that most natural of urges. So successful was I in this regard that I think I permanently inflicted upon myself psychological, erectile dysfunction which is sadly convenient today given the sorry state of my marriage.

Janet decided after having her two children it was time for a 32 year service and overhaul and so she decided to go with some breast implants and extensive liposuction. Personally, I was very disappointed, not just at the cost of well over $15,000, but due to the fact I simply did not approve of such superficiality. Additionally she would be in significant pain and would require extensive assistance from me for a couple of weeks which I resented given the elective nature of these surgeries. She chose a very well-known and highly regarded plastic surgeon, Dr.Mark Gilliland, who himself some ten years later would feature prominently in the news.

Apparently, while intoxicated, he sped in his Mercedes onto a sidewalk in the Galleria area, just a mile or so down Sage from where I was then living, and ploughed into two young British ladies who were both very seriously injured and hospitalised for quite some time but I believe eventually fully recovered. Gilliland fled the scene at speed, in spite of a shattered windshield which one of his victims had been flung into, but was apprehended and arrested by police outside his nearby apartment. He did express remorse when he heard how seriously he had injured the two young TV show producers. Obviously he was charged with a number of crimes and eventually went to trial which in itself had quite a dramatic twist. The charges he faced carried a potential penalty of a serious number of years. During the trial, witnesses described how he had mown down the two British ladies actually flinging them like rag dolls "high into the sky". Clearly having been intoxicated things did not look good for the Doctor. While the jury was deliberating Gilliland's legal team decided that it would probably be best to negotiate a swift plea bargain with the prosecution as their client was most likely looking at a decade or so behind bars. Now I believe the following all happened incredibly quickly and almost simultaneously as once a plea deal is agreed the jury no longer needs to deliberate. However, as a deal for two years prison was agreed, at the same moment the jury foreman emerged ready to pronounce their verdict. The jury had somehow found the defendant not guilty. What was the basis for this decision I am not sure but this was Texas after all. However, Gilliland had just, moments before, agreed to serve two years and that plea deal carried the day. What a charade, yet at the end of the day justice appears to have been served, albeit in a dramatic fashion.

On a slightly more humorous note around this time I had a late night out with a couple of industry colleagues from Amoco and Mobil. We enjoyed a few martinis and I partook of one of the first cigars of my life. I blame the cigar for what was later to happen. After a short drive home I entered my house and in the hallway had to stretch to step over a child gate at the foot of the stairs. As I did so I'm afraid I lost control of my bodily functions: the world dropped out of my bottom (as opposed to the bottom dropping out of my world as was far more typical) and I dreadfully soiled a brand new Valentino suit that I happened to be wearing. Somehow, after a thorough rinsing, my wife summoned up the courage to take it to the dry cleaner's the following day. For some reason I have been forever plagued with being caught short. I even recall years earlier in London when taking the tube home, sometimes hopping off the train, dashing down a tunnel to a quiet spot where I could relieve myself, run back to my platform, and take the next train home.

Shortly after this unpleasant incident I paid a reciprocal visit to Amoco in Chicago where we took in a Bulls basketball game, complete with Michael Jordan. I had just come off a diet where I shed about 15 lbs so I let myself go by having a 48 oz steak the first night and a 24 oz steak the next night followed by a large room service hamburger at the hotel: no wonder the weight did not stay off.

I soon developed quite a taste for the odd cigar now and then but would never touch a cigarette but once. This was probably due to the fact that in a drunken haze one night I did try a cigarette but inserted the already lit end into my mouth with most unpleasant consequences.

After Janet had fully recovered from her surgeries she was very proud of her now "perfect" body, so much so that she even commented to me why would someone with such a body want to have sex with someone like me. Now I was by no means Charles Atlas but neither was I Quasimodo.

At work the crude group was overall having an OK year but I would frequently argue with the two Pauls in London about our approach to CFDs. The market still traded pretty much as I saw it and had not yet switched to the "brute force and ignorance" approach that they favoured and would ultimately prevail. We used CFDs mainly to hedge our dated exposure that stemmed from our various dated related crude oil purchases be they Iranian, Russian, North Sea or West African. I think the two Pauls had the impressive record of losing money on perhaps 100% of the CFDs they traded but this did not appear to register with them.

Greenslade paid Mickey and me a visit around this time primarily to engage in a discussion with his old boss at Shell, Bob Brand, over a relatively small dispute we had concerning a loading at the Bonny terminals in Nigeria which Shell operated. If I recall correctly the dispute was for no more than $200,000. Bob was a congenial, greying, pleasant chap: obviously no match for Greenslade. The three of us headed over to the Shell building in Houston where we sat down with Bob. After exchanging a few pleasantries Greenslade went into his planned dishonest diatribe that was scarcely credible but it seemed to befuddle Bob sufficiently for him to give in to most if not all of our demands. Mickey and I barely said a word during the meeting and when we left I must admit I felt a little embarrassed. I suspect, but cannot be sure, that Mickey felt likewise.

Somewhat similarly, whenever we needed to spin a barely credible yarn to Platts about a dated Brent trade we had executed or had claimed to execute, I would almost always let Greenslade call Platts, even late in his evening, as obviously being a pathological liar was beneficial at such times.

One of the benefits of working in Houston was that we had four floor seats to every other Houston Rockets Basketball game. These were great: if you stuck your legs out you could trip over one of the players, not that I ever tried or would recommend doing this. The tickets were of course closely guarded by Neil Kelley, the keeper of the tickets, and one had to have a special client in town in order to get to use them. Luckily for me when Ian was visiting Houston I would have the privilege of taking him to a game and chauffeuring him around the city.

I was pretty much perpetually shrouded in the cold fog of depression despite still being on Prozac. When in this state I felt as if I was totally alone in a wilderness devoid of joy or the possibility of joy. I spent a great deal of time with my son who of course I loved deeply yet I found my entire existence an almighty strain. In the office I always appeared intense but would at times lose my temper a little with the phone answering girls as they passed the myriad of broker calls on to me. "No brokers" I would shout, which alleviated some of my immediate stress. Ian would call me most days early in his Singapore day and was often in a bad mood himself. I actually thought I performed a valuable service, to a degree, in letting him vent his anger on me. I had enough anger inside already, what was a little more.

My responsibilities still included submitting offers to the monthly ENAP and ANCAP tenders. We actually won the ENAP tender once or twice with a Nigerian cargo. ANCAP appeared to have taken a liking to Iranian Light but we, and other traders, had an understanding that we would not offer Iranian in tenders as this was the realm of NIOC. However, I had the bright idea that surely we could offer Iranian Light out of the strategic storage in South Africa. That was Iranian that was already out in the market place and it was not a direct offer from Kharg Island. Ian and Greenslade agreed that it seemed a reasonable idea and so they arranged for the SFF to back us on an offer of Iranian Light from South Africa delivered to Montevideo. Of course the journey from South Africa across the South Atlantic was much shorter than that from Charge Island so we won the tender with ease, and a decent profit margin. The offer was of course meant to be strictly private and confidential but unfortunately it turned out that the Coastal representatives in South America found out what had happened and they informed the Iranians who were furious. This caused quite a headache for poor Ian Taylor but as it turned out our long running crude for products exchanges with the Iranians were coming to a natural end so the damage was limited. I think we had to pay the Iranians at least the profit we had made so as not to be blacklisted so it was a disappointing end to what I had thought was a clever move.

As had been the case when I was previously in Houston I did a great deal of business with Exxon who coordinated all global activity through their head office in Florham Park, New Jersey. I had an excellent relationship with their trader, Jim Adams, who though from England had been in the US for a couple of decades. I sold them many North Sea cargoes and cargoes of Iranian and Urals both into NWE and into Lavera in the Med. Exxon was the main equity holder of the Australian Crude Gippsland. If ever they offered this to us it was always with the understanding that we would never show it to another Australian refiner: we would have to take it out of the region which was never easy. One time Jim called me and said they had a Gippsland cargo they simply could not place and we could take it any place we pleased including Australia. That night my Singapore office placed it at a decent profit into another Australian refiner. The following day Jim called me up all flustered. He apologised profusely but said he had made a terrible error and he should NOT have told us we could sell it into Australia. He had even gone so far as to tell his boss Jerry Staffen that he had told us that the normal conditions applied, which he recognised was not true but he had to cover himself. We were placed in the unpleasant situation of throwing my main contact Jim, under the bus, or allowing his boss to be furious at us and to call Ian and ask for compensation for our deemed transgression. We decided to protect Jim but poor Ian had to sit through several long "fireside chats," as we jokingly termed them, with Jerry Staffen who demanded that we apologise and pay an appropriate amount as recompense, which we did. Fortunately Ian did not blame me for either incident but it was no surprise he had no hair.

In December our second baby was born, a beautiful little girl that we named Camille Elizabeth. Fortunately for us Camille was an easier baby to handle than John had been. I was still severely depressed at work and my overall stress level was obviously increased by less sleep. Janet recalls seeing me giving Camille a bath one night staring blankly into space and I told her I was still depressed. Understandably this had a profound effect on Janet seeing me like this with our precious new baby.

As 1995 rolled into 1996 and bonuses were awarded I was given my lowest bonus ever: it was only $75,000. I was shocked and insulted especially as I had shown loyalty to Vitol by not leaving to join J. Aron. Ian explained that money was tight and I had not had a particularly good year but my new year was already shaping up very well and I should make a point of coming knocking on his door in a year's time.

1996 was indeed my best trading year at Vitol but perhaps because of that arguably my most painful. It was a very bullish year for WTI and I played this well throughout the year by buying large front to back spread positions coupled with large long WTI-Brent spread positions. I augmented this with regular WTI put shorts which always expired worthless. I managed this position solely on my own and very intensely. Even though I was doing well I was profoundly unhappy and most evenings when I got home I would go up to my bedroom and cry on the bed for a while and then write in my diary how I felt. I would write that I hated my life and desperately wanted to escape my living hell, but how could I? I was still a failure and always would be (even though I was making good money). When would I ever be free? I felt I was serving an endless prison sentence. Any slight market turn against me would fill my body with chest-crushing anxiety. The agonies I felt were physical as well as mental. I regretted yesterday, hated today and dreaded tomorrow. A wretched sorrow engulfed my soul as I fell back into my dark cellar. My diary deliberately made it appear that it was work that was solely responsible for my anguish and feeling of being in prison but in reality it was my entire existence.

Meanwhile in London the two Pauls expanded our dated Brent trading. Still almost all if not every CFD they traded lost money: it was quite uncanny. On my own volition I would trade the odd CFD early in the year, less than 10 in number, that were obvious money makers and each one indeed was. I'm sure this irked the London traders. In an effort to foster greater team spirit I decided no longer to cherry pick CFDs that would make money but would pick up on their strategy and point these trades out to them. I found a trade that should be good for a 40 cts loss which London loved, so I executed it. In fact they loved it so much I did another. It turned out my 40 cts/bbl loss was a little low as it lost 80 cts/bbl.

"Conscience is an inner voice that warns us somebody may be looking".   H.L. Mencken

Greenslade was increasingly focused on Nigeria which from a trading standpoint was still largely dominated by Arcadia and Addax. Nigeria was one of the most corrupt countries in the world and is till today by all accounts. In order to get a contract you had to pay something of the order of 18-20 cts/bbl, i.e., close to $200,000 per standard 900,000bbl cargo. This "commission" was obviously used to take care of people all the way from those at the loading terminal to those in the clerical office to the much higher ups all the way up to the Head of NNPC and PPMC (the Products and Pipeline Management company) and even to the President of the country himself. It was a question of having the right people connect you with the right people. Greenslade arranged for Vitol to buy out the Chevron half of the Calson joint venture, a Bermuda registered firm that traded crude for the joint benefit of Chevron and NNPC. It was through Calson that we would over the next decade plus earn many hundreds of millions if not billions through bribing the right people. If you had the right people in your pocket you might get an extra 2,000 or more barrels loaded onto your ship after the meters had been disconnected and thus did not appear on the final bill of lading figures. With the right contact in the clerical and contractual office you could have your pricing dates changed to significantly lower the price you paid for your cargo. All of this cost money but the investment paid out many times over. Greenslade also set about establishing several Bermuda based front companies, with the help of Secretary Fransen. Two of these were Sunshine and Mansell. In this way when NNPC awarded contracts it would not seem so obvious that they were giving them all to Vitol.

Nigeria was in the odd situation of producing around 2mmbbls/day of crude oil and owning several refineries. Thus it would appear they could process much of their own crude and supply products into their own domestic market. However, the refineries never operated. Traders such as Greenslade, allegedly, would make hefty payments to the Nigerian senior executives and politicians to maintain this absurd status quo. The traders would proceed to make obscene profits on the products cargoes, usually of dubious specifications, but certified by a cooperative inspector in Nigeria as if they were on specification, which they sold to Nigeria. Vitol and its fronts including Calson would grow to be the largest lifter of Nigerian crude. This had the added benefit of giving them huge dated Brent exposure which they would profitably optimise by buying at ridiculously high prices or selling at ridiculously low prices cargoes of dated Brent to affect the Platts dated quote to suit their exposure. Sometimes this would require the aid of other traders, so the Mayfair Pub in Mayfair London, became notorious as the location where the future short term path of the dated Brent price would be agreed. Vitol's typical partner would be Arcadia whose lead trader Marcus Green sadly passed away in 1999. He died on a Monday from cancer that he had kept secret from his colleagues and even his wife. He had been at his desk working on the Friday before his death. Marcus was succeeded almost seamlessly by my old friend Peter Bosworth. Peter was a real expert in Nigeria spending much time down there and even learning to speak in some of the local pidgin dialects.

In 2001 Mr. Obaseki, the Head of PPMC, was in Houston attending an oil conference. Greenslade, allegedly, needed to get some cash, $100,000 to $200,000, to him so he asked Mickey Barrett to deliver a suitcase containing such cash. Mickey, cognisant of the Foreign Corrupt Practices Act in the US, wisely refused. Greenslade, allegedly, according to another Vitol London crude trader, flew to Houston and made the delivery himself. The trader who told me this also told me how "The Chairman" had recently become a vocal critic of Bob Finch which to me was utterly unbelievable and beyond the pale.

Vitol was so engrained in Nigeria that by 2003 they needed a trusted man of their own on the spot and Ian and Greenslade chose their old friend, a gruff, Rugby loving South African named Rod Gavchon from the Finnish company Neste to move under very lucrative terms to Abuja and to take care of matters as necessary on the ground. On hearing this news I sent my old friend and colleague, Mickey Barrett a cheeky Yahoo instant message (IM), joking that they now had a new "bag man" for Nigeria. Mickey curtly replied via IM, that he traded futures in Houston and had no idea about Nigeria. That was news to me.

At a similar time I received, in error obviously, an IM from Mickey one afternoon around 3pm saying essentially, "Watch out: WTI is about to get very expensive". Clearly this was meant to be just sent internally as an alert to his colleagues that he was going to aggressively bid up WTI in the Platts window to aid in the pricing out of swaps or physical crude that they had that evening. I did not respond to the IM.

In 2013 a massive scandal gripped Nigeria where they suddenly announced that their country had been robbed essentially of some $6B dollars by dubious oil trades between NNPC and trading companies, including the likes of Vitol and Trafigura. The traders obviously said that this was nonsense. The scandal has appeared to go away, presumably in the usual fashion of applying grease to the wheels that required it.

Obviously Nigeria is an incredibly poor country due to the corruption. Much crude and product is stolen by locals and sold on the black market. The crudest example of this would be when people would try to tap into a gasoline pipeline and steal the gasoline. Clearly this is very dangerous and on several occasions massive explosions would ensue killing hundreds of people. From the sanctuary of your comfortable West End office, who would bother make the connection between your corrupt actions and these human tragedies.

As 1996 progressed I continued to do well culminating in the June WTI expiration when I had kept around 1mmbls of length going into the last day convinced that it was going to expire very strongly. I was right and probably added another $1m to our profitability. Bob Finch emailed me a short congratulatory note. That day so happened to coincide with our 30th Anniversary and though now with more employees than ever the whole company set off for a grand two day celebration again at the Forte Village in Sardinia. I was mentally exhausted. Some time had been set for a "Trading Committee Meeting" the morning we arrived at Heathrow before taking our charter flight to Sardinia. For the first time I was invited to this meeting which was great.

On the flight over, exhausted and relieved from the successful June WTI expiration, I proceeded to drink far too much as I sat chatting next to our Houston ship charterer, John Curtin, a very pleasant ex-Shell Englishman. I became so drunk that before we landed I vomited all over the place, including on myself. I was a total mess. John kindly suggested that I must have become ill after eating the prawns that were served. Unfortunately I was in no state to attend the Committee meeting which had always been a goal of mine, and instead sneaked off behind a sofa and attempted to sleep.

"A deception that elevates us is dearer than a host of low truths"
Alexander Pushkin

Shortly thereafter our Houston Gasoline Traders were involved in an amazing act of chutzpah. China had slowly but steadily been increasing its activities in the International Oil market and at this stage they were still a net exporter of products. Our Singapore office would do business with them and move cargoes within the region. The Chinese desperately wanted to move a cargo of Gasoline to the United States and ideally California. Now California has the strictest gasoline specifications of any State and only one or two refineries outside of California could make gasoline of the required standard. Nonetheless our gasoline traders told the Chinese that we would buy a cargo of their gasoline delivered into Long Beach. The Chinese were ecstatic. A number of Chinese officials joined a number of the Vitol gasoline traders at the port of Long Beach to witness the momentous occasion of a cargo of Chinese gasoline being discharged into a Californian tank. Celebratory drinks were had by all at the terminal before everyone departed once the discharge was complete. At this point Vitol brought in another vessel, reloaded the gasoline and promptly took it down to Mexico where it was sold, and rightly belonged.

Another interesting China story involved a mono-buoy that we had towed to China all the way from the UK, I believe from Stanlow, to use offshore China. Now this buoy was to be used to allow large ships to come alongside and moor while they discharged their cargo. As such it was obviously very firmly fixed to the sea bed. It also was equipped with some sophisticated electronic equipment. The "firmly fixed" bit seemed to escape the attention of a group of Chinese pirates who decided they wanted to steal the buoy. They encircled it in a large chain but of course it would not budge. The Chinese coast guard soon got wind of their escapades and a high speed boat chase to the Chinese coast soon ensued. The pirates were captured and immediately executed.

It was in 1995 or 1996 that the busy buzz of activity in the trading room was broken by a cry of "What the Fuck!" from a furious and worried Neil Kelley. Neil had given a sensitive fax to one of the girls in the office to send to our contact in a national oil company in South America. She had mistakenly sent it to the general trading fax number in that office instead of the private fax of the intended recipient, the boss of the group. For a number of years the boss, we'll call him Juan Valdez, for sake of privacy, had a "mutually beneficial relationship" with us. The fax of course contained sensitive information as to how he was going to make sure we won a certain piece of business. Fortunately, after a couple of hurried phone calls, Neil apparently managed to defuse the potentially dangerous situation and no harm was done. Juan would appear again in my life some years later under quite different circumstances.

Throughout the summer of '96 despite my success I was in total despair. I vowed to myself that life could not go on like this: I could not cope with the stress of my job, every slightest twist filling me with petrifying anxiety and a sense of failure, and the stress of a marriage that was constantly strained plus bringing up two children. The only thing I could do was retire and seek out a quieter, peaceful life which at that time meant returning to Jersey to become a lawyer. In actuality I think returning to Jersey would have been a nightmare given the fact a short period with my parents brought on a profound state of depression and I was not sure how Janet would adjust to the Island, although a totally different proposition to Bermuda. I thought it would be a great place to bring up and educate the children so this became my plan. During that summer I would send emails to myself, time stamped so that they would not be delivered until February or March of 1997. The emails detailed my mental agony and anguish and told me not to be shaken from my plan. On one occasion I did actually send an email to Mike Loya and maybe Ian saying how devastated I was by my day's losses, to which Mike replied "We all have bad days". If only I could have had or indeed have that attitude.

In November of 1996 my son John turned three and we had a very pleasant and enjoyable party at home, complete with clown for the kids, and beer and wine for the adults. For one brief moment that night I thought I might be able to continue this life a little longer but it was a fleeting thought.

"Woman inspires us to great things then prevent us from achieving them". Dumas

Janet for some reason had never liked this older house in River Oaks so around Christmas she conspired with our usual agent, Betty Carpenter, to sell it. I did not want to but with my usual strength of character rolled over and agreed. I did not want to sell it for two prime reasons: besides being premature, I still wondered if I really needed to retire and secondly I did not want my colleagues to see us sell the house and move into rented accommodation, which we did, as they might think I was planning to leave and therefore screw me on my bonus.

The start of 1997 was not as good trading-wise as had been 1996. However, as Ian suggested I called him saying I hoped I would get a good bonus as the crude group had had a great year and I was roughly responsible for about $19m of the $50m we appeared to have made, much to my amazement. Overall the company had done very well trading but we had large write-offs thanks to Euromin, the refinery and the Cuban business. Bonus money would still be tight. As I'm sure most of my colleagues did, I hated the wait up to mid-March to find out your bonus. It seemed counterproductive to me to make the traders go through this period of high anxiety for almost a quarter of the year because you always feared that a mistake made prior to bonus time would rightly or wrongly affect your prior year's bonus. Management explained that they did it this way so that bonuses were paid only when the accounting books had been firmly closed for the prior year. In Houston our Chief Accountant and CFO was Keith Swaby. He would always have a number of questions about last year's dealings, as he sought to close the books. He went through the Houston crude books with me and we showed about a $10m loss, which was about right. At this time he made a comment that struck me as odd: he half chuckled as he said well obviously we made about $19m on pure trading but we managed to move about $30m of profit to Geneva through our Brent "tax optimisation". I responded. "yeah, but that's just following the "at cost" rules is it not and obviously a great benefit". "Well, I hope we never get audited," he replied. I never could quite understand this as, as far as I understood, we were doing nothing untoward.

It was in late 1996 I believe that Ian sent out a note to all the traders detailing what we were doing in Yugoslavia, as war raged in the Balkans. It struck me that we had been providing the diesel fuel to Slobodan Milosevic and his army so that they could continue their massacre of the Bosnian Serbs. I mentioned this to Ian the next time we spoke and he fumbled an answer in the affirmative. I think one convenient delivery was made just before the massacre of some 6,000 Serbs at Srebrenica, but "stuff happens" when you don't discriminate. I was appalled that we would stoop to such a low level and would like to say that this was one of the reasons I resigned but that was not the case. It did not impact my decision. It has been well documented how Vitol used the notorious Serbian war Lord, Arkan, to settle a dispute in Yugoslavia and paid him $1m to do so.

I would have the occasional chat with Greenslade as bonus time approached and he said it looked like we had made close to $50m overall so that he and I, as de facto heads of the group, should be looking at a pretty decent bonus of the order of $1m. Ian had always told me never to discuss my bonus with anyone. In fact on at least two occasion he had told me to act disappointed even if I was not when chatting about it to my colleagues. I of course obliged. I was amazed at the $50m figure Greenslade mentioned we had made overall. I did not see how that was possible since very close to 100% of the many CFD trades transacted by London had lost money. $30m seemed a more realistic figure in my mind. Then shortly before bonuses were to be announced a bombshell dropped: the $50m figure was indeed incorrect and a $20m discrepancy had been found in the very complex crude books and accounts. When Greenslade told me this my heart sank as he went on to say, well we all did well on WTI last year so we should all be ok. He was trying to slime his way into taking credit for the work that had almost killed me. I received my bonus from Neil Kelley; it was $900,000. Neil explained it should have been more but money was tight due to all of the massive non-trading write-offs we had. I called London to see how they were feeling about things. I spoke to our genial Mediterranean trader, Gilles Chautard, who told me to be careful as the two Pauls were furious at their bonuses, and at me in particular, as Ian had told them what mine was as it obviously exceeded theirs by quite a margin. Thanks Ian. Now I had no say at all in who was paid what and thus the fury aimed at me by the Pauls was absolutely unjustified. Greenslade had never hesitated in London to screw Simon, for instance on a bonus, to his own benefit. I had simply done nothing, I was extremely disappointed in Ian, especially after he had always told me never to discuss my bonus, he then trumpets it to all and sundry at a particularly sensitive moment. Still what was done was done. For a few weeks now I had been getting these random emails from myself, written some 6-9 months ago, telling me how much I hated my life and I had to retire. This was pretty eerie and I got flustered every time one popped up should someone be looking over my shoulder.

So after one final discussion with Janet we agreed that we would follow through on the plan and later that summer move to Jersey. I telephoned Ian to inform him of my decision. He was furious. "How could I do this after receiving such a great bonus? I would be sorry and live to regret it". I was quite upset by this but lamely said nothing more than, "Please accept my decision as it is what I wish to do. I want to retire". I could not bring myself to tell the truth. I was sure Ian was right in that professionally I would be sorry, were it not for the fact that I felt I had to do what I was doing to save both myself and my family. It was not a pleasant conversation and it further hurt me to depart on such terms with Ian, a man I had respected and held in such high regard for nine years and considered a great friend. He did ask if I could just delay telling anyone else about my decision as he had a lot of people to deal with who were unhappy with their bonuses and it would further complicate things if the person, i.e., me, who got the best bonus, was leaving. Again I could not believe he had revealed my bonus to everyone.

About a week later when Ian sent an email out to the company saying that I was retiring and "hanging up my boots" I received a number of phone calls. The first was from Greenslade who, with his usual lack of sincerity, said if anyone deserved a break it was me and he wished me luck. Bob Finch, often a man of few but well-chosen words, also called. I had a deep respect for Bob and really liked him. He was by any estimation the greatest trader we had and had done more for the Company than anyone other than perhaps Ian. I told him I was simply burnt out and had no more to give. He suggested I take a 6 month break and then come back which was probably the most sensible suggestion of all but I explained that I was going to move back to Jersey.

I then had a sit down with Neil Kelley who made a cryptic comment that what I was doing was very smart. I had no idea what he meant. I was pretty amazed that no-one had the slightest inkling of the massive mental torment and anxiety I endured coupled with near suicidal depression. I had obviously kept that hidden very well.

Life after Vitol

My children, John and Camille, were now a mere 4 and 2. We made a trip to Jersey to look at houses which were all quite expensive as it is a desirable location and, rather like Bermuda, a tax haven, or as the Jersey government prefers to say, an Offshore Finance Centre. We found a house and prepared to buy it, negotiating over the phone from Houston.

That summer we spent partly in our rented apartment and partly in our house in Santa Fe, New Mexico that we had bought a couple of years earlier. I absolutely loved Santa Fe. On returning to Houston and with the house negotiations dragging on I was invited to lunch by my old friend Steve Hendel and Mike White, formerly of Catex. Hendel and his partner Steve Semlitz had recently left J. Aron and established a trading company inside Amerada Hess, termed HETCO. Amerada Hess was still primarily owned and run by its aged but active owner Leon Hess with whom Hendel, and indeed Hendel's father, had been very close. Hendel had employed Mike White, after receiving a recommendation from me, when Mike left Catex-Vitol as he felt grossly under compensated, which he was. His departure sadly sent Catex-Vitol, as it had been known after we purchased 51%, into a tail spin. They had tried to replace Mike with a couple of cowboy traders who ultimately turned a great little money-making venture into a massive financial liability. Hendel was a very persuasive, slightly eccentric, and likeable fellow. He told me I was too young to retire and should come up to New York, rent a house in Westchester County where he lived, and work for him at Hess Energy Trading Company (HETCO). The idea did sound appealing and I was feeling less stressed as doubtless Bob Finch had expected, so I mentioned it to Janet. She actually preferred the idea greatly over moving to Jersey which she was never really keen on. I accepted Hendel's offer. Perhaps I should have first called Ian and or Bob and offered to come back, duly rested, but such had been Ian's anger when I resigned I did not feel comfortable so doing. I did call Ian to tell him I was joining Hess and he pretty much said, "Fine". Not only had I left Vitol that April but so had Bob's closest friend and fellow fuel trader, Mike Metz, who joined Koch in London. Dale Snyder our West Coast fuel oil trader, joined Westport, Paul Butcher went back to J. Aron and Bob Borrowman a senior LPG trader went to Trammochem. Their reasons of course were all different to mine.

New York

Once again we were on the move. With two children in tow we made a trip to Greenwich, Connecticut and the main towns of Westchester County to look at houses to rent. Larchmont, where Hendel himself lived, was our favoured destination, as it was a mere 32 minutes on the train to Grand Central from where the office on the Avenue of the Americas was about a ten minute walk. We found a house about 15 minutes from the station and signed a year lease. For a couple of months I would commute up to New York from Houston for the week and return at weekends before the house was ready for us to move in.

When the family was all ready to move up in December we made the journey with our Houston based baby sitter to make things slightly easier. Upon arriving in New York Janet and I got into yet another argument and I quipped "Oh no. This was a mistake". That comment struck a chord in her head but she somewhat misunderstood it. I had meant going back to work with a stressful marriage and young children was once again going to be more than I could take. She simply thought it was the work aspect. I was simply unable to combine the two roles and it caused me sheer unending mental agony.

HETCO traded in a very different way to Vitol. They did have a London office but each trader simply speculated on futures and Brent as he saw fit. The first couple of months I did pretty well but soon the stress of trading plus a stressful home life was again taking its toll. Janet had to find schools, which she did, for the children and although a relatively mild New York winter it was very unfamiliar and inconvenient for us to be constantly bundling and unbundling the children. Once again we were not happy. I enjoyed working with my new colleagues who were generally a pleasant bunch most of whom I knew. Of course, there was Mike White making his customary fortune on Natural Gas.

Like most companies, HETCO, had the odd private source or two that they hoped would once in a while pop up with a nugget of precious information. One such source for the Steves was a mysterious Middle Easterner who would now and then call with some essentially worthless piece of Middle Eastern gossip. The Steves, however, explained to me that once in their J. Aron days they had received a call from him and he said, "Listen. I am about to read you the official Opec communique set for release, as the meeting has ended". "How come?" they obviously asked. "Well, I am reading it over the guy's shoulder as he types it!". This was of course incredible and explained why they continued to speak to him for a number of years just in case another such golden nugget could be mined.

I actually enjoyed working with Hendel in particular who was a very interesting fellow: he had the odd habit of walking around the trading room sticking small pieces of sellotape or sticky tape all over his face including his nose and ear lobes. He was very much into the New York Art scene and some ten years later had success in producing the Broadway musical hit "Fela!".

Unfortunately, during my time there I never had the chance to meet the late Mr. Leon Hess, who started this company so many decades earlier. He was by all accounts quite a character. Our senior products' trader cheekily asked him if he thought there was any truth to the rumour that Jimmy Hoffa was buried at the Meadowlands, which Mr. Hess owned. "Truth is sometimes stranger than fiction," was the enigmatic response. I did have the opportunity to meet his son, John, who succeeded him as Chairman, and he was a charming gentleman.

I used the train ride to and from Larchmont to read a great deal: "Anna Karenina," "War and Peace," "Crime and Punishment," "Into Thin Air" and the aptly named "It's been down so long it looks like up to me" come to mind. I would often ride in with Hendel. The trains were incredibly efficient compared to those back in the UK and I always had a seat. In about ten months of commuting there were only two days when we suffered any form of meaningful disruption.

The blackness of depression was always knocking at the door and after a bad day it would turn to utter despair. I did learn more discipline, trading with HETCO, and over the year I managed to make a reasonable amount of money.

Given my fragile mental state I did seek out a therapist and recall making an appointment one cold winter's evening. As I walked from the Larchmont station, I had forgotten the address but thought I could remember the street. So I walked down the street I suspected and found what looked like a therapist's office on the lower floor of a house, with the lights on. I walked in and sat down on a comfortable coach, typical of those found in therapists' offices or rooms. Soon a pleasant, elderly gentleman came in and, as he sat down, without any introductions, we began to discuss my life and my problems as I saw them. After an hour or so he essentially said that my wife and I needed to work together and formulate a plan of action that would work for both of us as clearly my current path was not working for me and probably not for her either. I stood up, thanked him and left. We never exchanged names. I did not pay and I have no idea if he was the therapist I had made an appointment with or even if he was a therapist, though I strongly suspect he was.

Around September a couple of old traders I knew who were consulting for Enron's oil trading division in Houston called and asked to meet. Wyatt and Clive were a couple of old semi-retired former traders who had both made a lot of money. They talked to me about how Enron needed more in-house crude experience and how they knew it must be hard for my Southern wife to settle in to the cold of the north-east. Now Enron had never had much of a reputation on crude oil, perhaps since the InterNorth debacle back in the mid-late 80s but I mentioned this to my wife. Janet jumped all over it. Great she said. Let's go back to Houston. I'll arrange a trip to look at houses and we will move as soon as possible. Well, I guess that was that, sort of.

Now Wyatt and Clive were slightly older than me and both had very interesting stories. Wyatt had started at Sun and soon moved to Phibro where he made a name for himself as a very successful products trader. I had been told that he had been a massive mover of product up the Colonial pipeline from the Gulf Coast to the north-east. If the cost of transportation was 5 cts/gallon say, obviously what you bought in the Gulf Coast you had to sell at slightly more than 5 cts over to cover your costs. Wyatt somehow would sell at something like 4.5 cts/gallon over the Gulf Coast and moved vast quantities in this way as other traders and end users would voraciously gobble up his barrels which he, in their eyes, was moving at a loss. Now the thing was, apparently, there was a fault in the Phibro trading system. Freight, whether seaborne or pipeline tariff, was not always correctly allocated to the product that it was moving. This was especially the case on the Colonial Pipeline. Wyatt's trading did not reflect the 5 cts/gallon pipeline tariff. This ended up in some unallocated freight account that presumably got pro-rated over all traders at the end of the year, or was otherwise dealt with. So with no freight effectively to pay Wyatt was making 4.5 cts/gallon on vast quantities of product which amounted to many millions of dollars, off which he was paid some very handsome bonuses.

This was not Wyatt's only claim to fame. After Phibro he had gone to a prior iteration of an Amerada Hess Trading company, along with his Phibro colleagues, David Murphy and Mike Gamson, the latter two were now at Vitol in Houston. Wyatt and Clive both explained to me that they were only consultants at Enron working about 2.5 days a week as they were not permitted to trade by virtue of their disability insurance settlements that they had received. Wyatt apparently had about 5 long term disability insurance policies and while at Hess he suffered some health problem and 3 of those five policies went on to pay him extremely handsomely long into the future. He, of course, did not want to trade to jeopardise these payments. He told me that as a child his father had been seriously injured and was unable to work but did not have any disability insurance: he vowed that the same would not happen to him. I think he was advising me to think of doing likewise but of course I did not. Somewhat similarly Clive was supposedly hit by a brick or slate falling off a tall building in Houston and this affected his mental sharpness so he too collected on a nice disability policy. If anyone actually needed such a policy I would suggest it would be yours truly but of course I never had the good sense to take one out. As was obvious to anyone who knew me I had very serious depression and anxiety issues and that trading was about the worst possible thing I could do for a living given my obsessive nature and absolute petrifying and paralysing fear of failure which I felt every time the slightest trade went wrong.

"Et tu, Ian?"

Right after, I received a surprise email from Ian Taylor titled something like "Ground control to Major Tom," as often in the past we used to joke in such a manner. Ian said he was in Boston but could fly down to New York tomorrow to meet me to discuss my "Re-entry". Obviously I was thrilled. We met the following evening at the Bull and Bear Bar in the Waldorf. I was delighted to see my old friend and mentor, especially, clearly on good terms. Ian said he wanted me to come back and that Mickey, my old colleague, was very keen on the idea. In the last year Neil Kelley had been replaced by my old friend Mike Loya as head of Houston and he too was keen on the idea. I told Ian that it was unbelievable timing in that Janet was adamant, right at that time, that she wanted to move back to Houston. I could not believe this apparent break of good fortune. I was becoming accustomed to only ever having bad luck, or thinking that I did. I told Ian that I had actually been approached by Enron but that obviously I would rejoin Vitol. He also mentioned, not to be repeated, that Mike Metz was going to leave Koch and rejoin Vitol in Houston early in the coming New Year. Before leaving he mentioned that Vitol's 1998 profit roughly cancelled out their loss or "unsufficiency" as it was oddly termed, in 1997 and thus resuming my old 1.5% shareholding would not be a problem. We did not have much time and as he left he said he'd get it sorted out and be in touch shortly.

That night I excitedly told Janet and she was pleasantly surprised. She was already in full Houston mode and was indeed planning to move at the beginning of October and I could commute for the last three months of the year. She made a house hunting trip to Houston and we chose to buy a house on Cedar Creek just off San Felipe and Post Oak, adjacent to Tanglewood. Though I had not seen it, it sounded nice so we went ahead. We moved all the furniture out of the Larchmont house, just leaving one bed for me, and she and the children moved back to Houston. I intended to see out the rest of the year of our lease and my year at HETCO but would keep my move confidential.

"It is easier to forgive an enemy than to forgive a friend."
William Blake

A couple of weeks later Ian called me, presumably to tell me that all was sorted out. Excitedly I took his call and he told me that in addition to Mickey and Mike's support Bob was very keen. However, and here I was utterly stunned, the two Pauls, Butcher having just rejoined from Aron, did not want me back and thus the move was off. I could not believe it. Why would Ian, the President of the Company, care what these two thought? As has been discussed Greenslade was known as an amoral, self-important sleaze ball, though good at his job and of course would be jealous of my relationship with Ian. Butcher's opinion should have mattered for nought. "Why?" I asked. Ian said after I had left they had found a $400,000 error in my 1996 profit numbers. I was astounded. Who cares, I thought? It was entirely possible and indeed probable that such an error existed but heck, so what, if they wanted they could start me at a negative $400k if it meant that much to them. I did not say any of this but weakly said, "Oh. Ok," I was truly devastated. Just when I felt I had a stroke of good fortune it had all crumbled to dust, as would be a frequent pattern in my future life. After putting the phone down I thought about calling Greenslade but decided not to. I just accepted it and in fact I effectively blocked it out of my mind for the next couple of years. It was truly devastating news. I could not believe Ian would allow me to be betrayed in this way. Bob Finch did not even tell his fuel team that Mike Metz was joining, together with his Koch colleague, Mike Winstone until they were ready to come on board. Bob would not have been bullied by his subordinates in this way. I suspect the truth was Greenslade, not only resenting my friendship with Ian, was still annoyed about the 1996 bonus situation which of course was none of my doing and, had Ian followed his own instructions that he always gave to me, he should not even have known about. Ian, I believe, did not even have the courage or decency to tell me the truth about the real reason the Pauls were against me, presumably as he felt responsibility for this. I was devastated by this apparent betrayal by a man I had looked up to and admired for so long, and who I considered a true friend, and to whom I had been incredibly loyal. It was a very bitter pill to swallow.

That night I told Janet that I guess it looked like Enron. I paid a visit to Enron and agreed terms to begin as a senior Crude Trader in the second week of January. For a month I would stay in my Larchmont house during the week and then fly back to Houston for the weekend. My landlord discovered my situation and said he would set about finding a new tenant for the New Year. Our lease expired Dec 31,1998. He actually found a family from France who wanted the house effective November 1. It was almost the end of October but in an effort to help the landlord I said I'd move out at the end of October and quickly found an apartment near Central Park and 5th at a slightly greater rent. When I asked the landlord to return my two months deposit he refused, saying of course not as I had broken the lease by moving out early! I could not believe it. For the next two months I kept up the charade at HETCO that I was still living in Larchmont and did not tell the Steves that I was going to have to resign until the week of Christmas. I explained to them that my family had already moved back to Houston. They did not want me to leave and suggested I work four days a week in New York and one in Houston and commute in that fashion. I thanked them for their kind suggestion but explained that my children, especially my son John, really missed me and I would have to move permanently back to Houston. This they understood and so I was set to join Enron around January the 7th, 1999.

Return to Houston: Enron

Even though it was early in the New Year the Enron books for 1998 had not yet been closed and signed off on by their auditors Arthur Andersen. Clive and Wyatt involved me in a discussion which involved a 10mmbbls of WTI three way exchange whereby two Enron entities, aided by Morgan Stanley, would basically just swap the barrels between themselves with no one making a profit, other than a small one for Morgan Stanley due to their cooperation. The aim was to put an extra $100m on to the end of year books of Enron Capital and Trade, the entity for which I worked. The deal was clearly a sham, as I said, but Clive and Wyatt said not to worry as Andersen would pretty much sign off on anything. They told me that a couple of years earlier the electricity, or power, trading group needed $200m extra earnings to meet their target. The then head of power, simply moved the forward power curves to create a fake $200m and the situation was taken care of. These forward curves were often based on very thinly traded markets so it was not easy for auditors to find their true value. Additionally, with the aid of some complex options shenanigans the waters could be further muddied to confuse auditors. A friend of mine, Kevin Hannon, who moved to Houston at about the same time as me, served two years for his apparent role in the Broadband debacle. Kevin had in happier times told me that Enron had almost been named Eneron. The latter sounded too much like a suppository in my opinion and they had made the right choice.

Now Enron was a hugely and highly profitable Natural Gas Trader but their oil group was not regarded highly. Much of their business was market making to the likes of airlines and producers, business for which they competed with the banks. This created a very large long term book of business which I was to manage along with their other two traders Marc Horowitz and David Rosenberg. They also had a couple of domestic traders, Don Schroeder and Pete Smith who traded a huge P+ book, made up mostly of options that they bought and hedged with WTI spreads on the NYMEX. Enron was heavily into the complexity and minutiae of options, for good reason I was soon to find out.

I had a pretty good compensation package at Enron but I had no idea how long I would last. A month later most of us Enron traders headed over to the London IP week where, a long time Phibro trader, Malcolm McAvity, for the first time in my experience referred to Enron as a giant Ponzi scheme. He was not entirely wrong. Enron had a habit of doing large complex option deals, marking them to a meaningless model at a huge profit and then taking that profit into earnings. When the deal played out and was ultimately a loss maker they would have to effectively do double that type of deal to make up for the earnings short fall, and so on. In this way it was rather Ponzi like. Many people made a lot of money selling things, whether a Brazilian power plant, or a Houston cogeneration plant, for far more that it was worth to Enron as Enron would then use complex but flawed options analysis to create a grossly inflated value for such asset and take it as earnings.

"Betrayal is the only truth that sticks".   Arthur Miller

That IP week we of course had a number of meetings. Somehow, having blocked out the betrayal a few months earlier, I had pleasantly arranged a meeting for several of the crude oil contingent to meet Paul Greenslade. Greenslade called me that morning saying unfortunately he could not make it as Ian had summoned him to something more important. I did not give it a second thought but years later I mused that perhaps Greenslade was not totally without conscience and had decided he did not wish to face me after what he had done to me. Or maybe I am giving him too much credit as a human being. In London I ran into a few of my old Vitol colleagues such as Gilles Chautard and Simon Boddy and had very pleasant conversations. I learnt that not only had Mike Metz rejoined (and Butcher for that matter) but so had the LPG defector Bob Borrowman and perhaps more significantly two gasoline traders, Dennis Crema and Guy Montgomery. Dennis and Guy had gone to a direct competitor and yet were welcomed back with open arms. This news had the effect of greatly increasing the sting I felt by Ian's betrayal.

On the flight back to Houston I happened to sit next to an old Vitol colleague, the Venezuelan Antonio Maarraoui: in his native Venezuela he was known as "the Toucan" because of his prominent nose. In talking to Tony, and as Ian had intimated in New York, Vitol's fortunes had turned around and, as a company, was now doing well. The previous autumn the oil market had been stunned and many people caught short by a surprise secret meeting one weekend in Madrid between the Oil Ministers of Saudi Arabia, Mexico and Venezuela. I recall that time very well and on that Friday the market appeared to be acting a little strangely and I had the odd idea of placing a call to Antonio, which I never did, to ask if he knew something. I did not make the call. Tony told me that in actual fact my strange intuition was indeed correct. That Friday he had received a call from an old friend of his from Maraven who worked in the office of the Oil Minister Ramirez. His friend called Tony and said he did not know what it meant but he had just been given a plane ticket to fly to Madrid with the Minister where they were to meet with the Saudis and the Mexicans and that this was meant to be top secret. Tony of course shared this with his colleagues who deduced that it could mean only one thing: Opec, and Mexico, were about to announce production cuts, as indeed they did. Vitol therefore went very long with this information and were about $4/bbl to the good come Monday. Oh how I wished I had called Tony that day, several months earlier, but I doubt he would have told me anything.

I also enquired of Tony as to how the refinery was doing. Tony said it had been decided to bring the management of the refinery back to Houston and directly involve all of the Houston traders. This of course made sense and the refining results began to improve. Still ideally they wanted to sell it.

Now, with my black cloud removed, Vitol's luck just seemed to get better and better. In 1999 they agreed to sell the refinery, at least covering their costs, to YPF, the Argentinian State run company. This would be a great relief. However, before the deal closed YPF were bought by the Spanish Oil Company Repsol who decided they did not want the refinery in Newfoundland and so the deal was never closed. This no doubt was a short term disappointment to Vitol but, as luck would have it, refiners' margins began to improve and as did their profit. Then in 2000-2003 margins positively exploded on massive worldwide product demand growth. Previously a margin of $4/bbl could be deemed mildly profitable and acceptable but during this "golden age of refining" margins exploded to around $40/bbl. This was way beyond anyone's wildest dreams. Vitol made an absolute fortune, probably 2-$3B over that period and then in 2003 sold the refinery to a Canadian Oil Royalty Trust, Harvest, for around $1.4B, a nice $1b profit. Shortly thereafter, the Canadian Royalty Trusts lost their tax advantaged status and had Harvest known this they would not have paid anywhere near the $1.4B. Their good fortune further benefitted from the disaster that had been Euromin. Once the aluminium mess had been untangled and massive losses taken they discovered they actually owned a zinc mine in the middle of Russia that was now immensely profitable. It certainly appeared that Vitol had been right, no matter how cruel, not to take me back as there was no way I could envisage my being part of these massive strokes of multi-billion dollar good luck.

I also asked Tony whatever happened to the potential Venezuelan Crude oil deal that had been presented to Vitol in early 1997 by a certain Jose Marquez when I was still working there. I sat in on only one meeting with Marquez and he claimed he could get us a long term contract for Leona crude oil at $5/bbl below the prevailing market price. I assumed of course that this was utter nonsense. Tony explained that Marquez had been very insistent and adamant and partly to placate him once and for all Tony agreed to fly to Caracas and with Marquez meet the Senior PDVSA executives who, obviously heavily incentivised, were going to give Vitol the deal. The Head of Crude Oil Sales at that time was Klauss Graff and Tony recalls waiting outside his office with Marquez but unfortunately, due to a late scheduling change, Graff had to postpone.

Tony was slowly becoming convinced by the story so Vitol forwarded Marquez some money which was obviously to be used to grease the necessary wheels in PDVSA. However, after receiving the money Marquez effectively disappeared. The whole thing had been an elaborate scam to defraud Vitol, even down to creating fake offices with the name of Graff and his title on the door. Somewhat to my surprise Vitol pursued Marquez with some success through the judicial system and got some of their money back. The reason I was surprised they pursued him was that clearly they were collaborating in a potential scheme involving bribery but they managed to navigate the issue with some success.

The crude oil market in early 1999 was seriously depressed, around $10/bbl. I felt things were clearly about to turn and we could well approach $20/bbl by the end of the year. I persuaded my colleagues to sell a lot of the low price put options we owned and to take a very large front to back position. This position within a few short months was about $7m to the good. The then overall boss of trading, Greg Whalley, a big, brash, former marine tank commander in the Gulf War, was also bullish and made a great deal of money trading his own book with outright length. He was truly a brilliant trader by any estimation having cut his teeth running the main Natural Gas book for Enron which made a fortune. Greg was quite surprised but impressed that such spreads on crude could make such good money. I was much happier expressing my view via spreads than naked longs or shorts though they were essentially tantamount to the same thing. On one side of me sat a very tall, extremely loud and funny, Harvard graduate named Pete Smith. Pete traded a huge P+ options book which was always way beyond my comprehension, however, he never ceased to show very handsome profits.

On one particularly miserable day I recall having had enough by around noon and simply stood up and left the office, telling no one of my plans. I went to watch a film which happened to appropriately be called "The Gambler," starring Michael Gambon as Dostoevsky, telling the tale of how he wrote the eponymous book. I had the entire theatre to myself.

Around this time I was still bullish on the crude market and so took an absolutely ludicrous and reckless 7 million barrel short position. Clearly I can only have been seeking to harm myself. I would frequently during my trading career take positions opposite to what I not only thought but essentially knew was correct. I was inherently a contrarian but when I was most convinced of something I would, in an effort to self-destruct, trade contrary to my better instincts. I recall at HETCO Steve Hendel once telling me to stop swimming against the tide and to "be a banana — one of the bunch". It was unbelievably difficult for me to do this given the internal struggles going on inside my head. In my early days at Vitol I was very often simply wrong, reliably so, about the market direction. After a while I picked up on the fact that Bob Finch realised this and would often ask me what I thought and use me as a contrary indicator. As my career progressed and I became a little more savvy and began to understand the market more I became less of a contrary indicator. However, Bob would often still ask me what I thought and by now I knew why so I would often tell him I thought the opposite of what I actually thought so that I would still be of benefit. Boy was I a mess. Behind me sat the main products trader Dave Botchlett who was extremely knowledgeable and experienced and on the fuel oil side we had an old former Vitol colleague of mine Dale Snyder.

We had a beautiful large house, with pool, on Cedar Creek, my two children were happily enrolled in the Post Oak Montessori school yet of course I was still depressed. Camille, with her sweet, engaging personality, at this tender age was considered "The Perfect Montessori student". Little did the school know that she was also the class kleptomaniac, something which she both successfully kept hidden and soon outgrew. My relationship with Janet had seriously deteriorated to such a degree that we loudly argued almost every night as we drank a couple of bottles of white wine. This obviously could not be good for John and Camille. During one especially hostile argument Janet even spat in my face. It was almost as if Janet and I were addicted to this dreadful drug of fierce arguments that left us both seething with anger and sadness. Somehow this habit had to be broken.

I went to far as to call my old boss Steve Semlitz to see if there was any way I could rejoin them but work in Houston. He said unfortunately not: they did not like small branch offices. A couple of days later my LED phone messaging system said, "Call Marc Rich in Switzerland". Now the original Marc Rich company became Glencore in the early 90s when Marc was bought out. However in the late 90s Rich decided to come back into the markets with a new company called Novarco which he controlled from Zug. They had offices in Europe as well as Connecticut where his old friend Clyde Melzer was based. I actually had a good Swedish friend, Chris Glass, who worked for Novarco in London so I assumed the message was from him and he must have been in Zug for a couple of days. It was already late in Europe but I called the number and got an incomprehensible lady's voice in German. I decided to call back the next day. When I did the lady answering the phone said.

"Ah yes, Mr. Rich was awaiting your call". I was shocked as Marc Rich was a true legend and why on earth would he personally call me. The lady went on to explain that he was busy but could I call back in one hour which of course I did. Eventually I spoke to Mr. Rich who explained that, "A mutual friend of ours, Steve Semlitz, suggested I was unhappy at Enron and might be willing to relocate to Europe." Where he got the last bit from I don't know but nonetheless I felt honoured to be speaking to such a legendary figure. I explained I would not move to Europe at the present day but he suggested why don't I just fly over to Zug and discuss potential possibilities. For some utterly ridiculous reason I said that was not convenient right now. He said, OK then why don't you call Clyde and arrange to meet him when he is in Houston next week. I said I would so do but before finishing the call I had the nerve or stupidity to ask him if he still, after such a long absence from the market, had the ability to run a successful oil trading firm. He dryly said, "Yes" and the conversation was over. I kicked myself twice: once for not accepting his offer to visit Zug and secondly for my stupid, almost rude, question.

A week later I met Clyde Melzer, for the first time, in the Omni Hotel Lobby. We spoke for about three hours. Clearly there was no professional fit for me with his organisation but we just enjoyed the conversation and exchanging stories. He really seemed like a terrific guy.

On a funny coincidental note, a couple of years later my good lawyer friend Martin Hunt, who I mentioned earlier had come to Houston in 1990 as had I, was a partner at the legal firm Bracewell and Giuliani. Martin was based in New York. One morning he and Rudy had breakfast with Clyde Melzer the guy some 20 years earlier Rudy had so zealously sought to prosecute. They had a great breakfast and laughed heartily about their previous run in.

I was still on anti-depressants but they seemed to make little difference. One night after dinner at Ruggles, on my way out I bumped into my old friend and colleague, David Gould. I was a little drunk and when he asked me how things were I told him the truth: my marriage was on the rocks, I hated Enron (not that I would like anywhere) and if my memory serves me correctly for the first time I believe I mentioned I felt suicidal. Dave gave me a few comforting words and then told me that an old colleague of his, Steve Hill, formerly of the eponymous trading company "Langham Hill," that had long ago gone belly-up, was putting together a new oil trading team for the Charlotte based utility, Duke, but here in Houston.

Once again I sensed the chance of a change but I was forever running, without ever escaping my demons: I seemed simply to be attracting new ones. When would it ever end?

Divorce and Duke Energy

I quickly contacted Steve Hill who had previously worked at MG right around the time of its implosion. His boss at Duke was Al Mitchell, a younger guy who had worked at MG for Hill. Hill had already employed a Head of Products trading, Bill Adkins, from Coastal who was busy putting together his team. After a couple of further meetings Steve offered me the job of Head of Crude Trading, for which I would have to put together a team. I was feeling excited but Janet was pretty indifferent: what difference would it make. She was clearly sick of me. As much as I may have thought Janet was a bad wife I failed to realise what it must have been like for her trying to raise two small children with such an anxiety ridden and depression prone husband.

I resigned to Greg Whalley in mid-June just two weeks after receiving a $60,000 retention bonus as stipulated in my contract. Greg asked me why would I leave for Duke? Why not use all my experience from Vitol, etc to build a successful crude business at Enron. I did not have a good answer. Deep down I did not have the confidence to build anything as I thought whatever I did was doomed to fail and I was worthless. Going to Duke would get me through another year of life. Beyond that I had no idea.

I told Greg I wanted to leave and assumed I would have to respect the three month non-compete clause as stipulated in my contract. There is a common misconception that non-compete clauses do not apply in Texas but Enron contracts were water tight and the non-compete period was inescapable. Greg responded by telling me well no, you actually have a 9 month non-compete as the contract clearly states it is 3 months or 9 months after the receipt of any contractual bonus. The early June payment I had just received was one such payment and thus I was not going to be free to work until March of 2000. I thought this was ridiculous being that I had only been at Enron six months but so it was. Greg eventually compromised and said I could begin at Duke in early Feb, basically 8 months away. This turned out, as things tended to do, to be a disaster for me as it would cost me several million dollars but I did not know that at the time.

Duke prepared a contract for me to start in November thinking Greg may compromise further but this was not to be. As well as a salary and a bonus of 6-10% of profits I was eligible to participate in Duke's long term incentive plan or PEP (Phantom Equity Plan), This was a three year plan running through 1999 until the end of 2001. I would sneak in at the last minute and receive a pro-rated share of my PEP allotment. However, when it became apparent that I would not start until February my contract was changed and I would no longer be in the PEP plan, not that I really knew what that meant. I would be awarded some other new and as yet undefined long term incentive. The Duke paperwork was not all finalised until the fall so I actually stayed working at Enron into October. I would then have three months off.

"Luck is what happens when preparation meets opportunity". Seneca

During this period of limbo I had lunch with my friend, and now head of the Vitol Houston office, Mike Loya. He said that Mickey and my replacement were not really taking on enough risk and he wanted me to rejoin. "What about the two Pauls?" I asked, "Who cares what they think," was his answer. Though tempted, I said after what happened last year and how badly I felt let down by Ian I could not. Now had Ian followed up with a phone call I would have almost certainly said yes but it was not to be.

One particularly depressed evening I was crying at home before getting ready to go out to a small function at a nearby cigar bar. Janet was especially unpleasant to me as I was leaving and I commented something to the effect of "Well, I may as well just go and kill myself". Unfortunately this was in ear shot of the children though I am not sure that they noticed. This was another thing that stuck in Janet's mind.

Over the next couple of month's Janet would go out with friends almost every evening treating me like the babysitter. She had once mentioned to me this bi-sexual hairdresser she went to see and I soon suspected, probably correctly though I am not certain, that she was having an affair with him. One evening she did not come home until well after 2am by which time I had called her close friend. Tricia, and asked if she knew where she was. Tricia replied she did not and she was terribly sorry. It certainly sounded like something was amiss.

For whatever reason my parents did not come over that Christmas. Janet had bought me a six day trip to Peru including Cuzco and Machu Picchu which I took in early January. I am sure she simply wanted to me rid of me for a while. I actually had a great time in Peru and in Lima met my good friend Alberto Valcarcel who to this day remains my closest friend. Alberto showed me around Lima and then before I left we took a trip down to Nazca to see the famous lines from a small airplane. Poor Alberto was violently sick as we viewed the astronaut and the hummingbird and goodness knows what else. I spent my last day in Lima walking half way across the City as I sought out major sites such as Pizarro's tomb and enjoyed the spectacularly beautiful wooden balconies for which Lima is renowned: Alberto thought I was nuts as many areas through which I walked were not considered safe for gringos armed with nothing but a large camera.

That New Year I decided to take a road trip with my now six year old son, John. We drove in the Discovery west along I-10 towards El Paso eventually making it to the spectacular Carlsbad Caverns. We then headed to White Sands National Park where we had barely an hour before the sunset. The night of Dec 31 I drove with John mostly asleep in the back, to Santa Fe and we arrived in our hotel room just in time to see in the new century as the Time Ball fell in Time Square. (Perhaps technically the new century and millennium began a year later but 99-00 was the big one.) After a brief stay in Santa Fe, where we had sold our house a year earlier, we headed back to Houston via Dallas. In Fort Worth we visited the zoo and were two of the very few visitors as it was freezing cold. That trip was certainly a rare high point in my otherwise downward spiralling life.

Shortly after I returned home Janet told me she wanted me to move out. She said she had been seeing a therapist who suggested we needed a separation and that I should see her therapist's partner as they worked as a team. Their methodology was that the woman was allowed to say and do whatever she wanted until such time as she was willing to hear the husband's side of things. I was both devastated and humiliated. I felt all this had happened because I had married Janet which I should never have done and now she was kicking me out. I really was in disbelief at what was unfolding.

I found a two bedroom furnished apartment just inside the LOOP on San Felipe barely half a mile from the house. After the initial shock and devastation I for once looked on the bright side: perhaps this was for the best and was actually what I wanted. We told the children it was just temporary and they spent every Wednesday with me, all three of us sleeping in one big bed, and every other weekend. On one of my first weekends off I travelled down to Guatemala to see the magnificence of Tikal. I almost felt a tiny bit like my old self.

"Bigamy is having one wife too many. Monogamy is the same" Oscar Wilde

I was still of course on Prozac but I decided to give up caffeine as I thought that might aid my acute anxiety. In the middle of February I started work at Duke, several miles down Westheimer beyond the Beltway, and I had already arranged for two traders I knew to join me namely Bill Taylor, who I had worked with at Vitol, and Matt Sandler, who had been at Neste for many years. Together we would trade crude futures speculatively and Bill would be the primary futures executor.

For several months Bill was going through a rather unpleasant grilling from the Department of Justice pertaining to his earlier time as head of gas and power trading at another utility, Avista. Apparently some traders who reported to Bill were accused of trying to manipulate the closing price of gas or power on the NYMEX by issuing an order to a broker on a taped line including the words "buy worst". In other words they wanted to buy at as high a price as possible so that the market would settle unrealistically high and presumably they would profit as a result of swaps they had pricing off that artificially inflated settlement.

Anyway, in my estimation Bill was a highly educated, slightly eccentric man of the highest integrity. He was extremely patriotic with a Texas and US flag flying in front of his house. He had also volunteered to serve in Vietnam.

Initially Bill would disappear for a few hours each Tuesday afternoon. He would report a little of his experiences which seemed comical. Bill had a habit of keeping expensive leather bound binders with all his trading notes and ideas covering a number of years. The DOJ were of course interested in his notebooks covering the period in question. Now, being eccentric Bill would write down famous quotes from various poets such as T.S.Elliot's "Wasteland" or from Shakespeare. When the DOJ officers read "April is the cruelest month …". They assumed this meant that something sinister was going to happen to or during April. This was both hilarious and, sadly serious. Poor Bill was pursued under civil charges for years after which he was physically and mentally drained and fined heavily. The process was not finished until long after he had left us at Duke.

I cannot imagine Bill doing anything dishonest. His boss at Avista and indeed friend, Neil Kelley, had told him at the very beginning just agree to something and settle. Bill refused saying he had done nothing wrong, and his government, of which he was very proud, would soon accept this. Sadly Bill suffered great mental anguish during the protracted process at the end of which he, a proud Vietnam volunteer, said to me "I think our government is evil". He explained he felt they did not care one iota about the truth: they just wanted a scalp, no matter what the cost to the individual singled out. I feel for sure there was a large amount of truth to this in the coming Enron debacle that engulfed similar companies. It seemed utterly a game of chance who was prosecuted and who was not and likely guilt or innocence were barely important in the overall scheme of things. Of course there were exceptions, where large and obvious scalps were involved, but when it came to going after lesser fish it did seem that luck more than guilt or innocence were the key determinants as to who was prosecuted. Such are the scales of Justice in the US corporate world and many would argue in the US in general.

For the next few months I attended therapy sessions hearing Janet complain while I was not permitted to respond. She brought up how I had been depressed when bathing Camille, how I had said moving to New York was a mistake and how I had just recently been crying in front of the children and said that I might as well go and kill myself. During this phase of the therapy we were allowed to meet for lunch, if Janet wanted, but I was otherwise not to contact her unless it was about the children. During one of our sessions I mentioned how fundamentally unsuited to trading I was: it was akin to making an alcoholic a barman. If I had followed my own inclination all those years ago, or perhaps had the ability to do so, so much pain and suffering could have been avoided. However, it was not to be. By March I was totally sick of this nonsense and decided that I would be better off divorced. I told my therapist about how I had always known it was a mistake to marry Janet and that she was incredibly moody and that I wanted a divorce. Janet had the amazing ability of being able to switch from a seemingly pleasant mood into a fuming rage in a nanosecond. It was quite amazing but unsettling. She also had most of what I would soon discover were the classic symptoms of a "crazy-maker". The next time we met as a group of four I blurted this out and said I was going to file for divorce, which I promptly did. I used a vicious lawyer named Wendy Burgower, that a friend had recommended to me. She was very blunt and to the point and explained to me that my clearly defined separate property was mine but that everything else would be split 45-55% in favour of Janet. My 1990 Vitol "shares" were my most valuable and only real separate property. Janet employed a painstakingly slow and thorough lawyer but in the interests of cost we quickly agreed terms and the papers were filed. We were not divorced until April 2001.

As divorce approached I had decided to write to Ian Taylor to ask if he would be so kind as to pay me my extremely modest amount of "shareholding" as obviously the divorce would be financially disruptive. Ian scribbled back a note saying that it would not be possible then, but that in any event, I would more than likely be receiving it in the next couple of years as the Company was doing well. In my opinion the note should have ended there but Ian saw fit to turn the knife and add, "Imagine how much you would be worth if you were still here now". That spiteful comment really hurt: I had always thought better of Ian and was surprised that he would write something so callous to me. He had also conveniently forgotten that it was due to his cowardly betrayal a couple of years earlier that I was no longer "still here". In fairness to Ian, he did not know the mental agony and anguish that I had fought with desperately for the last ten plus years during which I was almost permanently teetering on the edge of a major breakdown. On several occasions,

I did fall into the yawning chasm of despair yet usually managed to claw myself back up to the edge by my fingertips. With regard to his betrayal I suspect that Greenslade may even have gone so far as to threaten to resign if Ian were to have taken me back. This of course would have been a hollow threat given the infrastructure that Greenslade had built vis a vis Nigeria. However, prior to about 2001, when his courage was bolstered by a bulging personal and corporate balance sheet, Ian had a habit of backing down in the face of a threat or contractual dispute. I must confess, after receiving that note for quite some time, as unhealthy as it was for me, "Every time Vitol (a friend) succeeded, I died a little," to paraphrase Gore Vidal. To be fair to Ian, had Greenslade left, and I am only hypothesising that that was indeed raised, it would not be easy to find a Nigerian expert with his pathologically dishonest, sociopathic personality.

A young fuel trader had a relatively short but personally profitable career at Vitol. He was let go primarily for bringing a cargo with dangerously high levels of hydrogen sulphide into the HOFTI terminal in Houston. Now dangerous levels of this gas could be handled if sufficient notice was given and the necessary precautions taken. The trader had omitted to warn HOFTI of the nature of his cargo but through some stroke of luck they were made otherwise aware and no harm was done. Still it was a dreadful oversight on the trader's part. Someone at discharge could have been killed.

Indeed to show how serious the issue of hydrogen sulphide is I recall two times during my Vitol days when we ran afoul of it. The first was harmless but expensive the second sadly tragic. During my early days in Houston I was determined to open up some new avenues of business. One such avenue was to deal with APMC (The Alberta Petroleum Marketing Corporation) in an effort to export some of their crude oil out of Vancouver, after traveling across the Rockies in the TransMountain Pipeline. After much effort I managed to secure a cargo of Rainbow crude and sold it at a decent profit to the refiner Tesoro who intended to take it to their refinery in Alaska. However, en route they ran into the fact that it was higher in hydrogen sulphide than they had first thought and thus their refinery could not take it. They ended up sitting the vessel, very expensively, for quite some time offshore whilst they decided what to do. Ultimately they sold it at a considerable further loss into China. That was my only foray into taking Rainbow crude out of Vancouver. After that, however, it was quite often moved in that direction.

On another occasion we in the crude group had purchased a cargo of Soyo crude oil from Angola. If my memory is correct, I believe I may have bought the cargo and one of my London colleagues sold it to Petrofina (now part of TotalFinaElf) to take to their Antwerp refinery. It was well known that Soyo had high H2S and required special handling at loading and discharge. Fina were indeed familiar with this grade and had handled it before. However, for some tragic reason there was an oversight and the crude was not correctly handled at discharge resulting, I believe, in the death of an employee.

In the summer of 2000 with divorce inevitable Janet bought a small 3 bedroom house in West University and I moved back into the house on Cedar Creek. My mood was somewhat better and the next 2-3 years were my least depressed of the last 25. Of course I worried about the effect it would have on John and Camille but we co-parented the best we could. They soon moved to the public West University Elementary School where most of their friends also went.

My year at Duke proceeded reasonably well and I chose to trade focusing purely on WTI-Brent and WTI time spreads upon which I always seemed to have a pretty good handle. That year the group made about $16m of which I made over $9m. I received a bonus of $400k, 55% of which had to go to Janet, after tax. At that time Vitol were paying out my 1992 and 1994 US stock appreciation rights again 55% of which went to Janet but that did not entail a great deal of money. Just prior the divorce Janet suggested that maybe we postpone it and try to work on things but in my mind things had gone too far and I was feeling better than I had in over ten years. The divorce went through in April and I received the standard visitation rights.

My parents were deeply shocked by the news but also very supportive. For two weeks each during the summers of 2000 and 2001 I took John and Camille over to Jersey to see my parents. Unfortunately, John seemed most affected by the divorce and could at times be surly and difficult. Spending this amount of time with my parents also brought back many bad memories and I was on edge and feeling depressed for most of the visits. I was glad to get back to Houston.

I actually attended a Vitol crude dinner at the 2002 IP Week in London. Greenslade, in his after dinner speech even gave me a mention in that it was a pleasure to see me back. Hmmm. Ian also gave a speech in which, as I told him later, he appeared to be asking the main Platts dated Brent journalist present, to give up on being so strict on the way he quoted dated Brent and let the "manipulation" continue unimpeded. Ian said that was not at all how he intended to come across. I must say it felt sad and odd talking to my great friend and mentor now that I no longer worked with him.

In 2000 and 2001 we added several more traders to our oil group. One of these was Pete Smith who approached me and asked if he could leave Enron and bring his P+ business to Duke. After all, he said, you have seen how profitable it is. I was a little nervous but brought him on board thinking he would not screw a friend. However, I instructed our chief analyst to keep a very close eye on his book. A year later, in late 2001, I decided nervously to take a detailed look myself at his book which was showing an $8m profit. My curiosity was piqued by the fact that he had been offered a better position at another "power Ponzi," as I termed them, to trade P+ by an old Enron colleague of his. When I looked at the detail I simply looked at what options he owned and then asked brokers to quote me market prices for those options. When I did so the $8m profit turned into about a $1m loss. I was mortified. Basically an option say bought for $1.30, now worth $1, was marked to market at $2. Obviously volatility was a key component of the value of these options (as indeed was common sense but that was always overlooked) but to further muddy the waters instead of messing with volatility Pete would value the options using correlation and he would report daily the correlation to be used by the analysts in their options valuation model. By tweaking correlation he could make his book look as profitable as he liked. I am not even sure what variables he was correlating but it worked. Quite why the analysts did not simply value his options against a list of options quotes from brokers I will never know. Clearly I had a problem and had to confront Pete. Before I had barely said a word Pete said, "Don't worry, I understand the true value of these options better than the market and I will take my book of business as it is with me to this other company for $8m". I could not believe what I was hearing. He was going to have his new company pay Duke $8m for some load of options that were worth about negative $1m. Somehow he pulled it off. His new firm paid us $8m and the trades were gone. Duke, and more importantly for me the crude group, had dodged a $9m bullet. I can only assume at his new home he tweaked the correlation to make the book worth a few million more. I must say however, I do greatly appreciate his not screwing me. His new firm meanwhile was busy "Enronising" everything in sight, such was the zeitgeist of that era, taking huge nonsensical options profits on pipeline capacity and storage and anything else they could get their hands on. The charade at his new home collapsed soon after Enron collapsed and the parent company itself, like Duke, appeared threatened with insolvency. However, both parents pulled through and are thriving to this day.

After Pete had left Enron and with the foundations starting to crumble I believe the P+ book was greatly expanded. Tens of millions of barrels of options would be purchased and then, via correlation, marked at a huge profit thus creating tens of millions of fake dollars of profit. However, their problems were of course far bigger than that.

Many other similar companies, Dynegy, El Paso, Aquila and others all, I believe, operated in a similar fashion and traders were paid tens of millions of dollars for essentially losing hundreds of millions, if not billions. I am amazed that no one at these other companies was ever prosecuted. Through his brother-in-law, I learnt that the CEO of one such company was extremely worried, but he skated by, unscathed. Perhaps the Feds did not fully understand what was going on, or Enron was deemed sufficient. One poor Junior Accountant at Dynegy was prosecuted probably for doing nothing other than what he was told, and got 16 years for his troubles but I believe that sentence was subsequently dramatically reduced.

"Beware of Greeks bearing gifts".   Proverb attributed to Virgil

When the Head of Duke International, Bruce Williamson, left Duke to become CEO of Dynegy the above was my parting advise to him. It was after all the massive and bogus use of options which use many Greek terms, theta, gamma, delta, for example, that essentially created the era of costly confusion that engulfed and nearly destroyed so many of the Enron "wannabes".

2001 continued to go quite well and I was managing to cope with the stress of trading. However in mid 2001 an industry friend of mine forwarded to me a bunch of photographs taken at Vitol's recent 35th year Anniversary. The site of Greenslade's smug face brought back the memories I had managed to largely suppress since late 1998 and I was filled with hatred for Greenslade and despair for myself. All my worst feelings came back in a flash, as though they had been waiting for an opportunity to pounce on me again. Unfortunately, from that moment on, for several years I would dwell on how Greenslade had deprived me of what might have been. How I hoped he would one day get done for all the egregious market manipulation and alleged bribery that he had conducted but it was not to be. Those thoughts would haunt my mind for years to come and I began to think I was cursed, for the first time thinking back to my rain affected cricketing career at Oxford and all else that had befallen me since.

I worked for a small group called Duke Energy Merchants (DEM) which traded crude oil, gasoline, some heating oil and some ethane and propane. We also oddly enough had a fertiliser trader. The fertiliser and LPG traders were haemorrhaging money but the crude and gasoline groups were profitable.

At the end of 2001 my performance was rewarded with a promotion to Senior Vice President of Crude and Products Trading. At this time I had a brief chat with my old friend Mike Loya who said it was pretty easy being the boss of traders: you just told them to do more of what was making money and less of what was not. Mike was always very direct. He also told me that the main thing he had gained from his Harvard MBA was not any great knowledge but confidence: he would never be intimidated by anyone in a business setting. This was also very candid. Among his Harvard classmates were Meg Whitman, Jim Hackett of Anadarko and Jeff Skilling.

I sensed that my more senior role would give me a chance to get away from day to day trading which was, I thought, my ultimate goal. I attended a meeting in London with my boss and the Duke International people in Europe whilst still having quite a few crude trades on over which I mentally agonised. Not being able, as usual, to stare in a teeth-grinding trance at the NYMEX screen gave me horrendous anxiety such that I called my crude colleagues and asked them to liquidate everything I had at a negligible profit. Had I simply not been so anxious my positions would have paid off handsomely but I simply could not mentally cope with their existence.

On another occasion I attended a meeting of all the senior Duke International people from London, Australia and South and Central America. We operated a couple of oil burning power plants in Central America and so I approached the gentleman responsible for buying the oil, explaining that we could now supply the oil from within Duke. He was very amenable to the idea. However, as soon as he returned to his office he was impossible to deal with and I did not pursue it as I sensed that a Clyde Meltzer/John Barnes type of situation, as discussed earlier at Enron, was in play. Interestingly the same fellow was later involved in some serious litigation with Duke. He and some cohorts had purchased a small power plant in North Carolina and then sold it to Duke at several million dollars of profit. All the time this chap was a Duke employee. Apparently, this power plant case did go to court but was settled before the conclusion of the trial with the Duke employee essentially paying back Duke any excess profit "earnt". Now interestingly this chap, Joe, had for some time before this power plant case been selling, along with his cohorts, spare parts to Duke at an inflated price with prior knowledge, of course, of what types of parts Duke would require. The manner of how Joe's schemes were discovered by Duke is quite amusing. One day he was looking at pornography on his Duke computer in his office. Like most companies Duke had safeguards against what they considered improper use of company computers. As such, when the porn came up on the screen the computer froze. Now Joe had also been looking at a couple of documents pertaining to his spare parts scheme. The IT representative of Duke had to send everything that was active on the computer to the head of Duke International, Richard McGee. Richard, therefore saw the incriminating documents and the game was up.

Duke Energy Merchants sat in the same building as the far bigger Duke Energy North America or DENA which was a massive unregulated gas and power trading group. They had contracted to build numerous gas fired merchant power plants which were supposedly all very profitable. Their numbers ran into the billions of dollars and their apparent profits were the main reason that the Duke utility share price had soared over the last couple of years. In a sense they were the Enron inside Duke. That year we were allowed to take up to 50% of our coming bonus, for 2001, in the form of at-the-money 10 year Duke Energy call options. I was very comfortable at Duke and had just been promoted to be Head of Crude and Products and so I elected to take 50% of my bonus as options. As an incentive we were given double the amount of options you would ordinarily have received. It was around this time that I began to realise the significance of the Long term incentive plan. Basically it was a plan tied to the share price of Duke Energy effective March 1, 2002. I also discovered that the Executive Committee of Duke had a similar plan tied to the share price on the same day. Thus all efforts were made to boost earnings in order to boost the share price by March 1. Rather like Enron I discovered DENA used similar tools to boost their earnings. In early 2002 Enron began to unravel and in my new more senior capacity I was invited to meetings with the senior DENA management and traders. I got to see that they had some $9B of accrued profits in the "accrual book" that would roll onto the relevant years accounting books as time went on. It was an unbelievably rosy picture, that was indeed too good to be true. Duke Energy Merchants actually posted a loss in 2001 and as such we were technically not due a bonus. This was especially galling for the crude team and the gasoline team as we have made roughly $30m and $6m respectively. My contribution had been over $19m. Unfortunately our profits were dwarfed by losses in LPG and more so fertiliser. Since we were not due a traditional bonus our options election technically should have been disallowed but unfortunately it was not. Duke elected to make special discretionary bonus payments to us oil traders but still gave us our requested options. This was a disaster as I had invested $600k in $41 call options which was roughly the highest Duke had ever traded as it rapidly fell, along with the unfolding Enron debacle, to well below $20. I simultaneously discovered that had I been included in the original PEP plan, which I would have but for the onerous non-compete clause with Enron, I would have received over $4m. My long term incentive, while decent, amounted to a little over $440k for the three years 2000-2002. As Enron collapsed so did much of the forward gas and power market. Duke's exposure was only a few hundred million dollars to Enron which paled in significance to the $9B they had in accrued profits. Except it didn't. Those accrued profits were, in my opinion, all fictitious and when valued correctly showed forward losses running into the billions. So huge were the losses that the solvency of the massive Duke utility itself was called into question. The DENA traders, the executive committee and those in the PEP scheme had all received many millions of dollars in bonuses and incentive payments that were based entirely on fictitious numbers. The head man in the London office, who had paid $200m for an essentially worthless gas trading business, even received $11m.

I did my best to continue trading in 2002 but felt utterly demoralised as I had been duped, along with all the other Duke shareholders into effectively buying Duke stock at $41 via my options. Like Enron, Duke had used bogus options analysis to grossly inflate the value of their gas and power positions and indeed of their merchant power plants many of which were cancelled before being completely constructed. Some of their power plants were duel fuel, i.e., they could run on natural gas or fuel oil depending on the relative price of each commodity. This so called optionality was assigned a nonsensical value and in one case they assigned a value to a plant that did not even have duel fuel capability. As I explained in a meeting, under their methodology, if crude 12 months out was $20, you could analyse history and say that there was a high probability that say 4 times in the next year it would move either a $1 up or down. Thus, in their methodology, it was reasonable to assume that you would capture at least 2 moves of 50cts. Thus crude purchased at $20 was really worth $21 and if you bought crude at $20 you could mark to market it at $21 making an immediate $1 profit. Obviously this was nonsensical but it was essentially, in my view, what Duke did to its more esoteric gas and power deals. Anybody would be laughed at if they tried it in the simple example I have outlined but it is the same thing. Now a key component of any option price is its volatility: the higher the volatility the higher the options value. Volatility was traded in gas and power in over the counter markets. If Duke (or Enron or any of the similar companies using the same dubious methods) wanted to boost the apparent value of the options within their book of business they would need to boost volatility. To do this, Duke would often engage in options wash trades at a high volatility with a cooperative counterpart so that they could point to the clearly established higher volatility and mark to market their transactions accordingly.

Wash trades got a bad name in the Energy business around this time and the SEC and CFTC went after several gas and power companies for executing such trades but I do not think they ever truly understood the nefarious purposes behind many of them. Wash trades, as stand alone, have little impact or meaning. In fact many people may do a wash trade if they buy something they quickly regret and immediately turn around and sell it. There is of course nothing wrong with that but if you are doing it to set a false benchmark against which you can inflate your so called profits that is a different matter. I could not believe all that Duke had been up to and not only did it cost me a lot of money it would undoubtedly cost me my job. After their handsome payments courtesy of the fictitious DENA profits the executive committee in Charlotte declared all traders crooked and slowly started to unravel DENA and undoubtedly soon DEM.

That year, 2002, I made about $4m but I had little hope of receiving a bonus. Furthermore we had recently taken on an options trader from Chicago who created such a huge crude oil options position that it exceeded his allocated daily risk limits by a factor of 50! He did so much business that there were of course unsubstantiated rumours of broker kickbacks but I have no idea if that was true. It seemed that that enormous bomb was going to land on my desk and I became very nervous: I did not want to be attached to it in any way.

Two Duke traders, one of them a friend of mine and who has children the same age as John and Camille, were indicted and prosecuted but just for a very small supposed manipulation of the profit/loss accounts by $50m in order to boost their bonuses. Both bravely went to trial and were acquitted. When I say bravely, it is because I believe if you go to trial your chances of being convicted are higher than 90%. However, rather like Enron, where the Feds went after the relatively trivial "Nigerian barge case" all the big multi-billion dollar scams and commensurate unjust payouts seemed to be ignored. While the two Duke traders were being prosecuted their boss at DENA, an upstanding pillar of the local church and community, mysteriously moved with his family for a couple of years to Canada but after the acquittals and the coast was clear he returned home to his pillar like duties. There were also rumours at Duke that they had to have two allegations of sexual harassment against some members of DENA management hushed up. Perhaps, if true, those involved have a future as Republican politicians.

Susan

After my divorce was finalised in April 2001 I felt a definite sense of relief and freedom. I enjoyed greatly having John and Camille over on Wednesday's and every other weekend when we would spend much time in the pool or simply messing around. John, however, was clearly upset by the situation and I wished so much that I could make things right for him in his mind. Obviously both his parents still loved him dearly but I know children of a certain age especially do take divorce very hard. He could often be deliberately difficult to deal with and generally contrary and this would result in my losing my temper which did little to improve the situation. I told myself things would improve over time.

I had been separated since the beginning of 2000. I was not involved in any serious relationship or barely semi-serious until the week of September the 11th, 2001. I had previously met a somewhat younger English girl, also an Oxonian, who I really liked but I did not sense any prospect of a real future especially as I had John and Camille to consider. Not that I ever planned or thought things through very well, I was aware that were I to become seriously involved with someone they would have to be an effective and loving step-mother to my children. Janet I believe was still involved with the hairdresser George who spent quite some time at her house with the children, a situation with which I was not particularly enamoured.

My friend and colleague, Kurt, in London, found my going out on pre-arranged "blind-dates" completely hilarious. It so happened that his wife shared a hair dresser with Nicole Kidman in London. Kurt met Nicole at a party held by the hairdresser and began chatting to her about blind dates since she had just recently separated from Tom Cruise. He actually persuaded her to take my phone number and she said she would call but I have been waiting ever since.

The Saturday after the horrific tragedies of September 11, 2001, was the 13th. My friend Alberto, who worked for Duke in Lima, was in town and we were both invited to a party at my neighbour Erica's house. She explained she had a friend she wanted me to meet named Susan, who had previously worked at Telerate, and to whom she had already mentioned that I was coming to the party. I recalled Susan from a brief meeting about 7 or 8 years prior when she, in her mid to early 20s, came into our office as our Telerate news service representative. We actually shook hands and she was strikingly beautiful. Given what traders are like she received a huge amount of attention from the pack of hungry wolves but the alpha wolf of the group at that time had the courtesy to show her around the office and then escort her back downstairs. They were together for about two years.

Upon arriving at the party I immediately noticed Susan who appeared as beautiful and young as ever. She was in the middle of an anecdote with some guys that involved pump action shot-gun type hand gestures and noises and a "Take that, mother fucker". "Hmmm, Feisty, I thought".

At an opportune moment I went up to Susan and reintroduced myself. She remembered meeting me all those years before. After a pleasant chat, absent any excessive expletives, she gave me her phone number in order to arrange to meet for brunch tomorrow. She later told me she thought that was a bit swift on my part but she knew that I had children and obviously this weekend they were not with me.

We had a very pleasant brunch and then went to an afternoon movie. I obviously found her very attractive but she also seemed very nice and interesting and we got along extremely well. I learnt that she was 32, some six years younger than me, was from the middle of nowhere in southwest Texas and had been in Houston about the same time as me. She had subsequently moved from Telerate to software sales where she had a brief but successful period of time at Oracle before being poached by a smaller rival, WebMethods. She was very proud of her career achievements and the fact that she could look after herself, armed or not.

**"All women become like their mothers. That is their tragedy.
No man, does, and that is his".
Oscar Wilde**

I must disagree with Mr.Wilde on the latter point: it was my thinking much like my mother that led to a great deal of the tragedy in my life. However, I am sure my wife, and indeed myself, find his first point utterly terrifying.

We spent the next 4-6 weeks getting to know each other and going out probably twice a week. I learnt that she herself had quite a tough upbringing with a particularly crazy, evangelical type mother who had contributed to Susan being estranged from her birth father and her step father who raised her from 5-15 years of age. She had been very close to this old west Texas rancher and was clearly hurt by their estrangement which was due in no way to her but sadly to the manipulative actions of her mother. She had a sister 9 years older who ran a successful specialty advertising business with her husband in Houston but who she seldom saw and a brother who lived near her mother in a tiny town west of San Antonio. Despite her mother's "craziness" Susan had decided to maintain a relationship with her, something her sister chose not to do. Susan's formative years with the old rancher had seen her grow up in a family that was well-off and not wanting for anything but in a very simple way.

"In this world of sin and sorrow there is always something to be thankful for: as for me, I rejoice that I am not a Republican. H.L. Mencken

Fortunately, Susan had not inherited her mother's extreme political views epitomised by what I like to call the "Tea Pot Taliban". Susan, to her credit, is in fact a recovering Republican.

We clearly liked each other and after about 7 weeks I invited her to Asheville, in North Carolina, for a weekend which she gladly accepted and we had a terrific time staying at the Biltmore. Not one to hang around I then invited her to Phoenix for a weekend which she again accepted. We were becoming quite attached and the relationship was approaching a more serious phase. Although she had very limited world experiences and knowledge she was very interesting, and although seemed tough and aggressive at times, clearly had a softer and more vulnerable centre. She had not met John and Camille to whom she thus far did not exist. I had no intention of introducing them to anybody unless I was pretty convinced the relationship would last. I decided it was time to ask how she felt about having her own children: I most definitely did not want anymore. She said she was unsure and that perhaps being a stepmother would be more than enough to satisfy any maternal cravings she may have. I thought then about ending the relationship. I did not want to as I was extremely fond of her but obviously having more children was a huge consideration and at this time I was 100% against. However, not wanting in my heart to end the relationship, I convinced myself that she was not really the motherly type. Her stories growing up, usually unsupervised in the country, made me think of her as somewhat wild and uncivilised or undomesticated. She made me think of the following quote attributed to Clemenceau:

"America is the only nation in history which, miraculously, has gone directly from barbarism to degeneration without the usual interval of civilisation".

Hopefully she was not too degenerate.

She was seriously proud of her career, as she would repeatedly say, and to be honest she struck me more as mistress material rather than wife and mother material. In fact a couple of years prior to her meeting she and her friends would hang out with a couple of old rich guys and one had offered her $100,000 a year to be his mistress. He was unmarried. Susan did not find him attractive in the slightest so turned him down. I felt offended, on her behalf, which she found quite chivalrous of me.

And so our relationship became much more serious and we became virtually inseparable, as long as the children were not around. She hated me communicating with my ex-wife Janet who would have an annoying habit of calling me unnecessarily seemingly just to disrupt our relationship. My parents met Susan that Christmas and liked her personality a lot. The feelings were mutual. I was impressed by Susan's positive attitude and felt that it might rub off on me and lead to a turnaround in fortunes. So much for that glimmer of hope.

Six months into the relationship, that is around March 2002, I decided that it was time for her to meet John and Camille. This was obviously a huge step, both for the children and Susan. We met at my house and overall it went well. Camille immediately took a liking to her and latched on to her like a barnacle. John was less taken but still liked her. John, I think, really felt bad for his mother and I believe his mother played on this which was obviously very much to John's detriment. Once John and Camille had met Susan, Janet would make it clear how much she despised her and would frequently curse and swear about Susan in front of the children. She would also have heated phone or key slinging arguments with her boyfriend George or some new guy John which I am sure was deeply unsettling for John and Camille. We learnt all this from Camille. Quite why Janet was so against my involvement with someone else I don't know: we had been separated for over 2 years, and our relationship had been a disaster for years before that. Susan believed she just wanted to continue to have control over me which she would exercise through the children primarily using guilt and manipulation to which I must admit I was vulnerable. Janet would frequently be rude, dismissive and hostile to Susan, something of which I was not entirely aware but this greatly upset Susan. When Susan did mention this to me I offered to speak to Janet about it but Susan said she could take care of it herself. Janet's behaviour really was inexcusable as Susan was trying to be a loving stepmother to John and Camille, a responsibility she took very seriously, and this was not at all helped by Janet's meddling and hostility.

Susan had no children of her own and taking on the role of stepmother to an eight and six year old is by no means easy. There were of course certain misunderstandings and differences of opinion between Susan and me such as when I gave the children hot chocolate before bed, something she vehemently disagreed with, and when I would take a quick shot at pool for John when he could not quite reach and she felt angrily that I was infantilising him. Obviously most parents have such minor disagreements and simply sort them out the best they can, as indeed did we, if we overlook the unjustified vicious tongue-lashing I received on each occasion.

When Susan and I were on our own we got on like a house on fire. She truly seemed to care deeply about me and me about her. She would comment that the only time we seemed ever to argue was when Janet interfered or over something that the children did or did not do. This was correct. I felt happy with Susan and saw her as someone I loved and with whom I could enjoy the rest of my life, travelling and involving the children.

Camille became really attached to Susan so much so that she asked her if she could call Susan "Mom". Susan said that was very flattering but that it was probably not a good idea. Camille then went on to say. "You know, mom and Dad, love John more than me". This of course touched Susan and it deeply touched me and I was so sad that Camille somehow had that impression. Perhaps it stemmed from all the attention John got from playing Little League Baseball, with Camille always in tow, though she actually soon overcame that issue and came into her own. Susan even went so far as to say to Camille that she was one of the reasons she was attracted to me. This of course was very kind but perhaps a bit of a sleight on yours truly.

As 2002 progressed my relationship with Susan blossomed as my career at Duke plummeted thanks to DENA.

Towards the end of 2002 there was a very unpleasant incident at our house when John and Camille were there. John ran upstairs to Susan's closet (that Janet had once but briefly used) and began throwing Susan's clothes all over the place, screaming "This is my Mom's closet! Get out". This was very disturbing for Susan and me and my heart bled for John as to why he was so upset. Though we were close he would never talk to me about what was on his mind. I desperately wanted to help. Our suspicion was that Janet put him up to the act but why on earth she would do something so destructive to a young mind was beyond me.

As previously mentioned, I believe Janet had several "crazy-making" characteristics : for one, she would quite easily flat-out lie. One quite amazing and totally ridiculous lie involved a trip to Telluride she was going to take with John. They were going to ski with friends there. Meanwhile Camille would stay with us. On the morning of their trip, all flustered and in a state of near panic, John and Camille called saying Susan had to rush over immediately and pick up Camille as John and his mother had to dash to the airport to make their flight. Now I happened to know, and I double checked quickly online, that there is only one flight to Montrose/Telluride each day and it is in the early afternoon. Susan had to wake Amelia up from a nap and drove over to Janet's where Janet calmly said that she had managed to switch to a later flight and there was no rush. This of course was totally false as she would not pay the excessive change fees for one thing, were there a later flight, and, as I stated, there is only the early afternoon flight which they were of course booked on all along. I have no idea why Janet would pull such a foolish stunt especially as it was obvious she was lying and more so it had distressed John and Camille. Some things simply defy a logical explanation. Secondly, she also had the habit of being nice, to draw you in, and then quickly turning nasty to totally confuse you.

Susan would insist that Janet was essentially delusional, living in a "world according to Janet". While I could see that she often had unreasonable expectations and could lie without compunction, I never felt she was delusional and always found this idea of Susan's a little odd. Upon reflection, perhaps we had a little pre-emptive projection at play.

Susan was, and still is, a huge fan of therapy. She had been going for years to a wise old lady named Sarna in Houston. She explained how Sarna had greatly helped her and she decided that it would be a benefit to us as a couple and to me as an individual if we went to see Sarna, especially to discuss issues that arose from parenting John and Camille and how to deal with Janet's negative interference. We would continue to do this well after we were married. Typically if we argued Susan would yank me to Sarna's office and with her assistance we would iron out the issue. I must say over 80% of the time it seemed to be that Sarna was trying to explain to Susan how she had overreacted or misunderstood something. I also recall Susan mentioning to me that when she first met Sarna she felt fragmented, like a broken mirror, and Sarna helped her come to terms with this.

Susan also decided to accompany on one of my appointments to see Dr. Bakes, who, for some reason, Susan took an immediate disliking too. On my next and, I believe, final appointment Dr. Bakes advised me not to remarry as I may well end up in a similar position as I was then, with an ex-wife and two young children. I'm not sure if her insight was based on her understanding of me or her one meeting with Susan.

Though the children were involved with Susan she would never stay overnight when they were with me and always go back to her small house in the Heights. I did not want to set any bad examples, not that I hadn't already, and felt that once, as was becoming inevitable, we were engaged then Susan could move in permanently and we would sell her house.

"Too many people spend money they haven't earned to buy things that don't want to impress people they don't like"
Will Rogers

The above is one of the things I dislike most about America, along with their idiotic addiction to guns and the belief that universal health care is somehow evil. The masses are brainwashed into buying all sorts of utterly unnecessary rubbish which brings no happiness and just leads to another buying fix and a cycle of debt and misery. What other country, after a massive terrorist attack like 9/11, would tell its citizens to go shopping?

That Christmas the children had the benefit of two houses full of presents, both of course to excess, which apparently I am told is one of the positives that children see in the bleakness of divorce. Susan and I made a point of never talking negatively about Janet in front of John and Camille. By now I was totally used to the massive orgy of mindless consumerism that is Christmas in America. I found it quite offensive but simply accepted it: yet another value I abandoned.

As 2002 rolled into 2003 I was becoming increasingly concerned with the goings on at Duke as were my close colleagues Matt Sandler and our London representative, Kurt Rohner, who I had known for years. We agreed that legal action was likely going to be necessary but Matt and Kurt wanted to wait until after March to see what, if any, bonus we received. I struggled to see the merit in waiting that long.

Kurt at one time had executed a small product trade that lost maybe $30k but it really seemed to bother him. Being his boss, and not wanting to see him in distress over such a relative trifle, I volunteered to take the trade, and the loss, from him. He was absolutely stunned. He said never in his over 20 years of trading had he seen anyone do such a thing. It was no big deal to me, however. Kurt so happened to be married to the ex-broker with whom I had done my "chicken pox" trade some 15 years prior. She had told Kurt that I was always such a happy fellow when she knew me. But as we know that person was long since dead.

Susan meanwhile had been totally unjustly fired from her job at WebMethods. She had grounds for a suit on numerous grounds including unfair dismissal and sexual harassment given the myriad of disgraceful comments that were said about her. She actually was doing a great job so much so that she had four deals lined up almost ready to close when she was fired. Those deals would have earnt her a six figure commission. After firing her, her boss closed the deals and took the commission himself. She said she did not believe in legal action. Neither did I, if it was frivolous, but in this case it was absolutely warranted, but she nonetheless refused.

With the massive options bomb heading my way at work and the rapidly deteriorating conditions I decided I could not wait till March to do something. I proceeded to make a serious tactical blunder that would again cost me a lot of money. I went with Matt to meet a couple of lawyer friends of his who were amazed by our revelations. They thought we would have a very strong case, mainly for having our options replaced by cash and for a bonus and suitable severance. I retained the lawyers and had them send a letter to Duke on my behalf that said I wished to receive full value for my options and bonus and a suitable severance and would like to sit down with them to arrange this in return for which I would not disclose any of the massive irregularities that I discovered. Duke promptly sent me home for two weeks. Two weeks later Duke told me to report back to work and if I failed to do so I was effectively resigning, Foolishly I did not return to work and thus I resigned. I thought I would still prevail in a legal case but I was not acting sensibly. My lawyer was basically milking me, thus far of about $14,000 and when I asked him to file a suit he refused. At this point I should have reported him to the Texas Legal Board but instead I sought just to sever my contract with him. Susan and I paid him a visit where Susan tore into him and he agreed to cancel our contract. On the way out he somewhat cheekily warned me that I should be careful if I intended to marry "that one".

Meanwhile Matt, Kurt and I were looking to move as a team to another company. There were few opportunities as the energy trader market was seriously oversupplied with traders being let go from Enron and all the similar companies. Through a broker we ran into a small London and New York based bond trading company named Mako, after the shark. After several meetings we struck a deal with them to join as a team and started to look for office space. I obviously had plenty of time to do this while Kurt and Matt were still at work. We took a small office in the Regus suites just down the road on San Felipe. Mako sent a guy to set up our systems and prepared to send a young analyst from London to be our assistant in Houston. We would not start work until Matt and Kurt had left Duke.

"By all means marry. If you get a good wife you'll become happy; if you get a bad one you'll become a philosopher."
Socrates

Around this time I decided the time was right to propose which I duly did at home to the sound of Beethoven's "Ode to Joy". Susan and I were both delighted and we began to prepare for a wedding towards the end of July. When we told the children Camille was thrilled but John less so. We told them that they would both have an important role in the wedding which was to be held at St. Martin's.

Kurt and Matt were both given a modest bonus and then let go with a decent severance. I had nothing and my phone calls to Duke were being ignored. I was becoming increasingly concerned that I had made yet another blunder.

At Duke, before the meltdown, I slowly saw how I was being moved into management and I was pleased at the prospect of no longer having to trade. Now I had accepted a purely speculative trading job with no base salary and a 30% bonus but with very tight position limits. Once again I was getting myself into a mess. What was I thinking? I felt I had no choice but this was yet another example of a dreadfully self-destructive decision. Susan initially was not at all supportive of my decision to sue Duke despite my trying to convince her of the massive irregularities of which I was aware. She rather angrily said I was just upset for buying a losing stock. This lack of support was of course disappointing though she later came more around to understanding my point of view.

In our first week at Mako the three of us were uniformly bullish and placed some trades accordingly. However, a small market move against us set off the Mako alarm bells and we were stopped out of our position. A couple of days later the market assumed a very strong bullish trajectory that we had anticipated but we were not in it. My old demons came to the fore. I had a hollow feeling inside me which I recognised as the demon of depression, waiting to strike. After several especially depressing days, one evening Susan found me lying naked on the sofa downstairs, crying and violently pounding the pillows. She was quite alarmed yet set about comforting me. The stress of my clumsy Duke exit coupled with my new Mako position had brought me back down to the depths of despair. Susan told me if the wedding was going to be too much for me we could cancel or postpone it but nothing would have to change in our relationship. This was of course very thoughtful of her but it was in no way our pending nuptials that were worrying me. The creature inside me, with which I had fought all my life, was back in insidious action, trying to destroy me.

Somehow I managed to pull myself together and we soon made a little money at Mako. Susan and I started to prepare for the wedding in earnest. We decided to sell her house which was about $30,000 under water. After quite some time trying to sell it we ultimately gave up and put it up for auction where of course it did sell, but at a loss of over $30,000. I also discovered that Susan owed a good $10,000 on her Mercedes C class in excess of its value and she owed about $18,000 in back taxes and penalties. I had no issue with any of this, as it made me feel additionally important and of value to her, as she clearly was to me. Though her personal finances were a bit of a mess, there were no signs of Susan being a spendthrift. In fact Susan helped me reduce my monthly expenses by changing my home insurance company and my landscaper.

We of course moved all of Susan's possessions into my house on Cedar Creek. These included two pistols and a small shotgun which I had my quail-hunting friend Dan inspect once they were at my house. Dan was amazed to find that all three were loaded but much to his alarm, not only was the shotgun loaded but the safety was off. That had been a disaster waiting to happen as we had driven across town. He unloaded all the guns and told us to put them well away, which we duly did.

"Men marry women with the hope they will never change.
Women marry men with the hope they will change. Invariably
they are both disappointed".
Albert Einstein

We were married on July 26, 2003, at St. Martin's Church followed by a reception at the Forrest Club. Alberto was my best man. John was suitably attired in a tuxedo by my side and Camille wore a white dress at Susan's side. It was a beautiful day and we took extra special care to keep John and Camille heavily involved. My parents of course came over. It was the first time they had experienced a summer in Houston.

As a humorous aside a couple of years later I would be standing outside this church with Cindy Sheehan and her cohorts waving my anti-Bush banner. The Church was attended regularly by George H.W. Bush and his wife and James Baker and I believe they both contributed significantly to the construction of the magnificent new Church that now stands grandly on the corner of Sage and San Felipe.

After a short honeymoon in St. Maarten, which was terrific, we returned home to start our new life together. We discussed all manner of new ideas that would not involve my trading as this clearly caused me massive mental duress but we were unable to arrive at a satisfactory solution.

Such was my frustration and unhappiness at Mako, I would act furiously in the office and frequently keep very short hours, much to the concern of Matt and Kurt who were relying on me to lead the group.

At home, quite understandably Susan wanted to make some changes to the house as it basically reflected how Janet had set it up. It was furnished with a mishmash of old, but high quality, furniture from Santa Fe and other more traditional pieces we had bought in Houston. We sold a few things, bought a new bed and some new sofas. Susan then decided she wanted to decorate. She brought over a friend of hers who was training as a decorator. Her friend came along with her boss and had a look around. The first thing they wanted to do was paint all the downstairs moulding, for whatever reason, a shade of taupe. Currently it was white. Quite why this was so important I failed to understand and when they quoted me a price of $18,000 for the work I nearly dropped dead. "Oh no, what have I done?" I fearfully thought, at the same time trying to suppress this unwelcome negative notion. I told Susan there was no way I was going to do that and that led to an argument about furniture and paint. I tried to explain that at Mako, so far, we had made no money, so let's be a little sensible in our aspirations. This would be an ongoing theme throughout our marriage.

I decided to pursue my Duke situation and was recommended an extremely good securities lawyer, Eric Fryar. After explaining the circumstances of my complaint and all that I knew I asked him if he would take it on contingency, mainly due to my previous waste of over $14,000. A couple of days later he agreed and then set about preparing an initial complaint which he duly filed. Duke obviously took it seriously as they employed the renowned Houston Law firm Fulbright and Jaworski to rebut the case. They immediately filed for "summary judgement, i.e., for the judge to kick the case out. Eric said this was always possible but hopefully unlikely. We prevailed and the case was not kicked out. Eric then prepared an incredibly detailed complaint which to me was a legal masterpiece. Before filing he sent it to Duke's lawyers at Fulbright and very soon they requested mediation.

By coincidence, one of my colleague Matt's brothers worked up north for one of the largest class action attorneys in the country. Off the record, Matt forwarded a copy of my complaint to his brother. His brother was amazed. He said if my complaint was correct, which it was, this case could be huge. However, being the lead plaintiff in a class action case was no fun and did not guarantee me anything.

The mediation took all day and was a pretty tedious process with the mediator bouncing between respective parties once we had both had a chance to lay our cards on the table. Eric did a great job of explaining my complaint. Fulbright then had their turn to rebut the case which I found amusing. They almost appeared to be agreeing with everything I said but that it would be very hard to prove. This strengthened my resolve. Eric mentioned that it was definitely a winnable case but it could take years and that the Bush Justice Department was basically in the mode of turning a blind eye to large corporate frauds, other than a few headline cases like Enron and Tyco, and that that would further hamper my chances.

We started very far apart and by around 9pm at night we agreed on a settlement that was about one-third of what they really owed me. I was very disappointed but what was I to do. I did not have the desire for a long legal battle and Duke to a degree did not care as they had a whole host of in-house lawyers who would be more than happy spending their days trying to prevent me from getting paid anything. The thought did occur to me that for the greater good we should file my detailed complaint and then join forces with a large class action firm but Eric said while we could, it would probably not be to my benefit. Thus the settlement was agreed. At least I had a little more money to cover the fact that our Mako gig was not going as well as we had hoped.

Susan too was disappointed when I told her of the outcome but she agreed it was the best we could do, under the circumstances.

We were managing to eke out a small profit at Mako but I absolutely hated it. I had recurring thoughts of how Greenslade's vindictiveness was in large part responsible for my plight, as news filtered through on the grapevine, that Vitol continued to flourish, while I struggled in my usual state of despair and crushing anguish. Had I returned to Vitol, back in 1999, my "shareholding" alone, would by now be worth well over $60m, largely thanks to Repsol cancelling the YPF refinery purchase; by 2007, it would have been worth well in excess of $100m. Since 1999 every year my compensation at Vitol would have exceeded my entire nine year earnings there by a factor of 2 to 4, with the possible exception of 1999 when I may have earnt a mere $4m or so. Traders and support staff alike were making tens of millions of dollars year after year, frequently through no fault of their own. I struggled to come to terms with the fact my great old friend Ian's betrayal and weakness had deprived me of some of this and condemned me to a life of utter wretchedness and suffering. The money would not have cured all that ailed me but I suspect it would have helped as ironically the life I now led was, and would become, even more stressful than any I had previously encountered, certainly much more so than my potentially resumed Vitol career would have been. However, that is an easy assumption to make and one that in no way can be verified.

One evening in early November Susan came to bed in tears. "What was wrong?" I asked. "I'm pregnant" she cried. I was speechless. Oh my: I comforted her and said it would be fine and that John and Camille would like to have a younger sibling. Clearly our lives were soon to take yet another dramatic turn.

That fall the rugby World Cup was held in Australia and England were favourites. All the games were in the middle of the night, but I would insist on getting John out of bed to watch them with me or even take him to the pub, in the case of our semifinal victory over France. The Wednesday before the Final my friend Martin Hunt told me that he was going to Sydney for the Final. He was crazy, I thought, but what the heck, why not? Susan fully supported my decision which in hindsight was very generous given my near apoplectic fit that I had thrown over the prospect of spending, admittedly very large sums, on decorating the house. I hurriedly, Thursday morning, bought two tickets from Houston to Sydney, via LA, for John and myself returning the following Sunday from Sydney. We would only spend one night in Sydney. I had an old Duke friend in Sydney who I emailed overnight and asked him to get me two tickets and to find me a room. I called him from LA and he had managed to do both. John was obviously thrilled to be going, and I thought I was a little crazy to be dragging him all that way. However, after England's famous victory, it was thoroughly worth it and we had a fantastic couple of days in Sydney before heading back on the Sunday night. That certainly was a trip that John and I will never forget and for a week or two it actually lifted my spirits. John and I also attended the World Cup Final four years later in Paris when unfortunately we lost to South Africa. Of course we spent a couple of days taking in the main sites of the city, entirely on foot, such that by the end of the second day John was thoroughly exhausted. I had an old familiar problem from the past: I desperately needed to go to the bathroom but lacked the coinage and time to use one of the odd Parisian toilets. So, I am ashamed to say, in front of my 14 year old son, I ran into a doorway just off a major thoroughfare and managed to pull down my pants before the world once again fell out of my bottom. From Paris we paid a quick visit to my parents in Jersey which was especially nice for John as my dad did not have long to live.

Immediately after it was Thanksgiving and Susan and I took John and Camille to Disney World where we had a thoroughly superb time, all wearing our England World Cup winning T-shirts. That was certainly a great couple of weeks. Susan could not go on many of the rides due to her condition but we told John and Camille that she was prone to motion sickness. We had decided to wait until Christmas until we gave them the news.

Destiny: "Everywhere man blames nature and fate, yet his fate

is mostly but the echo of his character and passions, his mistakes and weaknesses". Democritus

Throughout this period and for a good few more years I would see Sarna both on my own and with Susan, the latter being to sort out parenting issues and problems with Janet, still interfering. Sarna recognised that I was clearly depressed and she explained to me the effect growing up with an alcoholic parent can have. I was not aware of this so was pleased to receive this new information. Although it did not provide any relief it did perhaps shed some light on why I was the way I was. She further explained the significance of "inner dialogue" and how we could change that as we were, after all, in charge of it. This interested me too but I have seldom, if ever, been able to fight off the demons inside my head when they are in full voice. More than that, I am not sure if I learnt much. Sarna would often say I needed to stop feeling sorry for myself and having a pity party. That was not particularly helpful. I was not so much feeling sorry for myself as hating myself and everything that I had become and was utterly drained by all my problems and disappointments and failures. I felt utterly hopeless and helpless. She felt that there must have been some positive payout for my constantly repeating actions that would result in making myself wretched. I'm afraid I could not see anything positive: it was maybe more like an addiction where I was addicted to trying to succeed and simply never would or could and was condemned to repeat this tortuous cycle. I told her that no matter what I felt or did I would always fail and that ultimately my destiny was to lose everything and I knew one day that I would.

My behaviour at Mako was becoming all the more erratic. Unlike my previous jobs this was such a small and intense environment that I could not shield my despair from my colleagues. I would even frequently at work search the internet and read articles about suicide. I could hardly bare to go into the office. As well as the obvious pain it would cause my family I had serious religious misgivings at this time over such a desperate course of action. I felt like the hyperconscious mouse in Dostoevsky's "Notes from the Underground," plagued with doubt and vacillation and unable to do anything but "creep ignominiously back into its mouse hole". Such was my obvious despair that Kurt flew over to join us for dinner and he and Matt told me that I should quit as clearly it was driving me insane. I appreciated their candour and perhaps concern. Matt in the meantime had already been looking for another job, I heard from an industry friend.

That Christmas, with my parents over, we told them and John and Camille that we were expecting a baby. My parents and Camille were excited and even John was to a degree. That was positive I thought.

The final straw at Mako occurred when we had established a fairly large spread position that was slightly underwater but we were supremely confident that it would work out. Because of the tight leash that we were on one evening management stopped us out. I was devastated. If we had just hung on a few more days we would have made $1m, my share of which would have been $200k. I could not believe it and would not take it anymore. I called management in New York and resigned which they understood. Matt and Kurt hung around until they could find new employment. Matt eventually returned to Neste and Kurt joined Nexen in London. But what about me? What was I to do? I did not want to trade but what else could I do. Susan for obvious reasons did not want me to trade either.

I was talking to the large Connecticut and Geneva based trader, Sempra. I really thought they were going to offer me a job but they strung me along for a couple of months and in the end nothing happened. I was very concerned, as I would be seemingly for the rest of my life, about money. I did not want to start spending my hard earned savings which, on Susan's sensible prompting, we invested in Municipal Bonds paying 5%.

I needed somehow to make money and so I put $400k in a Refco account and started to trade the WTI futures market myself, using my old friend, Richard May, as my broker. This was a risky high stress venture: just what I needed. I started fairly well but then took a nasty loss which sent me into a deep suicidal depression. Sarna sent me to a ten day out-patient treatment program which was again, for a very short period, quite helpful, but the effects soon wore off. Obviously this was a concern and a strain for Susan but she remained steadfast and did her utmost to help me through my increasingly frequent and dark periods of despair.

During 2002 and 2003, often in the depths of a Mako induced depression, Susan and I would spend quite some time playing casual tennis at the Racquet Club. We usually ended up hitting with Latin Americans and Middle Easterners. There was one late middle-aged Latin American who I particularly liked: he was clearly very intelligent and well educated and we often enjoyed brief conversations about various topics including oil.

Now as Christmas approached that year I was shopping with my parents in Central Market when I bumped into the Latin American chap and his wife. We started a conversation during which it became apparent that both he and I had been involved in the Oil Trading business. I gave him my name and told him that I had worked for a long time at Vitol. He told me he knew Vitol well, especially Neil Kelley and Bob Finch. He then told me where he had worked and that his name was "Juan Valdez". At this moment we both had an embarrassing epiphany that we did our best to cover up. He clearly knew that I knew and I knew that he knew that I knew he knew. We glossed over it and he explained that he was now a very senior executive at a large well known company here in the US. He told me to call him and have lunch. I duly called and left a message which was never, perhaps not surprisingly, ever returned. He was clearly embarrassed but in no way did I have any negative feelings towards him. After all we had "mutually beneficial relationships," with several people.

Throughout this period I would regularly see Sarna and she persuaded me to switch psychiatrists as maybe a different medication would be of benefit. My new Doctor prescribed 300 mg of Venlafaxine (Effexor) per day which I have been taking to this day. Effexor actually did appear to be a positive improvement but so much of my depression, as well as resulting from chemical imbalances, stemmed from external stressors and triggers. I could be triggered by a certain song or news story on the radio or by perfectly innocuous comments that people made to me but once that trigger was pulled a bullet hit me straight between the eyes.

On one particularly dreadful day at Mako I drove the short distance home in great despondency. My life was simply cursed, and a total failure: why must it continue, I thought to myself. As I pressed the electronic gate opener to open the gate to our house Winston, as he did, poked his head through the slowly opening gate as he prepared to bolt off down the street. With just his snout poking out the gate suddenly stopped opening and started to close, potentially crushing his snout. He yelped in pain. I jumped out of the car and ran and pushed the gate such that it continued to open. Winston was fine but on rushing out of the car I had neglected to put it in park. My Mercedes therefore slowly rolled forward as the opening gate scratched along almost the entire length of the left side of my car making a dreadful mess. By the time I had made sure Winston was ok I ran around the back of the car and jumped in the driver's seat to stop the car just as it collided with the basketball hoop at the end of our drive. Although funny in hindsight, and I retold this story to the delight of many of my friends, it just added to my overall feeling of total despair. Nothing would ever go right in my life.

Winston did not have a great deal of time left and was eventually put down with a variety of ailments including the inability to stand. His last destructive act was to rip out the entire cat door in our house and make a dog-door large enough for himself in the sheetrock. With his face covered in sheetrock he proudly walked around the house with the cat door draped around his neck, like a medallion.

Shortly after Winston's death we decided to adopt another dog from the local animal shelter. I went with Susan and young Amelia to see

Jonathan Ford

what they had and soon found myself attracted to a shy-looking golden dog that looked like a smallish dingo or perhaps a cross between a labrador and German shepherd. Anyway, I persuaded the family to take her and save her from the fate that many of her fellow inmates would soon have to face.

When we arrived home I attempted to get her out of the back of the car but she viciously snapped at me, her saviour, of all people. I tried again, but realised it was not a good idea so I let Susan take her out of the car. Clearly she had something against men but this had not been apparent at the shelter. Inside the house I kept my distance from her but at night she would go and lie protectively by Susan's side of the bed and basically keep me out of my own bedroom. We solved this problem by tying her leash to the leg of the bed.

Obviously we decided to take her back to the shelter but for some reason we procrastinated and then my parents were over for Christmas. Penny, as Amelia had christened her, loved my dad and so my parents actively walked her every day until after a few weeks she was even tolerant of me. So we decided to keep her and she became our somewhat temperamental and unstable pet for about the next 9 years until she too passed away, after a couple of very expensive ACL surgeries I might add.

It was in March of 2003 when my Mako situation was coming to an end that Susan and I went to the theatre to see "A Conversation with Spalding Grey". We of course expected an entertaining evening of witty repartee between Spalding and various members of the audience who he would invite to join him in one of the two arm chairs placed on stage. However this was not to be. The most exciting moment of the evening was when he made a mild criticism of the very fresh invasion of Iraq which led to a number of members of the audience to stand up and leave in protest. His conversations with audience members, were slow, laboured and lame. He went into a monologue about why he seemed so down: "because he could not dance (with his son)". He explained that while driving relatively recently on an extremely quiet road in Ireland, where barely another car was seen, his vehicle had been smashed into by another vehicle and his leg and hip had been badly injured. He could no longer dance as he put it with his young son as he pathetically attempted a little shuffle across the stage. I recognised so many of my own symptoms in him yet there he was parading them in front of an audience for all to plainly see while I fought daily to hide them from all but a very select few. Susan and I exchanged a few words with him in the foyer. Susan attempted to tell him that she knew a massage therapist/kinesiologist who might be able to help his condition. Spalding half smiled but said it was more serious than that, which it undoubtedly was. Upon leaving I told Susan that he was clearly extremely depressed and I would not at all be surprised if he was to commit suicide, such was his despair and lack of hope apparent to me. About 14 months later on the radio we heard that he had indeed killed himself by drowning. It was very sad.

Somehow through 2004 I managed to make an overall profit of $400k. How I did so I don't know but the effects on my health could not have been good. I do recall after one of my few moments of success Susan commented that I appeared manic. I essentially ignored that comment as I had never considered myself bipolar and whenever questioned by a doctor I would always say that I did not experience manic episodes. Those words would over ten years later take on, albeit probably too late, some considerable significance.

In February of 2004 my best friend Alberto was to get married in Lima, Peru. Of course I would attend. Susan being about four months pregnant was not overly keen to go but she did not wish to disappoint me as she knew how much I wanted to travel and how important it was to me. After a splendid couple of days in Lima we flew home. Immediately on the plane, fortunately we were in business class, Susan became violently ill and spent most of the flight in the toilet. When we arrived back in Houston we went straight to the hospital as she was severely dehydrated and feeling dreadful. Obviously we were worried about the baby. They kept her in the hospital for a couple of nights and ran a variety of tests. She had a whole smorgasbord of infections including botulism, e.coli and clostridium difficile colitis (c.diff). Because she was pregnant they used a strong antibiotic, vancomycin, to treat the infections as it apparently was not transferred through the placenta. Susan recovered in several days but remained on the vancomycin through the term of the pregnancy mainly to keep the c.diff at bay. She was of course constantly worried about any possible effects on the baby but the scans and the amniocentesis all said nothing was to be concerned about. Eventually on July 11 she gave birth to a beautiful, healthy, little girl that we named Amelia Grace. Unfortunately Amelia was born with hip dysplasia so immediately on being discharged we headed to the orthopedist who told us this was very common but Amelia would have to wear a contraption that kept her legs in a frog like position for the first few months. We were of course a little disappointed but it could have been worse and after a few short months she was ok.

Camille and John loved their little sister who was from a very early age full of life and personality. I found having a new born much less stressful than I had feared and in fact much easier second time around.

Amelia was an extremely spirited little girl from a young age and

Susan and I enjoyed traveling with her to Mexico and even to Rome and Paris where the locals really took a liking to her.

There were a couple of occasions early in Amelia's life when Susan's "lack of civilisation" did reveal itself. Both were harmless but did pay testimony to her rather wild and untethered upbringing.

The first was In the fall of 2003 when we decided to take a short trip to New York with Amelia and Camille. John had baseball practise so could not come. I of course knew New York pretty well having spent a full year working there not that long ago. The forecast was for drizzle so I prepared to take my trench raincoat, with lining if it were cold, that I had always used when commuting in New York. In my closet hung a brand new cashmere overcoat that still had the labels on it since I had purchased it back in 1998. For some reason Susan insisted I take this coat. Why she was so bothered I do not know and I tried to explain that my raincoat was far more suited to the weather that was to be expected. However she would not relent and, as usual I gave in. At the airport, while I was buying a drink, Susan and my two daughters waited near the gate. When I returned to them I found they had spread my brand new cashmere coat on the floor and were eating snacks on it and basically using it as a cheap blanket. I was both stunned and furious. I simply could not understand why Susan would do that. It was such odd and inappropriate behaviour, in my view.

We did have a few good days in New York, seeing some of the typical sites and eating at Serendipity at Camille's request. My coat, of course, was totally unsuited to the constant drizzle we encountered.

As 2005 approached I was still in need of employment and had no good leads. I did not want to leave Houston as Camille and John were still young and in Middle School, for which I paid. Fortunately, in early 2005 a good friend of mine at BP, Nick Wildgoose, called me. He was not a native American, as his name may suggest, but in fact hailed from Manchester, and was their head crude trader. I was actually in the process of returning from quite a successful quail hunt that I would from to time enjoy with my sharp-shooting friend Dan, in Mexico, just over the border from McAllen. Nick explained that BP was looking to staff a new group of "Originators" to develop longer term business with market counterparts in both crude and products. The word "Originator" brought back memories of Enron where I had first heard it and I never liked it. Nonetheless, with his advice I contacted the man spearheading this venture, Aidan Mills, and soon found myself being interviewed in both Houston and their main trading office in Warrenville outside Chicago. I was offered the job which paid less than I was accustomed to receiving but it was not bad overall.

On the subject of quail hunting Dan and I once made our way down to MacAllen, from where we would cross the border with our Mexican guide, in style, as Dan had invited an elder friend of his, Bob, who flew us in his private twin-engine turbo plane. Bob was a charming and fascinating fellow. He was a close personal friend of George HW Bush and reluctantly admitted that he had long known "Dubya" and he had always been "worthless". We joked that it had taken the Texas Rangers over 10 years to recover from Dubya: if only America could be so lucky. Now Bob made his money in the banking business. He and his associates would find a suitably located, quiet bank that did very little business and then arrange for hundreds if not thousands of their "friends" to open accounts at that bank. They would then, after a suitable period of time, show the bank and its stellar growth to the large major US banking groups who would buy the rapidly growing bank at a hefty price. With a nice profit in hand Bob and his cohorts would then arrange for all those new accounts to close and they would move to another suitable bank and repeat the process. He admitted he was amazed at how many times he could do this but it beat working.

BP
"An oil well is a hole in the ground with a liar on top".
Attributed to Mark Twain

BP was the most aggressive of the oil majors in terms of trading, as it had indeed been since the 1980s. Their traders were extremely well paid, maybe ten times what their equivalents were paid at other majors because they apparently made a huge contribution to BP's bottom line. I wondered, if they made all that extra money trading and Exxon for example did not, why was their return on equity or capital employed so much worse than Exxon's who had a very small trading/supply group and ran a very tight ship. Were BP's physical assets so inferior to account for the difference?

I was based in Houston but expected to fly to Chicago at least once a month to meet the traders and discuss opportunities. I knew most of the crude traders already as well as one or two of the product traders and I soon befriended a sturdy English chap by the name of Keith Neal who was a long-time BP employee and was now a Products Originator. He explained a lot of the inner workings of BP and especially IST (Integrated Supply and Trading) where he told me "perception was much more important than reality".

The Head of this new group of Originators, Aidan Mills, was a young Northern Irishman who was extremely political and had recently had the position of "turtle" or executive assistant to one of BP's top executives, Vivienne Cox, and was thus very well connected. As well as taking people from inside BP he went on an aggressive hiring spree outside bringing on at least three new people from the industry in an effort to make an enormous splash into the market.

Interestingly, my friend Alberto moved over the years quite frequently between Houston and Lima as his parents, with whom he was very close, lived in Lima yet he was largely educated and brought up in Houston. I had earlier helped him get on board with Duke to cover Latin America for us out of Lima as Duke International had a small office in Lima from where they managed their South American power generation portfolio. After Duke imploded he had a couple of years at Pluspetrol in Lima after which he still wanted to stay in Peru but had few options. And so, during my early days at BP, I persuaded BP that they needed someone with his regional expertise, that they lacked, together with his impeccable integrity. Even though they strongly disliked lone wolves in remote offices, they agreed, on my recommendation, to take Alberto on for at least 3 years in Lima before moving to Houston.

I was immediately assigned the task of working with Enbridge, a company with which we did a great deal of business, to jointly put together a bid for the St. James, Louisiana crude oil terminal owned by Koch that was being put up for sale. Part of BP's crude strategy at that time was to acquire crude oil tankage along the Gulf Coast and St. James was an especially strategic location given its access to Capline and its potential LLS blending capabilities. I soon learnt at BP that attitude (perception) was very important. You always had to give the impression that you were screwing your counterpart as we, BP, were so much smarter than everyone else. Therefore my easy going often jovial attitude did not always fit in too well with the likes of Aidan who always was serious and very businesslike. The traders were more of a jovial bunch and pretty much acted and did as they pleased but still they had to give the impression that anyone who dealt with them would get the wrong end of the stick. I often thought that BP people, like Paul Butcher who had started there, were the most well balanced I had met, as they had a chip on both shoulders.

Aidan explained to me that we knew exactly how Enbridge's MLP (Master Limited Partnership) economics worked and so could work out exactly how much they could bid for the St. James terminal. The idea was they would buy it backed by a long term lease from us. Quite how we knew their economics I did not know but we were BP and cleverer than everyone else. I think his assessment was based on a pipeline deal that we had recently concluded with them. He also explained that their economics could be boosted by some tax advantages that hung over from that pipeline deal and thus we could really exact a pound of flesh from them when we put together our joint bid. Some way to treat a partner I thought. I had to sit down with the crude traders and get an estimate of what they thought owning the terminal would be worth for them in terms of trading revenue. Based on that we could make a deal with Enbridge and then present the bid to Koch.

I had numerous protracted discussions and at one time a veritable summit meeting with Enbridge and a couple of my colleagues from our affiliate BP Pipeline. It was soon apparent that there was no way we were going to come to terms with Enbridge that would allow us to make a realistic bid on the terminal. We seemed to have more interest in screwing Enbridge than actually having access to the asset.

Finally Enbridge submitted their bid backed by our long term lease: we were out bid by a mile by NuStar. Now of course internally we had to lay the blame firmly at Enbridge's feet for our not winning the bid.

Another originator was given the task of lining up some long term ethanol purchases. This he successfully did with at least two counterparts for which he was handsomely rewarded. When the deals came to fruition they lost a fortune but we weren't going to worry about that. It seemed like I had gone back in time to Enron.

"The Power of Accurate observation is commonly called cynicism by those who have not got it" .
George Bernard Shaw

Back in the 80s BP trading had a reputation for basically just ripping off its affiliates, primarily upstream (the production side) and downstream (the refining and marketing side). I soon realised little if anything had changed.

BP product traders bought the products from the refineries at the appropriate Platts quote and could immediately turn around and sell it at the true market of a few dollars per tonne extra and be credited with making that money. Crude and product traders were at times given access to BP owned tankage to use in a contango market without paying anywhere near a market rate for the tanks and so were making free money, once again. The whole place seemed like an enormous farce to me that probably was more of a net loser to BP than a profit contributor yet the positive feedback kept flowing and IST was generally held in awe by the rest of BP.

BP traders were paid a percentage of what they made, most of which was simply free money off transfer prices. This could lead to 7 if not 8 figure bonuses. Being paid a percentage of profits could also incentivise bad behaviour as witnessed by the alleged propane manipulation case that was pending right around the time I had joined. BP ended up paying a fine for that as indeed they did for an alleged natural gas price manipulation game.

I decided to keep my head down and do the best I could. After the first year I was given my guaranteed minimum bonus which was fine as I had not concluded anything, though neither had anyone else other than the two massive money losing ethanol deals.

BP had for years, I understood, wanted trading tankage in Houston but had never been able to arrange a deal for whatever reason. For my second year this would be my primary focus. I Identified three likely candidates; HOFTI (or Houston fuels), Oil Tanking (OTI) and Teppco who had acquired an assortment of old tanks from Reliant that could be converted to crude use, but this was a far more complex and hairy proposition. After months of negotiations I concluded a deal for 1.6mmbls of new crude oil tanks to be built at Oil Tanking Houston and which we would lease for 7 years.

As an interesting aside the German-Singaporean gentleman with whom I concluded this deal was the brother of Singapore's chief executioner.

At the same time I was given the task of renegotiating our LOOP (Louisiana Offshore Oil Port) cavern deal, which I successfully did and I concluded a further deal with LOOP to have 3 million barrels of tankage constructed onshore Louisiana that we would use under a long term lease. I was on a roll! People realised that I could actually get things done despite the massive BP bureaucracy with which we were plagued and the fact we were always meant to screw our counter parties. Our traders ran into a problem with a Brent cargo they were storing at South Riding Point which I was asked to sort out and duly did. I even made a long term HLS sale to Conoco with the help of BP pipeline who had to install a drag reducing agent skid. Normally IST and Pipeline struggled to get anything done as of course they both had to give the appearance of screwing each other.

Keith and I later that year had dinner with some of the folks at Kinder Morgan with whom we did a lot of business but who complained that we were very difficult to deal with. At dinner they explained there was an obvious win-win deal to be done at their Carteret New Jersey facility and they could not understand why we would not entertain it. We basically could have knocked the deal out over dinner but it would not be done for a few more years after a Herculean effort by our superstar originator who finally concluded something that was staring us in the face for years. At that dinner the senior Kinder guy kindly offered that he would arrange a meeting with our boss, Aidan, to meet Rich Kinder. Now Rich Kinder was and is a legendary figure in the US oil business and it would be a great privilege to have a private meeting with him not to mention what business opportunities may result from such a meeting. When I mentioned this to Aidan he had no interest. I could not believe it. Again though, Aidan was too busy trying to look important internally and play politics rather than actually do anything useful. Once again perception won out over reality.

Now early in my second year, after much reflection, I think I found where I went wrong at BP. Despite getting things done I was not liked by my boss Aidan and it took me a long while to figure out why. I would have thought the fact that I had concluded a couple of very large and worthwhile tankage deals would reflect well on him but there had to be something else. At a NuStar party in San Antonio several of us BP originators were in attendance. Now the very political and astute long time originator, who brilliantly concluded the Carteret deal with Kinder, was TingGate Jue. He asked me what I thought of working with BP and how it compared with other companies I had worked with such as Vitol. I went on to say that it was great: there were so many opportunities and we had so many resources but it was also a bit like working for the civil service given all the bureaucracy. He agreed. At that point I should have shut up but I did not and thought we were just having a private chat amongst a few ex-traders. I went on to say that in my view "it was a bit of a scam" the way BP traders were paid what amounted to free money by exploiting the system whereas at a private trading company you had to actually make real money as there was no "system" to abuse. I am sure that scam comment went straight back to Aidan and my days were numbered.

We originators were given a target NPV (or net present value) of deals that we were expected to close in order to achieve our minimum bonus target. The value attributed to my storage deals was actually quite small but it was enough to reach my NPV target and thus to receive the minimum bonus. At bonus time in March 2007 I was one of the last to hear but I was not worried as everyone else, I understood, had been given their guaranteed minimum even though most of them had done absolutely nothing. You can imagine my shock when Aidan called and told me I was getting half of my minimum? I could not believe it. I argued with him strongly saying clearly this was a personal vendetta and in direct contradiction of the ethical standards we all had to sign. He proceeded to attempt to denigrate my deals, another violation of the ethical standards, and when I said well everyone else got the minimum without doing anything he said, "This is about you, not anyone else". The conversation ended and the following Monday I flew to Chicago to meet Aidan and our soon to be new boss Fergus. I referred to them as "The Thistle and Shamrock". The meeting quickly became ugly with my accusing Aidan of picking on me for whatever reason and I would take this up with HR. HR had obviously been briefed as they said all policies had been perfectly well followed. I was beside myself with anger.

I contacted my attorney friend Eric, who had helped so well with my Duke problem, and prepared a complaint against BP. In the complaint I detailed not just how Aidan had victimised and discriminated against me but also how in my opinion the entire BP trading establishment was a giant scam and a massive waste of shareholder money. Aidan also denigrated my work which again violated our ethical standards. To back this assertion up I cited numerous examples of ridiculous off-market transfer prices and the like from which BP traders profited. Some of the benchmarks against which BP traders were measured were even so ludicrous that I believe in some instances they were incentivised to actually lose money for BP. The main instance of this that comes to mind was what was known on the West Coast as the "Breakfast with BP" trade. Every morning traders from other companies would come into the office and try to buy the dirt cheap, below market piece of gasoline that the BP trader would sell on a daily basis over a long period of time. I suspect the purpose was to establish a below market price at which the trader bought all the gasoline from the refinery so that he could then sell the rest at the real market and show a huge "profit".

When my lawyer sent the complaint to BP in the summer of 2007 I dramatically cut back on my trips to Chicago as obviously I was a little uncomfortable with management knowing I had just called their entire operation a giant scam. BP said they would revert in a few days which indeed they did. Now BP had just settled a couple of manipulation cases with the US government for several hundred million dollars and further prosecution was deferred. Under those circumstances they deemed it appropriate to forward my complaint, with all its allegations, to the Department of Justice and soon I was summoned to Washington to be interviewed by members of the DOJ and various other Federal Agencies including the Bureau of Alcohol and Tobacco, the FBI and the Postal Service, who were responsible for mail fraud issues. BP had employed a defence attorney to accompany me. The two of us spent a couple of hours being interviewed about the contents of my complaint but since it appeared to contain no information of a criminal nature, and nothing further came of it, as far as I am aware. They also took the chance to ask me a few questions about my Duke lawsuit and the irregularities I believe I saw there.

The BP lawyers then contacted my lawyer and said go ahead and file if you wish, we have no interest in discussing a settlement. Now I believe they were somewhat bluffing in that they thought if I filed it would possibly be hard for me to find another job in the industry. On the other hand if I did not file I felt pretty safe in knowing that they would not fire me as that would appear as retaliation. I decided not to file.

One further similarity with Enron was the way BP used spurious options analysis to justify deals they simply wanted to do. For instance they would look at a certain tankage deal and imagine the "optionality" inherent in that deal in terms of the ability to, let's say go east or west, as market prices dictated, and then add the "extrinsic" value to the NPV of the deal to make it overcome the required internal NPV hurdle rate. I wish they had done this to my storage deals as they actually were money makers but I could have done with an extra $100m in NPV not that Aidan would have rewarded me for it.

In my last year at BP even though Aidan had moved on I knew my days were numbered and that I would not be treated fairly. Several originators, more on the financial product side, had already been let go. I did however do another nice fuel oil tankage deal with NuStar at our Texas City refinery which was of great benefit to our fuel oil trading team. This deal required the cooperation of the refinery business development unit which I managed to get.

The writing had been on the wall for the Origination group for quite some time as there was simply not enough business out there for a team of the size that we had assembled. However, my friend

Alberto was of value and they rightly kept him on.

Almost all the rest of us were let go around June 2008 with a generous severance package. My bonus for 2007 was $150,000 which actually surprised me but I was soon to learn that others had received far more. It is worthy of note that several people who actually did meaningful work within IST were shocked at my dismissal as I was the one originator who had done the most deals of real significance. Yet of course none of that really mattered.

Without a doubt there is a large element of "The Emperor's New Clothes" attached to the BP trading machine. Many people have made fortunes from that organisation some of whom have risen to senior management within the BP Group. In my view it makes BP all the more attractive a takeover target at the present time, notwithstanding other major issues, as the purchaser could immediately slash overheads by eliminating the bulk of this massively expensive group.

I also feel that BP's obsession with assigning everyone a yardstick or benchmark against which they were graded probably contributed to their two big disasters in recent years namely the Texas City explosion and the Macondo explosion: people were incentivised to cut costs and time which of course is not always wise in such a dangerous business. BP traders often had a superiority complex when dealing with industry counterparts and for sure the notorious "vampire squid" on Wall Street did not have a monopoly on referring to customers as "muppets". It always amused me how management stressed that, when we were dealing with counterparts, we had to be very careful to defend and uphold BP's reputation. I am not sure there was anything we originators could have said or done that damaged the reputation more than the various well publicised disasters and other lesser infractions had already done.

Despite my problems with Aidan Mills and the legal machinations, my 3 plus years at BP were work wise relatively low stress and I was pleased to not actually be speculatively trading: If only my personal life had been as placid.

In 2005 the extensive Volcker report into the Oil For Food deal that Iraq had with the UN was published with precise detail on all the corruption involved detailing numerous payments made by a variety of companies and individuals. Vitol were all over the report and I thought finally Greenslade might get his comeuppance: sadly this was not to be.The US authorities set about investigating numerous companies, including Vitol but appeared to focus on two US based companies namely Bayoil, run by Dave Chalmers and Coastal, run by Oscar Wyatt. Oscar was never very popular with the Bushes and had very close ties with Iraq. In 1990 before the US led invasion he had even made a trip to Iraq and brought home some

American hostages. The US government certainly had it in for him and he was prosecuted and sent to jail for about two years, at the grand old age of 81 or so. I believe he served 11 months. Dave Chalmers was also prosecuted and sentenced to two years in jail.

During the prosecution of Bayoil my old friend Dr. John Irving was indicted by the US in 2005 but he managed to avoid extradition and in 2009 paid a small fine. I have no doubt he had a few very unpleasant and stressful years during this time.

The US government were very lenient on Vitol and no individual was prosecuted and they were given a minor slap on the wrist and a fine of $17.5m which was far less than the amount of "surcharges" they had paid. Apparently their American trader in London, Robin D'Alessandro, who had previously worked for Chalmers and was intimately involved in the Iraq deals, was close to being prosecuted as indeed was David Fransen who was now in Geneva and signed off on many of the transactions but they both managed to skate by. Greenslade, as the Head of Crude in London, was the main man behind all these dealings but escaped unscathed. Vitol did, in 2007, have to plead guilty in New York to grand larceny but that was trivial in the overall scheme of things. I am left to wonder how I would have fared during such an investigation and maybe some of the other investigations to which, I believe, they have been subjected.

During my time at Vitol virtually nobody had heard of us outside of the oil industry. However, all that has changed with the advent of the internet such that they frequently appear in the news and Ian Taylor's views on oil are often quoted. Of course not all the press is good and their dealings with Arkan and in the Iraq/UN scandal are well documented and they feature in many articles about supposed Nigerian scandals, for example.

In 2012, because of Alan Duncan's obvious connections with David Cameron and William Hague, Vitol was given the highly profitable task of selling Libyan crude oil on behalf of the Libyan rebels. Vitol was by this time quite a controversial choice for the British government given their now widely known reputation and their conviction in a US court for grand larceny in relation to the Iraq/United Nations Oil for Food deal in which they and others paid massive "surcharges" to the Iraqi government. Perhaps what made it most controversial was that now after over 15 years they were the subject of an investigation into a major UK tax avoidance scheme as a result of them paying probably billions of dollars in compensation offshore, free of tax. It was in early 2012 that JP Morgan were fined for such a deal and Vitol entered into settlement negotiations with the exchequer over their similar plan known as the Vitol Employee Benefit Trust (VEBT) run by the Royal Bank of Canada in Jersey. Ian Taylor had actually mentioned such a tax structure to me as early as 1995. Much later I understood from a British trader that each senior Vitol employee in London would receive 100,000 pounds or so in salary and then a 25,000 annual bonus. In reality these bonuses ran into the 7 and even 8 figures so 25,000 pounds was a mere pittance. The trader then had an account, operated by the Trustee in Jersey, into which the bulk of the bonus was paid. Under trust guidelines money in the trust could only be used, via an interest free loan to oneself, for certain types of expenses such as education. You are not meant to use it to buy a Ferrari. However, such guidelines were apparently ignored by the Vitol traders: they must have had some very large education expenses. At the end of the day the loans could simply never be paid back, or at a suitable time, a trader could move to a tax free jurisdiction for a year at least, collect the contents of the Trust and bring them back tax free to the UK. As soon as I heard about it I thought it sounded too good to be true but Vitol apparently had it vetted by a Queen's Counsel (QC). Equally payments of 7 and 8 figures could result from the periodic retained earnings or "shareholder" payouts. These would in all probability go into the Trust or more likely, since they originated from overseas, either Rotterdam or Geneva, they would just go into a tax free account totally undeclared. The latter smacks more of evasion, in my view, than avoidance but the effects are the same. Foreign, i.e., non-British nationals were, I believe, permitted to have their bonuses paid directly offshore not even bothering with the Trust facade. In this way the UK Exchequer missed out on billions of pounds in tax revenue: perhaps Ian's 500,000 pound donation to the Tory party, coupled with a private dinner at No.10, was well worth it.

Vitol, in 2013 was prosecuted quite lamely in France, along with Total, for its role in the Iraq oil for food "bribery" case. Vitol employed a notorious French lawyer to lead their defence, Jaques Verges, known in France as "The Devil's Advocate". He had defended the Nazi war criminal, Klaus Barbie, Carlos "the Jackal" and numerous other notorious French criminals. During the trial the 88 year old lawyer passed away. Vitol was acquitted but the French authorities appealed the verdict and Vitol were recently ordered to pay a trivial fine of 300,000 Euros.

Financial Calamities
"When sorrows come, they come not single spies but in battalions".
Claudius, in Shakespeare's Hamlet

For John and Camille, as indeed for all children of divorce, the toing and froing between houses is a pain, to say the least. Invariably homework or an article of clothing is needed at one house but sits at the other. We lived about 10-15 minutes, in light traffic, from my ex-wife's house.

With the support of Sarna, Susan suggested that we move to West University so that we would be much closer to Janet's house and it would be better for all concerned. I was not especially in favour as I did not think the 10-15 minutes' drive was that onerous and I liked our house. However, I could see some benefit and so I agreed to the idea.

I found a new house that was to be built, by the same builder who had built my previous house on Westchester, on Edloe, near Bellaire Boulevard, in Southside Place. Southside Place was essentially a sub-section of West University. The house was not yet under construction so we made some changes to the plans and eventually agreed terms with the builder to build a house of some 5700 square feet that would have a far smaller back yard than we currently had. The house would take around 10-12 months to complete.

We began to prepare the Cedar Creek house for sale and were aware that it had a considerable slope from one side to the other. The single story attached study was some five inches higher than the other side over the garage. We had an engineer exam the house and we concluded that it was probably due to bad drainage by the study so we took some measures including installing a French drain in an effort to improve the situation. We hoped over time that would cause the house to level.

In 2006 Susan persuaded me that we should have another child and I thought why not. Soon she was pregnant and the baby was due in April 2007.

When we put the house on the market it was quickly under contract twice but both deals fell through because the slope had not been corrected: we must have had a more serious foundation issue though the slab was not visibly cracked and neither did the brick veneer of the house have any cracks.

We decided therefore that we would sell the now completed Edloe house. This was somewhat of a shame as Susan had taken great pains to design much of the interior of the house and had done a terrific job. It really was, in our eyes, a beautiful house. The market had risen considerably in West University and we soon found a buyer who was willing to pay some $300k more than we had spent. The buyer was just starting a new business and he said it would be at least a year until he was able to buy the house but would like to rent it for $8900 per month until then. This appealed to us as holding the house for 12 months would mean we would fall into the lower long term capital gains tax bracket.

The new young family with their three young, home-schooled children moved in. The buyer, however, was forever complaining about the most minor things such as a creaky floorboard or an unacceptable, in his view, temperature gradient in a certain part of the house. We had the builder take care of these but from time to time the buyer would still complain and we managed to take care of all his issues, no matter how minor.

Susan had an uncomplicated pregnancy and on April 6, 2007, our son was born. We named him William, with Philip as his middle name. John, Camille and Amelia were all delighted. He was truly a beautiful little baby boy. With William's birth I now had two beautiful little children and two fine bigger ones. I told myself that had I gone back to Vitol in 1999 Janet would almost certainly not have divorced me seeing how much money I was making and thus the birth of these two beautiful children was the positive side of my collapsing career. It was very much unlike me to try and see a silver lining but at least I tried. Arguably this was a rationalization that I used when I was consumed with regret and depression but I firmly believe it to be true. Susan, however, did not believe it which I found rather heartless of her. Very soon after William was born Susan fell and broke her arm such that she was not able to hold and feed the baby. I therefore found myself doing sole night duty as I slept with William feeding him every 2 to 3 hours or so. This was totally exhausting but I grew to like it and I believe it added greatly to our strong bond.

The following summer of 2007 we happened to be spending a few weeks in Avon, Colorado, with John and Camille and of course Amelia and little William. We came to love this part of Colorado especially in the summer. My parents were also with us in Colorado. My dad had to use an oxygen tank to cope with the altitude as he had six months earlier been diagnosed with lung cancer and had a tumour along with a large chunk of lung removed. At that time in Avon the Westin Riverfront Resort and Spa was under construction. We already owned a couple of time share weeks with the Westin in Maui and were very happy with these and with the Westin in general. The Riverfront was not a time share but a wholly owned condominium project that would be rented out as a Westin hotel when the owner of any condo was not using it. Such revenue would be split between the owner 55/45% with the management company. It appeared quite an attractive proposition but the units were extremely expensive. Susan thought it would be a good idea to purchase a unit as the Vail Valley property market was booming and we might even be able to sell our unit before it was complete as the complex was already some 60% sold out. The unit we took an interest in was on the back side, without a mountain view but had high vaulted ceilings and two balconies as opposed to the standard one. It was 1230 square feet and was priced at $1.2m. This seemed exorbitant to me and it was totally out of character for me to consider such a deal but consider it I did. I felt the units such as ours should be priced below $1m but eventually, in spite of my reservations, I agreed to place a deposit of $40,000, soon to be increased to $200,000 to secure the unit. Though the unit would no doubt be beautiful and a terrific place to take the family, financially it was yet another in my never-ending stream of catastrophic decisions.

"Advice is judged by results not intentions". Cicero

When it was time for our tenants/buyers to buy the house the buyer emailed me saying they loved the house and still wanted to buy it but they needed until Christmas, i.e., 6 months, until they were in a position to actually close on the house. In the meantime he suggested they would just continue paying the $8900 per month. This seemed perfectly reasonable to me and indeed to our agent. Susan, however, was not so pleased and did not trust the buyer/tenant as she had had far more contact with him over the past 18 months and had to deal with his almost incessant moaning. Susan turned to a mortgage broker friend of hers who, I believe, gave her some terrible advice that she unfortunately took to heart. Obviously he had no idea about the financial health of our tenants but he said, very assertively, that there was no way, if they could not buy the house today, that they would be able to buy it at Christmas. Quite why he felt this way, I don't know, but we took his advice and needless to say it was yet another financial disaster, plus the cause of a series of major time consuming headaches. Once again, I had rolled over weakly when confronted by a verbal barrage from my wife even though I knew, seemingly as always in these cases, I was making a mistake. Quite why I did this I am not entirely sure. Perhaps it was because I wished to minimise the domestic hostilities as I reflected back on my childhood. The tenant swiftly moved out but was absolutely furious and soon sent us a nasty letter from a sleazy lawyer threatening to sue us for damages incurred in installing curtains and for trying to sell them a substandard house, the same house that he had just said in an email that he loved and wanted to buy. We sent the letter to our lawyer friend Eric Fryar but pretty much ignored it thinking it was an empty threat that was totally without merit.

Meanwhile the Colorado trip was pretty stressful. John wanted to monopolise my time and my dad of course was struggling even though he had the use of an oxygen tank. We could seldom agree upon the simplest things such as where to go to dinner and so it was that I was feeling pretty despondent and on edge, as usual. We did manage to enjoy much of our trip such as the strenuous hike up to the beautiful crystal clear "Hanging Lake". During the hike young Camille noticed a man staring at Susan and asked Susan what could he possibly want. Susan replied that he was probably wondering how someone so beautiful could possibly be with someone like me, who was bringing up the rear, huffing and puffing and sweating profusely.

Once the trip was over it took us a month or so, and about $10,000, to refinish the wood floors in the Houston house that the tenant had badly scratched and to repaint the walls where he had removed the curtain fixtures. We eventually put the house back on the market and found a buyer in November to close in December. He was willing to pay a higher price than had previously been agreed so things appeared as if they were going to work out, but as usual they did not. The previous tenants sued us. It was an utterly frivolous suit but nonetheless they filed. When it came to finalising our new contract the agent, who was a good friend of Susan's, insisted, against my strong protestations, to declare the fact that the house was involved in a law suit. I explained that this would simply worry the new buyer and the suit was purely one over a matter of money, some $40,000, that a previous disgruntled tenant was trying to extract from us. I am sure a more experienced and savvy agent would have agreed with me, but she forced us to declare the suit. The new buyer raised this concern, as expected, so we offered the previous tenant his earnest money back if he would drop the suit. He claimed never to have received this offer by fax from lawyer to lawyer. To make matters worse my dad's cancer had returned and it was clear that he was dying. This was all happening as Christmas approached. With the suit unsettled the new buyer pulled out. I rushed to Jersey to see my dad in hospital before he died. I had one day in hospital with him, when we talked mostly about football, as we did. He was on so much morphine that he was suffering from hallucinations and saw rabbits in his room. The next day I returned to the hospital with my brother and mother but he was basically unconscious, just barely moaning. After a short while he passed away. I was thankful for the fact that he had been able to see his new grandson William, at least for a few, all be they tough, weeks in Colorado.

I spent the next two weeks with my mother as she had just lost her companion of over 50 years and despite their problems they had been inseparable. Even under these circumstances I had wanted to return home as I found spending such a long time with my mother very stressful. The Edloe house went back on the market. We hired a new lawyer and spent some $20,000 countersuing the tenants for making us lose a sale but under court ordered mediation, after fruitless negotiations, we ended up settling by giving them back their earnest money, exactly as we had earlier offered. What a painful and time consuming fiasco that had proven to be.

Prior to Christmas, with the Edloe house on the market we decided to bite the bullet and have our Cedar Creek foundation correctly rectified by Auchan, the main foundation repair company in Houston. We had tried, under the builders' warranty to hold the builder responsible as the foundation was guaranteed for ten years and I had only owned the house for nine. The builder, Lovett homes, denied any responsibility and during the stipulated arbitration process, during which the arbitrator assigned points to various criteria, we almost prevailed, but not quite. So we were faced with a total expense of around $100,000 to repair the foundation. We of course had to move out for a couple of weeks into a nearby apartment. All this was happening while my dad was dying and while the Edloe house was about to fall through. Amazingly, as if we did not have enough to deal with, Susan's birth father passed away suddenly at this time. To say we were all under considerable stress would be an understatement. Fortunately for me, Susan essentially took control of the foundation issue, which was quite a project.

The Auchan folks had to dig around 80 3ft x 3ft holes in the house, about two-thirds inside and one-third outside which involved jack hammering through the slab each time. The idea was then to very slowly, with men in around six holes at a time, jack the low side of the house up fully five inches and of course jack the interior up a lesser amount so as to ultimately level the house. Once the house was levelled new piers were installed in place of the jacks to make the foundation solid and of course each of the 80 plus holes had to be refilled with concrete to once again complete the slab. Amazingly, as they undertook this painstaking and delicate process, not a single crack appeared in any interior or exterior wall.

As the process was drawing to a close they had to examine the slab under the study and it was here we finally discovered the cause of the problem: the original piers had not been tied with rebar to the slab and thus the study had floated up. Clearly the builder had indeed been at fault. Susan and I by this time were so exhausted with lawyers and legal matters that we did not have the mental energy or will to call over our lawyer and reinstitute proceedings against the builder. Who knows if we would have won. The foundation was now at least rock solid and the house level and so we moved back in and put the house back on the market. We now had two large Houston houses up for sale. We would see which house sold first and live in the other one. It was early in 2008.

Now throughout 2007, knowing that my time at BP was going to be limited, I tried to find another job, not that I really wanted to return to trading. I had numerous interviews but all went nowhere. At Nexen and a Belgian bank I appeared over qualified for their needs. Merrill Lynch had a very interesting position but they filled it internally. I was recommended by my friend Wildgoose to the huge, Ken Griffin fund in Chicago, Citadel. The young chap to whom the oil group reported was an Englishman from Oxford so we had a lot in common. I absolutely did not want to leave Houston because of John and Camille but the Citadel opportunity warranted at least exploring. They had just taken on three BP product traders who put me through a pretty gruelling interview process as was BP's style. I was not offered the job. I replied to the Oxford guy that they were making a mistake: unlike the BP traders I actually had a successful track record of making money in the private trading or real trading world and was not simply picking up the "free" money that was the wont and privilege of BP traders. I stressed the fact that I had also been intimately involved in setting up a trading team and associated infrastructure at Duke and indeed to a much lesser extent at HETCO. Unfortunately for me, as the compensation would have been great, my fellow Oxonian was unmoved. I stopped short of telling him to call me back in 6 months when the ex BP traders had lost enough money, as surely they would. Perhaps I should have made this point as in roughly that time span, give or take a few months, they were all indeed let go, no doubt having been extremely well compensated. They all landed at large trading houses such as Vitol or Trafigura where of course they would have to make real money. Private trading houses, as discussed at length earlier, had the advantage though of largely being under the radar of the regulators and authorities and had the ability to play by a different set of rules, or almost no rules. Susan was actually quite annoyed with my failure to find a job, blaming my interviewing style, even though in the past I had been offered countless jobs. The fact was I was now a little older and the industry was not exactly flush with available positions. To this day she insists that I have never been able to get along with people with whom I work, something that is utterly baseless. She will point to BP where I did have a problem with one boss but that was for a very particular reason or personal vendetta. The actual truth was I was always very well liked wherever I worked and my colleagues were always sad to see me go. Susan suggested I have lunch with a couple of guys in the industry that we both knew, as they may have known of an unexplored and highly lucrative avenue in the Oil Business, other than trading, of which I was not aware. Not only was I more extensively experienced than these two guys, but after twenty years, I felt it was rather unlikely that a hidden jewel existed of which I was unaware. I had a couple of pleasant lunches, nonetheless.

My life was, seemingly as ever, one giant mess.

Over spring break of 2008 we all went to Maui to our timeshare at the Westin. Susan, Amelia, William and I went for two weeks while John and Camille joined us just for the second. It was on the whole a good trip but Susan still felt that John and Camille could be disruptive and was worried about their influence on her two little ones. Unfortunately, and much to my dismay, she did have a point. I desperately wanted everyone to get along, Rodney King style.

The second incident indicative of Susan's "wilder side" concerned our flight home taking us via Dallas where we had to take the inter-terminal train. We were all getting along, joking around and laughing when I must have made a silly off-hand minor joke at Susan's expense. She promptly threw an entire giant sized cup of water all over me which seemed a little excessive, to say the least. It rapidly brought the jovial frivolity to an end but I think it was simply a manifestation of her struggling to cope with her newly acquired extended family and the influence of my older children on our younger ones.

The Cedar Creek House soon sold at a price that more than covered our foundation expenses, relative to the two contracts that had fallen through over two years prior. And so we moved into the House on Edloe.

The fun would soon continue.

Leaving Houston for Colorado
"Oh what a tangled web we weave when first we practise to deceive".
Sir Walter Scott, from the poem, Marmion.

My life, and indeed that of the entire family, had clearly for some time been an utterly tangled mess. However, it was not until a little later that we were to be deceived in yet another failed financial fiasco. My mental state was permanently on edge and I struggled to deal sensibly with the slightest perturbation. Sadly, I continued in a state of natural pessimism as I had found that hope was always dashed upon the rocks of reality and just increased my disappointment.

The kinesiologist, Pepe, that Susan had mentioned years earlier to Spalding Grey was, to be fair, an expert in the muscle and ligament structure of the body. I had visited him on a couple of occasions. Once I believe I had a slipped disc in the neck which he popped back in with a violent yank on a towel behind my relaxed neck: a procedure a doctor later told me was very dangerous. Susan saw him quite frequently and one day she excitedly came back and told me that Pepe had invested in a movie deal via his step son-in-law that had yielded 30 times the original investment. Now that was a staggering multiple and of course I should have been far more skeptical but why would Pepe, a friend of ours, lie or perhaps, more likely, Susan had mis-heard. In any event a little simple research would have saved us from yet another nightmare.

Pepe gave us the contact information of the producers in Los Angeles and we called them. Joe Reilly and Tom Kelly had indeed just finished their second movie with the Sprouse Twins (of Zak and Cody fame off the Disney Channel) and were now working on a 3rd which was to be a romantic comedy titled "Lovesick," written and directed by their friend, Bobby Moresco, who had recently won a screenwriting Oscar, together with his partner, Paul Haggis for the movie, "Crash". Moresco directed and his daughter Amanda had written the second Sprouse twin movie, "The Kings of Appletown" that was now in Post Production. If we were interested in investing in "Lovesick" we should fly to LA and meet the producers and view the new Sprouse movie. A simple Google search at this time would have shown that Reilly and Kelly had numerous cease and desist orders against them in various States and were running the classic "Producers" scam, assisted by several sales people in a boiler room, as it were. We were total fools to get involved but the fact that Pepe had made 30 times his money was quite an endorsement, albeit a false one.

We still had a lot of balls in the air. My job search was going nowhere but I did not wish to leave Houston as Camille had just entered middle school and John was in his final year. However, Susan seemed extremely stressed at this time, thinking my older children were a bad influence on the younger ones. I did not fully appreciate the extent of Susan's concerns and clearly there was a failure to communicate effectively between the two of us.

Amazingly a "Head Hunter" from New York came up with an opportunity that was essentially written just for me. It was unbelievable. The opportunity was with the small South African, London and Houston based trader, Masefield, that I knew of quite well since my days at Vitol. After several long phone interviews with their people in London and South Africa and then a long breakfast meeting with their owner, Jim Daly, it was obvious that it was a perfect fit. They invited me over to South Africa to hammer out the details of my deal.

At lunch I told Susan of this great news. I had unsuccessfully been looking for a job for 12 months and suddenly along comes the perfect job, which would not involve speculative trading, with a company that intrigued me. I had also just been notified that my time with BP was to end around July 1 of 2008 but I would receive around 4 months' salary and an element of pro-rated bonus as severance. This seemed fair on BP's part. I told Susan I simply had to go to South Africa and agree final terms and we would be set.

Susan understood my obvious excitement at receiving such a seemingly attractive opportunity but, after initially exploding into a rage asking angrily what on earth I was doing thinking of taking a job, she then took the time to more clearly explain her concerns and the cause of her being stressed. She explained that it would be best if we put some distance between ourselves and my older children, and especially their mother. Plus we had the condo in Avon that would soon be ready, so why not move to the mountains and try a new adventure. I was somewhat shocked but we just about had enough money to live comfortably so we should have been able to make it work. Nonetheless, I felt we could confront the necessary issues if we stayed in Houston but Susan was not open to the idea. Additionally, I was not ready to stop working and I explained to Susan that if I left the industry now it would be almost impossible to find another job a few years down the road. She also added that John and Camille could fly out once a month and obviously have a great place to visit during Holiday periods and the like. I must admit I was disappointed to turn down Masefield, which I did, but I came around to seeing the benefits and novelty of moving to the mountains and so our new course was set. I was a little sad of course when I told John and Camille that we were leaving Houston but I stressed the positive aspects which softened the blow and they soon became excited at the prospect of flying monthly to the mountains of Colorado.

We put the Edloe house back on the market and in no time received interest in the house from an MLB Baseball player who had just joined the Astros. Unfortunately he did not wish to buy it but to lease it, furnished, for the substantial amount of $12,000 per month for 18 months. This suited us well as we did not need the furniture in Colorado.

"A fool and his money are soon parted". Proverb

Having had our heads turned by Pepe and a phone call with Reilly and Kelly, we flew out as a family to meet the movie producers and to view the recently finished movie, "The Kings of Appletown," which we thought was really good. Tom and Joe were very hospitable and after I foolishly wrote them a cheque for $150,000 for two units of the new movie "Lovesick" they just had, by chance, the need to raise a little more money for marketing "Appletown." As a special favour we could buy two units in that movie which we had thought had been fully financed. This we excitedly did at a cost of $70,000 thinking, what was the risk, as the movie was made and it was a very good family film. The next day Joe took us to meet Moresco at his house and we had our photo taken with him and his Oscar statue. I also told Joe and Tom that I could probably get a good few of my oil industry friends to invest in these movies and perhaps we could work out a mutually beneficial deal. The following day Joe and Tom said it was not their usual style but they would use me to help raise money and would pay me a commission of a few per cent. I excitedly and stupidly sensed a new opportunity that could actually turn into something positive. I subsequently invested another $110,000 in "Appletown," as if I was not already in deep enough.

As chance would have it, our new prospective tenants were at their Los Angeles beach house at that time so we paid them a visit and got to know them a little before heading back to Houston.

I brought several of my old Vitol colleagues into the movie deals and of course my best friend Alberto and one or two others. I raised around $450k.

The entire fiasco unfolded over some six years. The whole thing was a giant scam and we lost all of our money: in my case that was $350,000. The producers had made an excellent movie, The Kings of Appletown, for which they had raised over $12m but I later learnt from people with knowledge of such things that they probably spent less than $4m on the movie. The rest they wasted or squirrelled away.

As for Pepe, he received one tiny cheque for the first movie in which he had invested, a very low-budget film titled "The Prince and the Pauper". Where the 30x multiple came from, I have no idea. I spent hours and hours trying to attract investors to these projects, but fortunately was largely unsuccessful. Hundreds of people had been invested in the two

Sprouse twins' movies and we were able to salvage nothing. After Joe dropped a bombshell in

2010 that he and the movie were going bankrupt, a group of investors, including myself, stepped in, added some extra funds, and set about managing the various LLCs associated with the movies for around 4 years in an attempt to get some money back for all the investors.

We spent countless hours on this, including the preparation of annual K1 forms, and other required documentation. We ultimately gave up in 2014. It was after this bombshell that I fully understood how we had all been taken for a ride and how we had constantly been lied to. It was a total disgrace. The FBI has been looking at the scam for about the last three years but as yet nothing has come of this and I am not hopeful. I am all but certain Joe must have hidden millions of dollars. Joe died of a heart attack in 2014. I was actually suspicious when I heard the news of his demise but I obtained a copy of his death certificate from the Los Angeles Coroner's office.

Yet again I had become involved in something totally out of my comfort zone and stupidly lost a large amount of money and a great deal of time. This further added to my general sense of self-loathing and proof that nothing I did would ever turn out. As mentioned earlier, I had told Sarna that it was my destiny to lose everything and I seemed to be on my way to fulfilling this, deliberately or otherwise, I have no idea. There seemed to be something deep inside my inner being that wanted to destroy me yet at this time I was unable to fully conceive of what was, I now think, afoot. I was seriously troubled by my stupidity and my failure to do a simple google search on these characters. I was also embarrassed to have brought in a handful of my old friends and colleagues, but luckily not too many, and their losses were minor.

"The truth is incontrovertible. Malice may attack it, ignorance deride it, but in the end, there it is". Winston Churchill

After John and Camille had made a couple of weekend trips to Colorado, Susan told me she would prefer them no longer to come as they were still, almost more so, being disruptive. I would simply fly back to Houston once a month to see them. I understood where she was coming from and could not disagree: over the next five years I would fly once a month from wherever we were living, to Houston. Obviously this saddened me but clearly I could not allow my older children to be a negative influence, for whatever reason, on the little ones. Divorce and merging families is not an easy matter.

The condo lived up to our expectations as did the common areas of the resort. It was a truly first class building and it had a cable car for access to the mountain across the Eagle River once the ski season started. We were the only people in full time residence and we had the run of the whole place. We got to know all the valet staff and most of the people inside the hotel. It was a little bit like a quiet version of the "Suite life of Zak and Cody". Amelia especially liked the Westin Kids' Club where she would spend a great deal of her time.

After a couple of months in Avon I received a call from Chevron asking if I was interested in returning to Houston to work for them. I thanked them for their interest but said no. Susan to this day will accuse me of turning down numerous (this was the only one) job offers while we were in Colorado and that I could easily have taken advantage of one. This is utterly befuddling as we had just moved to Colorado, she said she wanted to spend time out here with her husband and family, and perhaps most of all, escape the other half of my family. At no time did she suggest that just she and Amelia and William move to Avon and I stay in Houston to work. This clearly would contradict much of the foregoing yet she stands by this falsehood to this day. Furthermore she would not have wanted me to be close to my ex-wife as she thought that was problematic. It was only just a couple of months since I had turned down the job that I wanted with Masefield so to think now in hindsight we would have turned back around, with our Houston house rented, is utter nonsense. The accommodation was a bit tight compared to what we were used to so as Christmas approached we decided we should let the condo rent out, which it did very well during ski season, and we rented a 4000 square foot house in Eagle Ranch, some 30 minutes west, down the Vail Valley. This was much more comfortable especially as we had decided to invite my mother over to spend three months with us as she was still recovering from the loss of her partner of almost 50 years.

While I was out on one of my periodic visits to my older children, Susan had her older sister come to visit for a couple of very snowy days. Susan, as discussed was under immense stress and I am not sure having her sister visit was such a good idea. On the morning of her departure her sister apparently was unable to book a taxi so she persuaded Susan to drive her to the Eagle-Vail airport, some twenty minutes away, in spite of the fact that Amelia and William, aged 4 and 2 respectively, were asleep in the house. Quite what Susan was thinking, driving for around 50 minutes on dangerously icy roads with her two young children alone at home, I do not know. When she returned home she found the children huddled together with Amelia doing her best to comfort her little brother telling him everything would be all right. The thought of this still breaks my heart. When Susan told me about this I was absolutely flabbergasted but tried to be understanding and just stressed that everyone was indeed, thankfully, all right.

Having my mum around was of course very stressful, made more so by her nearly constant twittering in my ear of criticisms of Susan. I failed to see what constructive purpose this could possibly achieve but it was relentless. It was also extremely rude given that Susan had been kind enough to invite her over for an extended stay. Sadly, I was too pathetically weak to defend my wife against this totally unjust criticism. For better or worse I shared much of my mother's comments with Susan which understandably upset her. The whole area was by now deep in snow and walking on the sidewalks or road was quite treacherous. My mother and I would often walk down to the coffee shop in Eagle Ranch and on one occasion I took a very nasty slip and fell such that I hit my head on the ice and was very nearly knocked out. My mother commented that I should be more careful as I could kill myself with such a fall, but perhaps that was what I wanted. I felt it an odd comment to make but ignored it: however it was true.

Around this time and after a winter dealing with many feet of snow we decided the mountains of Colorado would probably not work for the long term. Seeing the magnificent herd of Elk in Eagle Ranch, however, was quite something. We basically had the flexibility to move anywhere and one place high up on the list was Charleston, South Carolina where we identified two excellent looking schools for the children. For Amelia there was Ashley Hall, a very highly regarded girls' school where Barbara Bush had once been a pupil. William would also be able to attend Ashley Hall before likely moving to the boys' equivalent, namely Porter Gaud. In the spring we all made the long trip across country to Charleston and Amelia had an interview at Ashley Hall. She was accepted into the Kindergarten for the coming fall. Charleston was clearly a beautiful city with its incredibly historic peninsula, its rich civil war history and its beautiful nearby island beaches. Even during this trip my mother was constantly twittering in my ear. I felt utterly wretched.

Upon returning to Colorado, Susan planned a trip with Amelia to find a suitable house to rent in Charleston. Unfortunately every house she found seemed to get snatched from under her nose and she returned empty handed. We had decided we wanted to live in the quaint and unique sub division of l'On in Mount Pleasant, connected to the City of Charleston by the spectacular, newly constructed, Arthur Ravenel suspension bridge. We of course were not the only ones with such an idea so rental houses in particular went extremely quickly. The actual housing market was, however quite depressed, as the mortgage crisis was well underway and so I had the bright but foolish idea of buying a modest house in I'On especially as we could borrow money so cheaply. At that time we managed to live comfortably off our income from the rent of the house in Houston plus the interest we received from our portfolio at Morgan Stanley of municipal bonds and bank preferred shares.

Charleston

Susan had found an agent in Charleston and we used her as our eyes to look at a couple of houses that appeared suitable and were within our budget. We bought, site unseen, a 2650 square foot house, in I'on for $700,000. We then had to rent a U-Haul which Susan towed behind her Audi Q7 all the way to Charleston. The rest of us flew and we shipped my Mercedes. When we met up in I'On we were very pleased with our house purchase. It looked just as it had appeared on the internet and had a very pleasant if small back yard. It was roughly half the size of the houses we had previously lived in so we had to store quite a few of our belongings.

We settled into the house that we found very comfortable but shortly after my mother had returned to Jersey we discovered that almost all of the wood siding of the house was rotten. The sellers obviously knew this but did not disclose it as indeed they did not several other defects of which they had been aware. We had to have the house totally resided in the more suitable "hardiplank" which cost the best part of $50,000. We had the house painted a classic Palladian blue.

Amelia began her school life at Ashley Hall that August as did William in a 3 year old class. Both children greatly enjoyed it. I had previously thought Houston was the most humid place in the Universe but soon discovered, that summer, that Charleston had it beat. I really struggled with the weather as I did with the mosquitoes and the tiny "no-see-ums" which would bite me to such an extent that my arms and legs were in a frightful mess as I constantly scratched them. Thankfully these little midges were only a problem for a couple of weeks twice a year.

Charleston had a very old population of longtime residents coupled with a major percentage of imports from all around the country. On the whole we found the people very friendly and we soon had a small group of friends. I would continue to make my monthly flights to Houston to see John and Camille who were now in the massive local High School, Lamar, in the River Oaks area. This school had over 3600 children but many of John and Camille's friends attended and were in the IB (International Baccalaureate Program). John was still seriously into baseball and was playing at that time for the Junior Varsity but had his sights set on eventually playing at College, which was still a few years off.

My relationship with Susan was unfortunately a little strained partly due to the fact that we had essentially cut off my older children from the younger ones and partly due to my mother's previously incessant criticism of her. I have previously stated that I took the birth of my two younger children as a silver-lining to the dark cloud of my failed career. I especially enjoyed watching my older children interact with their younger siblings. However, due to a number of complex factors, primarily the previously mentioned disruptiveness and my ex-wife's interference, I was deprived of this pleasure. I accepted this but it saddened me very, very deeply and fed my "destiny delusion" in that nothing would ever work out for me.

Out of duty and obligation I nonetheless invited my mother back over for another three months which was slightly better than the previous time but not by much. In Charleston I failed completely to empathise with Susan and to understand that some of her odd behaviours were essentially due to her labouring under intense, frankly unspeakable, stress. Instead, I am ashamed to say, I put these odd behaviours in my mental box that I would use later to incorrectly condemn her as suffering from a variety of diagnosable mental ailments. My mother was aware of the stress Susan in particular was under but she continued to constantly criticise her to me, totally without any justification. This of course created great distress for me but I lacked the strength or sense to tell my mother to stop: we simply never had that type of relationship. I simply took it and said very little in response.

In I'On we befriended a couple with young children who had moved about the same time as us from Boston. The husband, Foster, was soon to become a good friend. He was in no way a brain-washed, jingoistic consumerist which I found many Americans to be. He worked in the software industry, as of course had Susan

"The truth exposes some people so deeply, their last defence is a carefree insanity".   Criss Jami

One evening at dinner with Foster and his wife, Susan and Foster were discussing the software business. Susan of course proudly stressed her Oracle career and how she was a highly accomplished sales woman, which she was. The conversation remained convivial. Foster asked her why she did not look for a job considering her considerable experience here in Charleston. He came up with a variety of suggestions and the conversation subsequently turned in a different direction. After what had been a perfectly enjoyable evening we returned home suddenly for Susan to unleash her wrath upon me. "I know what you were doing," she said angrily. Feeling tired and ready for bed I did not have the faintest idea about what she was talking. "I'm sorry," I said, "what did I do?" totally confused. "You put Foster up to that!" she yelled, "You told him in advance to try and persuade me to get a job. How dare you?". I was utterly stunned. There was not a thread of truth to this allegation and I was both disturbed and insulted by the fact she could possibly imagine me doing such a thing. I was never one to go in for game playing or manipulation but it made me have serious doubts about how her mind worked and why she was both so aggressive and paranoid and for want of a better word, delusional. I believe I managed to convince her that she had simply misunderstood the situation, as she many times did, and we went to bed. My mind, however, was still in a state of shock and utter disbelief.

Somewhat similarly I mentioned to Susan that I had heard on the news that many American companies, such as Apple and Google, paid very little in American corporation tax. Rather than engage in a conversation, as I expected, Susan immediately attacked me verbally, claiming that I was picking on technology companies since she had previously worked for Oracle. I was flabbergasted.

Another bizarre but equally disturbing incident occurred involving our house alarm system. For some reason Susan decided we should each have our own code and a third one to be given to anybody else who needed access to the house. As I entered the house from the rear screened-in porch one evening I triggered the alarm and could not for the life of me remember my new code. With the alarm sirens blaring, Susan was on her way down the stairs and I politely asked if she could give me the code so I could turn off the alarm. "No." she said. "I am not giving you my code". I stared at her in open mouthed disbelief. What possible reason could she have for this ludicrous act of defiance? I hastily explained that I had forgotten my code and she scoffed at me. Whatever was going on in her mind was entirely beyond my comprehension. The issue was a total farce. After some time she finally relented and told me the code and I turned off the alarm. I must confess I was extremely upset by the whole thing as I could not understand her behaviour. However, it was a manifestation of her righteous, if slightly misplaced, anger and I was totally unable to see this. Instead I stored it in my own mental box of what I perceived to be her delusions. Both of these incidents, I see now, can be put down to the dreadfully difficult situation that Susan was facing and though I tried to be supportive I failed to be truly empathetic. I too was enduring this exceptional mental anguish. Realistically our relationship at this point was all but irreparably damaged: we both were laden with heavy grief and sadness that we carried in our separate dark and lonely cellars. If we did try to communicate it would tend to lead to a misunderstanding which only made matters worse. It was truly a tragedy but fate had not yet finished with us and it would be a number of years more before I was unceremoniously dumped onto the scrap heap of life, having lost almost everything, and being essentially destroyed.

One day when I was out of town, presumably visiting my elder children in Houston, I spoke to my wife on the phone. She explained that an odd looking car had been sitting for a good while on our usually quiet little street. She was sufficiently concerned to call the police who told her that they were aware of its presence. Mount Pleasant Police would cruise the neighbourhood at night and had obviously noticed the car and were keeping an eye on it. However, the man on the phone said, "We see him". This immediately made my wife jump to the conclusion, which she excitedly shared with me, that the streets of I'On were all covered with hidden cameras so we could all be seen at any time. Sensing it would be futile to attempt to explain that this was obviously not the case I simply agreed.

To this day Susan claims that I would sit brooding, full of resentment and hatred aimed at her: this is entirely untrue and what I supposedly resented made utterly no sense at all. It reminded me of the words of Kate Mc Gahan: ""I see how you look at me," spits the hateful man. He thinks we are looking at him with the evil eye when we are not looking at him that way at all. We are just looking at him. It's because he can't accept the hate inside of himself that he projects it onto us".

On one such trip back to Houston to see my elder children I discovered that I had a two hour credit with our old therapist friend Sarna. I decided to use the credit and spent two hours discussing my marriage which to me was a shambles. Sarna found the above incidents quite amazing and wondered if Susan was paranoid. I explained that Susan was forever seemingly angry at me and was about as approachable as a prickly pear cactus. I even went so far as to say that I felt the best option for me would undoubtedly be divorce but I could not bare to do that to my young children. I would try to make things better for the sake of the family but this would prove to be an impossible and self-destructive decision. Sarna joked that I might have better luck a third time but I instructed her were I ever to contemplate a third marriage she was to shoot me.

At the end of 2009 our tenants in Houston were due to move out and we would no longer receive the substantial monthly rent check. This obviously put a strain on our finances so we put the house up for sale. Like the rest of the country the Houston housing market had taken a tumble. The house was worth considerably less than what we had previously almost sold it for. We had someone express an interest in renting it for $5000 per month but decided against it as a sale would just be cleaner though doubtless a painful experience. Susan, again to this day, berates me about the "fact" we only rented the Houston house as we always intended to return there. Well, here was a tenant who would fulfil that need but Susan was totally against re-renting it. Furthermore, when we initially rented the house to the MLB player it was only on the market for sale and not for rent. However, he offered lease terms that were so attractive that we decided to take them and then see how the market was down the road. At no point had we discussed returning to Houston, at least not until we left Charleston.

Meanwhile the market in Colorado had taken a massive hit and our condo was now worth a good $400,000 less than we had paid for it, a level from which it has barely recovered much to this day. At every turn we just dug ourselves deeper and deeper into financial difficulties and a host of other problems. As much as I tried I could not shake the horrid, hollow feeling that would constantly gnaw at me along with the voice inside my head that cruelly reminded me that my destiny would be fulfilled.

As soon as we relisted the house in Houston we received an offer some $270,000 less than we had previously had it under contract for. I knew the market had weakened but did not think it had weakened that much and I misplayed my hand. Rather than countering I simply asked them to come back with an improved offer. They did not and moved on to another house. It was about six months later and for about $90,000 less that the house eventually sold. What a nightmare that house had been. We invested the proceeds of the house in mainly bank preferred shares and continued to seemingly live within our means, quite comfortably.

In Charleston I would occasionally visit a therapist for my almost ever present depression. Once, after I had given her a brief but thorough synopsis of my life, she commented that she was surprised I was still alive and that there were three clear occasions when I might have succumbed to the temptation of ending it all. Sadly that total has now increased to five.

As the summer of 2011 approached Susan and I felt that we had a decision to make: should we stay here in Charleston which we had grown to like, despite the humidity and bugs, but where we had no long term friends or family, or should we return to Texas, where Susan has basically, other than these last three years, spent her whole life and felt most at home. I did not want to return to Houston where I still felt the old me had died and it would bring back too many painful memories. Susan did not aggressively push Houston and we both agreed to consider Austin, which neither of us knew well but about which we had heard great things. We decided to take a look.

Austin

The four of us flew to Austin in late June 2011 which turned out to the hottest summer on record with over 100 days over 100 degrees F and many over 110. We wondered if we were doing the right thing but we were assured that this was not the norm, which indeed it was not, and so we decided not to be deterred. This time the fact the property market had fallen worked in our favour as Austin house prices were down quite a bit. We put the Charleston house on the market and after the $50,000 on the exterior plus redoing two bathrooms we ended up selling it for a $150,000 loss: another great financial move. We looked at many properties in Austin over a long, hot two days and finally found one that appeared ideal in beautiful Steiner Ranch, about 15 miles to the west of Austin.

The house had been built in 2009 and was being sold by a couple from Utah who had moved to Austin but had been caught up in a well-known local fraud and were forced to sell. The 5700 square foot house seemed ideal for the way our family lived with its large open, hacienda-style downstairs. In hindsight we probably could have fought for a lower price but we concluded the deal at $1.1m. In fairness to Susan she did not really want to spend that much but I explained with the cheap cost of money and the fact that I would no longer have to fly to Houston monthly our expenses should be similar to those we had in Charleston. There was also a highly rated public elementary school nearby that should be ideal for Amelia and eventually William. Susan agreed to send Amelia there for first grade. We thought Amelia would enjoy riding the school bus from our neighbourhood and the school was very well run, modern and had high academic standards. William was enrolled in St. Andrew's, a private Episcopal school that offered a pre-k program. This school was expensive but we felt it would offer a more beneficial and nurturing environment. Amelia liked her school and made a few good friends but she did not like being yelled at in PE and actually did not enjoy the school bus experience and so we decided to switch her to the same school that her brother attended for the following year.

"I protect myself by refusing to know myself". Floriano Martins

For the first couple of years in Austin I underestimated how much Susan really disliked the place. We even went so far as to explore the idea of moving to Fort Worth on a couple of instances. However, I was not fully aware of her unhappiness: she later told me that she had basically cried for two years at her displeasure at being in Austin. On one occasion, after we had just moved in and before we had internet in the house, I asked Susan if she would mind dropping me at the local Starbucks which she was going to pass as she ventured out. "Of course I cannot," she snapped. "I don't have time for that". I was shocked. It literally would have taken maybe 30 seconds, if the traffic light was green, or no time, if red, to drop me off. I was planning to walk home. I can only assume she reacted in this way because of her dislike for our new home city.

Susan's elder sister, with whom she has a strained relationship and rarely if ever now communicates, paid us a visit shortly after we had relocated. As I sat outside chatting to her over coffee she made a statement that struck me as odd yet meaningful: she told me I must not let Susan destroy my spirit, which appeared to her to be the case, or words to that effect. I am not sure what precipitated this comment: little did I know how much more my spirit was to be destroyed almost to the point of non-existence but tragically so was Susan's.

Around this time I was invited to a rare gathering in Houston of Oxford alumni to a lunch at the St. Regis Hotel where the guest of honour was Chris Patten, formerly the governor of Hong Kong. Chris entertained us with several humorous anecdotes about his time as governor and I enjoyed being in the company of likeminded people, one or two of which I knew. After the formalities of lunch were over a general, open, social session was arranged. However, I could not face this and retired to my room where I openly wept for much of the remainder of the evening as I once again mourned my own death now over 22 years in the past.

In January of 2014 I did manage to attend another smaller gathering of Oxford alumni in San Antonio in honour of Professor Shearer (as in Alan, she said) West. I greatly enjoyed this gathering and indeed a small dinner afterwards with Senator Bob Krueger, the last Democratic US Senator from Texas and Lord Andrew Dunrossil, whose father many years ago, on behalf of the British Government, had smuggled books secretly to the newly imprisoned Nelson Mandela.

In the summer of 2014 the four of us took a trip to visit my mother, preceded by a few days in New York. Here Susan and I had the great thrill of seeing Kenneth Branagh's "Macbeth" in the magnificent and unique setting of the Park Avenue Armory. I had loved this play since studying it as a 15 year old. I had always been fascinated by its rich imagery of death and darkness. Little did I know that I would soon be "palled in the dunnest smoke of hell".

"Annual Income twenty pounds, annual expenditure nineteen six, result happiness. Annual income twenty pounds, annual expenditure twenty pound ought and six, result, misery".
Charles Dickens, David Copperfield.

After living comfortably for the last three years on the income generated by our conservative investments, our monthly expenditures for whatever reason seemed to rocket once we were in Austin and so I saw no option other than to invest in more risky instruments which effectively put me back into the role of trader, a role that had previously all but destroyed me and sent me to the limits of pain and torment. Rather like taking the Mako job why on earth would I inflict this upon myself and perhaps more importantly, those closest to me. It is quite a statement, given what has gone before, but so were to begin the worst four years in terms of mental instability and resultant marital stress in my entire life. The situation upon recent reflection horrifies me.

"There are only two tragedies in life: one is not getting what one wants, and the other is getting it". Oscar Wilde

Late in 2012 a complex oil production project I had been working on for several years finally came to fruition and I received in excess of $1m. I had hoped for considerably more but still this was a very nice sum and I had a sense of relief as this should have been more than enough to remove all of the recent financial pressure. Sadly this was not to be. Susan, somewhat understandably did spend a little extra after this windfall but the destructive creature inside me convinced me that this was a new and out of control pattern such that I would be forced to actively and more aggressively trade and invest. Only now, when it is tragically too late, but with more painfully gained information, do I see that this internal "conversation" also coincided with a brief, and relatively modest in magnitude, period of mania. This belief also provided a disastrous necessity in my mind: to engage in ever more risky investing behaviour. Rightly or wrongly I viewed Susan as a financial wrecking ball that was gaining momentum and would soon have my life reduced to a pile of rubble.

Discussions between Susan and me about money would always end in arguments. I asked her at what stage in life were women like her given the manual about how to make their husband miserable. That went down like a lead balloon, not surprisingly. A little later, I became haunted by two comments that Susan, presumably in a state of justifiable anger at my instability, had made to me over the last couple of years when we were discussing money and I had asked her to cut back on spending. One was that she "was sorry if I could not afford her" and another was "she had a lifestyle to maintain". Susan does not recall making these hurtful comments but obviously they had a very negative effect on my fragile mind. In a somewhat similar vein she once commented that I judged my personal worth by how my investing was going. This was partially correct but more precisely I was simply happier when the jackboot of financial stress was momentarily removed from my windpipe. She, on the other hand, valued herself based on how other people saw her. This reminded me of a David Foster Wallace quote: "you will become way less concerned with what people think of you when you realise how seldom they do".

Susan, however, does look amazingly youthful and age-defyingly beautiful. She is blessed with magnificent skin that she protects and treats religiously. Sometimes I wonder if she does not have a portrait, hidden away in a dusty attic, that is ageing hideously, like Dorian Gray.

> **"A successful man is one who makes more money than his wife can spend".**
> **Lana Turner**

She also once told me, much to my surprise, that she had to spend, to excess I presumed, so that she received her fair share given how much money I gave to my ex-wife and older children. Not only was this childish but utterly nonsensical. The only money I gave my ex-wife was the court ordered child support and I did pay for some extracurricular activities for my older children but in all probability I spent less on them than my younger ones. I was again lost for words.

As open-minded and logical I like to think I am, I failed to understand or barely consider things from Susan's perspective. Not only had she ridden the wild rollercoaster of my emotions for the last ten years but here was I telling her that the ride was to continue, and an ever more wild and uncontrollable ride it would become. Not that I was aware, but Susan was in a state of fear: fear of living with an oddly self-destructive, (manic) depressive lunatic. At times, as in Charleston, she would act a little irrationally and I would eagerly store that away in my mind as evidence that she was delusional and suffering from diagnosable mental ailments. I was persuaded of this to such an extent that it allowed my destructive self to convince me that I had no choice other than to aggressively trade as, I believed, Susan was incapable of working or partnering with me. The situation for me was not helped by Susan's tendency, perhaps jokingly, to tell her friends that I did nothing. I began to feel that she resented my not having a regular job even though I provided an extremely high standard of living for my family. It appeared to me, maybe incorrectly, that by spending more than we earnt she was trying to force me to get a job. After all anyone could make 15% after tax on their investments. When a couple we knew learnt how I made a living, the husband commented to his wife that Susan was killing me considering the stress I was under. I may have misunderstood but I was hurt by Susan's comments and such hurt would lead to more despair and hopelessness, a situation my destructive self thrived upon. Never did I stop to consider how much of her energy she had to devote to the children and to keeping a very calm exterior so as to protect the children from my emotional instability. She was remarkably successful in this endeavour which is a great testament to her strength of character and for which I am profoundly grateful.

As for me, I felt thoroughly trapped. I had to keep the bills paid but they simply would not stop coming. I felt had no choice but to take on considerably more risk so in 2012 I moved all my Morgan Stanley and Merrill Lynch conservative investments over to Etrade where I could trade more aggressively in order to make more money. I would spend every day essentially trading high dividend paying stocks and options. It was more stressful than my life had ever been at Vitol or HETCO or even Mako. I was living on an emotional roller coaster with many sharp down turns into despair and self-loathing. I seriously began to consider suicide. There was no way I could continue on this path and I convinced myself that it was impossible for Susan to conceive of cutting back meaningfully on expenses. That may have been a convenient excuse: my destructive self had total control and was well on its way to achieving its objective. I would spend all day focused on my market investments and most days were, in my perspective, bad. Somehow I had to present a happy exterior to my young children when they came home from school, often to swim together, but I was in absolute mental agony. My true self was desperately screaming out for help but into a vacuum. I was under the inexorable control of my destructive self, a control it would not easily relinquish as it sought the inevitable conclusion. Sadly the obvious solution: simply living a slightly more modest lifestyle off safe investments that would not require my trading was never discussed.

Upon reflection, and with the perspective added by some recent, excruciatingly, painful developments, I confess that I may have been, or probably have been, delusional. That is a terrible, heart-wrenching admission for me to make but if I accept it, it enables me to see everything so much more clearly and to make sense of a nonsensical period of mental hell. As well as the inner battle between what I consider my true self and the destructive animal, I am ashamed to say that I convinced myself 100% that my wife was utterly delusional. As above, I would store every act of irrationality in my mental box where I condemned her, falsely, as a delusional, narcissistic woman. My false self wondered, if it was a form of control: keeping me stressed and striving to pay massive bills. However, when I became really depressed and anguished Susan would support me and try her best to comfort me. While I appreciated this, in my sick mind I assumed it was all part of deliberate, capricious or crazy-making behaviour on her part.

"At 50, every man has the face he deserves" George Orwell

In March of 2013 Susan decided to throw me a 50th birthday party at our house. It was actually an immensely enjoyable and quite extravagant affair with many people in attendance. One lady commented that my wife must really love me to go to so much trouble. Sadly, and typically, I was not really appreciative at all: I was more concerned at the expense, which was perhaps understandable, since we were somehow, at the time, spending over $40,000 per month, on what, I have no idea. I met several very interesting and pleasant people at the party. In particular, I enjoyed talking to a Turkish chap who, in a previous life, had been a successful musician, touring all over Europe in a band. We discussed Turkey, Orhan Pamuk and eventually my perpetual desire to escape from it all, whatever "it" was. "Oh you mean kill yourself," he commented casually. I was a little taken aback as that was not what I had meant. I replied that I had simply meant escaping the traditional grind or "rat race". He had told me that his years of being on the road and dealing with a whole host of different types of people had led to him being very perceptive. Perhaps his perception detected something that was indeed deep inside me, though in no way had I been referring to it at this time. Alternatively, it could have been a simple misunderstanding. In any event, it reminded me of my conversation with Andy Tighe, almost thirty years earlier, when I had first mentioned my desire to "disappear".

Over the past four years we have taken many trips: to Colorado, Palm Desert, Hawaii and Europe. During every one I was consumed with my investments and, were it not for Susan's efforts at deflection and protection I would have ruined all those wonderful trips for everyone. So deep at times was my despair, not to mention my constant obsession, that for Susan to keep the trips happy and enjoyable for the children was an almighty and exhausting effort. Yet somehow she was successful but it was taking a heavy toll upon her. The trip to Palm Desert was especially stressful as I was having a particularly bad time and we were with another family from whom I had to hide my true state. This was exhausting but I seemed to succeed. Susan actually gave me some anxiety pills which helped a little: I assume she had them to help her to deal with living with me. Obviously Susan felt the strain of my depression and on the way to the airport she erupted into a massive expletive-ridden rage when I simply and quietly stated that we needed to turn left out of a gas station. I was totally shocked as indeed were the children. Such was her explosive wrath that even Amelia bravely told her that I had done nothing wrong.

In early 2013 Susan and I took a long weekend in Santa Fe, New Mexico, perhaps the only time we ever left Amelia and William with their grandmother. This trip happened to coincide with Ben Bernanke's first ever comment about possibly "tapering" the Fed's bond buying. With my usual luck I had just dipped my toe in the mortgage MREIT market and immediately lost 20%. I was devastated. My interest rate sensitive MLPs also took a hit but that was short lived. I really wanted to die. I moaned and groaned on the bed and tearfully went for a solitary sit in the park. The pressure was really proving to be too much. My destructive self must have been delighted: the mental torment I was suffering was perhaps the most intense ever. I can only imagine what Susan felt but we did manage to enjoy most of our time in the beautiful City that I really loved. As time developed I would occasionally make extra money from my trading, this being in addition to the dividends and interest off which we lived. However then I would be hit with a random loss out of left field for $100k, such as when Boardwalk Partners, an MLP, decided out of the blue to cut its dividend by 80%. Such events knocked me totally down and into a deep insidious, self-hating depression. I was still a failure and always would be. The world would be a better place without me and once I was gone my black cloud of bad luck would be removed from my family.

My first high risk foray was late in 2011 when I unfortunately decided to answer a late afternoon call from my Morgan Stanley account manager. He knew I invested for dividends and he had just had a presentation from an Oil Royalty Trust, the Chesapeake Granite Wash Trust (CHK), that at least for a few years would pay around 11%. This was not a dividend but more a return of your capital which you would receive and hopefully quite a bit more over the life of the trust. I read the prospectus and was pretty skeptical. Now for some silly reason I thought Chesapeake was a well-run natural gas producer, primarily, of excellent repute. From where I acquired this idea I am not sure but rather like the movie fiasco, a simple Google search and a little bit of research on the Company, especially its controversial Chairman, the late Aubrey "Swift Boat" McLendon, I would have run a mile. The offer price was $19 and I was uncertain if you would ever receive $19 in distributions during the entire 20 year life of the trust, the production of which had a very steep decline curve in the later years. I decided to invest $90,000. Within three of four weeks the price had risen to $25 or so. People must have been seduced by the apparent 11% yield. I told Susan and said, look we have about $25,000 of free money, let's take it. I don't know why I felt compelled to involve Susan but I did. She said, no, I'm sure oil will keep going up, to which I countered, well it does not matter as these guys are hedged for 3 years and after that their production will decline greatly. I agreed to wait. A couple of weeks later we had $50,000 profit on our $90,000 investment. I was an idiot not to take it. Again Susan told me to hold on but it was unfair of me to involve her in this. To make 50% on something you barely believe in over a few months is clearly a bird's nest on the ground but I refused to pick it up. Worse, as the price began to fall back towards the low $20s I decided to buy more thinking that there would be another flurry of buying by buyers who were seduced by the yield. This was not to be and when in March the 10Q came out showing a massive write down in reserves the trust plunged in value and I took a loss of $240,000. I was once again devastated. It was bad enough trying to pay the bills with the capital I had but if I lost capital then obviously I had to effectively make more with less. This was nothing short of a disaster which utterly shattered me for several days. How could I have been so stupid? I had a free $50,000 and ignored it and lost 5 times as much. To compound my misery I had actually read the 10Q just after the market had closed for the day. I planned to immediately sell but unfortunately the news was all over the market first thing the next morning and I was unable to avoid the plunge which added $100k to my losses. If I had only read the report a couple of hours earlier.

I realise only now that this purchase of CHK was my falling off the proverbial wagon. I was truly and destructively addicted to trading. I hated it and knew it caused me untold agonies but I had opened Pandora's box and it would not be closed until all the demons in my mind had wrought their destruction.

During these days in my dark cellar I was haunted by thoughts of my curse or my destiny and the fact that, once again, the only luck I had, was bad luck, and that I was fatally doomed.

During the summer of 2013 and 2014 we spent several weeks in our Colorado Condo. However, all day and every day I was obsessed with my investments and was constantly checking my Etrade account and trading on my iPhone. My destructive self was totally and utterly in control and essentially Susan could only watch in horror as I set about destroying myself. My addictive obsession totally removed any pleasure I could possibly have. Even when I would go for a cycle on the double bike with William, which he loved, my mind was elsewhere. Again only Susan's Herculean efforts kept the trip enjoyable for the children.

**"Of all escape mechanisms death is the most efficient".
H.L.Mencken**

It was during this summer of 2013 that I began to consider suicide more than ever before. I even discussed it in a matter of fact fashion with Susan telling her that it would be for the best and that she could tell the children that I had simply had an accident. They would get over it. This obviously had a negative effect on Susan which I underestimated. She was very concerned for me and did her best to comfort and console me. She tried to tell me that my young children especially really needed me and were so used to having me around that it would be a terrible loss. She even said she would miss me. To think I could talk seriously about suicide to my wife and not have it affect her is utterly unrealistic yet I was so consumed with my own mental anguish that I was, sadly, unable to appreciate the perspective or needs of anyone else. I felt that I was providing a good material living for my family but at what cost. I could have lowered my financial objectives and been a happier, more present husband and father though I am not sure my destructive self would ever have allowed me to be happy nor indeed allow me to be so in the future, no matter what I do, so strong is my belief in my destiny.

Later in 2013, back in Austin, with my portfolio back in the black, in addition to having kept the monthly bills at bay, Susan asked if I was pleased that I had not killed myself that summer. I actually replied "not really" as it was just a matter of time before I would once again be staring desperately into the bleak chasm of despair and financial ruin. Quite why, at this stage, we did not think a change of tack was called for I do not know, but we sadly did not. For whatever reasons we persisted along a path that brought me nothing but sheer mental agony and persistent thoughts of suicide, not to mention the negative effects it had on Susan.

In 2013 and 2014 I had entered the highly risky realm of upstream MLPs (Master Limited Partnerships) such as LINN Energy and Vanguard Natural Resources. These companies paid 8-9%, tax deferred, and were supposedly well hedged in the event of an oil price collapse. The fluctuations in the price of LINN in particular caused me monumental stress but the distribution came each month and I kept the ship afloat. I augmented the distribution from LINN and other MLPs such as Enbridge and NuStar with a strategy of selling puts on companies such as Shell and Total and AT&T at levels at which I was willing to own the stock. This on the whole was a successful strategy and when I was ever put upon I would be happy to hold the stock for its dividend until such a time as I could sell it at a decent profit. Much of this effort could be and was wiped out by my disastrous foray into MREITS and the Boardwalk fiasco which would wipe out 6 months of hard work in the blink of an eye and send me, once again, into a tailspin into the depths of despair.

Financial Disaster and Suicidal Despair

It was in the summer of 2014 when the proverbial wheels came off and I would crash down the hillside, in the bare chassis of my life, with sparks flying in all directions and nothing to seemingly stop me from going over the cliff into a bottomless chasm. I was finally going to realise my destiny. I was determined.

Meanwhile the young children were doing well at school, John had been awarded a baseball scholarship to Rice University, where he soon excelled as an outfielder, and Camille had won herself a place at the prestigious McCombs School of Business at the University of Texas, here in Austin.

With Camille, purely by coincidence, being in the same City, Susan decided that she would see if she could maybe reintroduce Camille, slowly and carefully, to our family. This did not go especially well. When Camille arrived in Austin she needed to purchase a few things for her room so I met her and we paid a visit to the Container Store and Crate and Barrel. For whatever reason this infuriated Susan who demanded to know why I was doing this as I hated shopping. I tried to calmly explain that I was Camille's father and since we happened to be in the same city it seemed quite an obvious thing to do. "Why can't her mother do it"? By this time I had virtually drained all of Susan's emotional reserves and she was running on fumes. She was actually a little hurt that Camille did not ask her to help and that was the reason for her poorly expressed yet understandable anger. I would have much preferred to have Susan help with the shopping, as most men would, and I would have loved to see the relationship between Camille and Susan re-established. Essentially, my massive instability had prevented this but I was unable to see it. I put this once again down to Susan's "delusions" and irrational tendencies.

On a couple of other days Camille came out to the house to see us but each went extremely badly. First off Camille explained to me, which I relayed precisely to Susan, that she would come to see us but she would not be sociable as she had a lot of homework to do with which she needed my help. When she came to the house she set about her homework, as expected, but once she had left Susan was furious that she had been so wrapped up with me doing school work. That did not help their relationship at all.

On the day of Camille's second visit I had noticed that Susan had done something to her eyelashes: she clearly had extensions put on, as I am not totally without any powers of observation and I felt a breeze every time she blinked. I had intended to ask her about it but it slipped my mind. That day Camille mentioned Susan's eyelashes to me which reminded me of my intent to mention it to my wife, and so I did. Susan, perhaps I should've expected, blew a gasket, "What do you care?". "You wouldn't have noticed if Camille hadn't told you?" "I don't want to tell you about it". "Oh boy," I thought. She then proceeded sadly to blame me for the break down in her relationship with Camille and accused me, falsely of course, of gossiping about her with my daughter.

Shortly thereafter Camille and I had lunch. Camille said she was not sure how easy it was going to be after all these years to re-establish a relationship with Susan especially because she was "bat-shit crazy" and fake. I did not step up as any self-respecting husband would and defend my wife who had stood so steadfastly by my side during periods of unimaginable stress and torment. Since I lacked the insight and understanding to realise it myself I could not explain to Camille what I had put Susan through and thus a certain amount of anger and apparent irrationality were the least one could expect. Sadly I missed a chance to positively benefit the relationship that Camille could have had with her stepmother, which was what I really wanted, but such was my mental state that it was utterly impossible. Camille went on to say that she resented how Susan had bad-mouthed her mother, Janet, when she was young, in an apparent effort to take her from Janet. Again I could have stepped up and explained that the vitriol with which Janet spoke about Susan totally eclipsed anything in the other direction, but I was not up to the task. Camille admitted that her relationship with her mother could at times be rocky especially when her mother had a glass of wine or three. They would have dreadful screaming matches where Camille could use every expletive under the sun. She said, although she had issues, her mother was her mother. Shortly after this Susan said Camille had "defriended" her from Facebook which brought her to tears. Camille though told me she had no recollection of ever having Susan as a friend on Facebook. Nonetheless, I had done nothing to prevent this heart-breaking misunderstanding, being too wrapped up with my own inner demons.

Camille then went on to tell me something that shocked me immensely yet, at the time, I lacked the perspective to fully comprehend it and as was my wont I went on to mischaracterize it as another negative about Susan. When aged 8 or so we were all in Hawaii and Camille and Susan were out swimming and chatting in the waves. After Camille had persistently asked why her mother and father had divorced, and would not let up, Susan eventually told Camille that basically I had never loved her mother and had only really married her because of the STD issue. In hindsight, Camille felt this was a pretty inappropriate thing for Susan to tell an eight year old girl. However, in Susan's defence, not only was Camille incredibly persistent in her questions, but Janet at this time was being especially interfering and would even show the children our old wedding photos and wedding video. She apparently told them that she could have me back any time she wanted, so this was of course very unsettling for John and Camille. Susan was really just trying to set the record clear in Camille's mind, under difficult circumstances.

This Hawaiian adventure had begun with me thinking that I was dying of kidney poisoning as it turned out that the night before flying to Maui, while watching John in a baseball game, I had been bitten by a black widow spider. I felt the bite thinking it was a nasty mosquito or perhaps a spider of sorts but not a black widow. 24 hours later I felt a bit sickly. I had overlooked the roughly 8 inch diameter flat but hard red circle on my thigh. That night my kidneys and diaphragm were agony and I tossed and turned all night thinking I had been poisoned, which indeed I had. In the morning Susan was about to head to the beach with Camille and leave me with Amelia but I suggested that might not be such a good idea. The hotel doctor sent me to the Hospital saying this did not look good. I had told the doctor but not the hospital staff about my bite. After several hours of blood tests and scans I finally told the hospital doctors about my bite. One of them immediately said it was a black widow bite and the neurotoxin attacks the diaphragm and kidneys, amongst other areas of the body. Since there were no such spiders on the Islands there was no anti-venom so I just had to pull through. I could tell I was over the worst so they packed me off in a taxi back to the hotel where I spent the next 24 hours in bed.

Another very odd situation had occurred perhaps even earlier than the one in Hawaii. When Camille was little she had a box in which she kept her most precious pieces of arts and crafts. She would look at it almost daily and then one day found, to her amazement, something totally new: it was the divorce decree pertaining to her mother's first marriage. She was too young to be upset but totally confused as to why, presumably Susan, had put it in there. I must confess I am pretty confused too but it must have been to do with Janet's constant interfering.

Not long after the black widow incident we had taken young Amelia for a terrific weekend to Acapulco where I managed to be stung by a scorpion on the back, with no ill effects. However, just a few weeks later I had a rather nasty run-in with some angry bees: clearly I was on some sort of a roll. I was at a BP industry golf outing in Scottsdale, Arizona, when doubtless inspired a little by alcohol, I decided to go off the beaten track on my way to the dinner destination and so set off through some modest undergrowth. Midway I felt the call of nature so proceeded to relieve myself on a convenient cactus. However, this appeared to greatly annoy a load of bees that proceeded to attack in number, so there I stood holding my manhood in my left hand and frantically flapping my hat in defence with my right hand. Finally, I beat a hasty retreat and made it to the dinner but I had sustained two or three direct hits to my face and left hand but felt none the worse for wear. The next morning, however, my left hand had swollen such that it would not nearly close and resembled a boxing glove and my face looked as if I had been on the losing end of a bare-knuckle boxing match. I was certainly the subject of much curiosity and amusement at breakfast that day. Fortunately that was the end of my hostile interactions with the animal kingdom, other than having a flock of wild turkeys surround me in my back yard at one time making a giant mess with all their poop.

Camille and I have been to Europe together each of the last two years. In 2013 we went to London for a few days before surprising my mum in Jersey with a visit for her 80th birthday. The following year I took her to Paris and Amsterdam for her senior year spring break. Both trips were terrific and we had a great time. Of course I was constantly checking my phone but I did my best not to let it detract from our enjoyment and was surprisingly successful.

At a recent Halloween, Camille had been at a friend's house while the parents threw a small Halloween gathering. Camille ventured downstairs to the party where she was greeted by an absolutely terrifying site: it appeared to be someone in a Ted Cruz mask. However, upon closer inspection she realised it was even more horrifying: it was Ted Cruz, in person. She retreated in shock upstairs and upon hearing of this I immediately insisted she attend intensive therapy to stave off PTSD which she duly did. Many in Texas, and indeed America, I am sad to say, have not been so lucky.

Thankfully Amelia and William were enjoying school and thriving. As parents we had subjected them to quite a few tests and educational therapies, whether needed or not, as we wanted to make sure that they were essentially not in need of any special assistance having experienced two serious failings in the past concerning the health of my children. Perhaps the most interesting therapy was biofeedback or neurofeedback. Both children would frequently go. Susan also went and eventually succeeded in persuading me to give it a try.

After the children had had their first QEEG, which was analysed by a specialist in Dallas, Susan and I sat down with the technician in Austin to discuss their reports. Apparently both had certain areas of brain activity that could use some neurofeedback but nothing of any concern. What was of concern, and one area where we had been greatly let down by the most expensive and wasteful health system in the world, was the fact that William did have a very slight speech impediment. For years we had known this and spent a fortune on having it treated with minimal positive effects. It so happened that one of Susan's friends had experience in such matters, and she suggested that it seemed pretty obvious to her that he might be slightly "tongue-tied. So, we took him to a specialist and this was indeed the case and after very minor surgery the condition was rectified. It simply appalls me that so many doctors and therapists had overlooked this relatively obvious and easily fixable problem. Susan, after giving birth to William, had even mentioned a typical, and in fact the most obvious, symptom of being tongue-tied to her nurse when infant William would struggle to feed. For a nurse specialised in new born babies and helping their mothers feed this struck me as an egregious oversight.

The second instance of being let down badly by the "system" concerned my eldest son and dyslexia. It was revealed in John's first year of College that he actually had a mild form of the disease and all his schools in Houston had failed to pick up on it. Being a student athlete at Rice meant they had many extra privileges such as access to good doctors and a psychological and educational evaluation. It was during this later process that is was pointed out that he had clearly always struggled with mild dyslexia and he was granted a little extra time when doing tests to accommodate this. Now this made me feel guilty and sad: when John was young I had frequently yelled at him for reading slowly and for procrastinating over homework: classic symptoms of dyslexia. I telephoned him to apologise which he accepted.

When my QEEG was sent to Dallas the technician called me in to discuss it. I was of course still on my 300 mg of Effexor daily. She commented that it was the quickest they had ever received back a report from the doctor in Dallas. This could have been pure chance or it could have been that my QEEG showed serious problems. I believe it was the latter. As well as, not surprisingly, showing major depression, my anxiety level was off the charts and I had signs of significant PTSD. I began treatment. Somewhat to my surprise the treatment seemed to greatly reduce my tendency to ruminate on the past. However, after maybe ten sessions I ceased going as my life was accelerating unimpeded toward the waiting abyss.

"All the things that one has forgotten scream for help in dreams". Elias Canetti

During my years in Austin, and some before, I have had several recurring dreams. In one I would have bitter shouting arguments with my mum. In another, a fairly common one I believe, I was back at College and about to sit my finals. However, I was my current age and had forgotten everything I ever knew about Physics and thus was filled with fear.

The third recurring dream involved Judith. I would be frantically trying to find her number or email in my iPhone but I never could find it and I could not even operate my phone correctly. In my dream I was desperate to reach her in Australia of all places. Now a couple of years ago Judith happened out of the blue to contact me on email. We exchanged a few chatty emails about our lives and I learnt that she was now a Prison Governor in charge of several open prisons in Kent. She lived in her original home town of Deal. These few emails have had the effect of stopping this dream, which was a plus.

Lastly, I would often dream about meeting my old Vitol colleagues, especially Ian and Bob. We would have extremely pleasant conversations and I would often stay at Bob's house. They would both apologise for not taking me back. Not surprisingly Greenslade often featured and usually I was successfully pushing him over a cliff edge or putting a bullet into his over-sized head. I actually fantasised about putting a bullet in his head when awake, too.

In the summer of 2014 by some miracle I found myself up about 10% on my overall portfolio, after taking all dividends and interest as income. I told my wife that we could take out $100k and use it to redo our back yard and install a nice patio, fire pit and outdoor kitchen area, something which we had both wanted to do when finances permitted. However, when discussed maybe nine months prior Susan made it clear that she felt we needed to fill in our swimming pool and build another as the current one was not ideally situated. This would have eaten up over $60,000 and seemed excessive to me: why not be sensible and work with what we have. We were unable to reach an agreement. Now the last few years had taken an enormous toll on Susan and though she was pleased, I think, at the news she knew I would doubtless soon be back in my dark cellar. Sadly, but perhaps not surprisingly, we suffered a breakdown in communication. I was terribly deflated by Susan's lack of excitement and enthusiasm: she appeared to scoff at me and seemed uninterested in the patio idea. I presumed this was because $100k would be insufficient should she want a new pool which I still thought was totally unrealistic. Unfortunately, this was a very significant and devastatingly destructive step. I became very sad and profoundly depressed. I felt even when financially in sound shape I would always be upset, if not totally in despair, and the brain crushing pressure would never be relieved as nothing would ever be enough. If it is possible to point to one particular incident, I would say that this was when the destructive wheels of destiny began inexorably and terribly to turn towards their inevitable conclusion. With my mind in a sad and fragile state the destructive me, or "the creature" sensed its chance for a major coup and pounced on me viciously when I was at my most vulnerable. The "creature" never went away and was constantly snapping at my heels but it had extreme cunning coupled with patience and realised that the best time to strike was when I was in a very fragile emotional state such as now. The "creature" made me shut down physically and emotionally and prepare to face my own personal armageddon.

'The Destiny of man is in his own soul.' Herodotus

At the end of September 2014 when my portfolio was still in the black but with the "creature" totally in charge I told Susan that I had a powerful sense of impending doom and that we were going to lose everything. I saw this enormous boulder coming crashing down out of the sky to flatten me. I had plenty of time to dodge it but for whatever reason I did not. I simply waited for impact. After all it was my destiny. I was finally ready to lose everything. At that same time I stopped my exercise program that I had been following 4-5 times per week for three years. I essentially shut down waiting for the end. Somewhat oddly, Susan has subsequently told me that this exercise regime, whilst the children were at school, was highly selfish. I happened to need a new car as my lease had expired. I bought a basic Porsche Cayenne, which I have greatly enjoyed, but I knew that the "creature" or the Universe would see that such an action would not go unpunished. A mutual lady friend of ours commented that it was nice to see me have a new car as I deserved it but Susan appeared to again scoff at this and I was deeply hurt. Susan may have been joking but sadly I took it as a very harsh sleight along the lines of how I "did nothing". This served of course to compound my belief in the inevitability of the coming armageddon. Over the preceding years I had often said that nothing I did was ever appreciated and that I received no respect. Susan would harshly respond that respect had to be earnt and I had done nothing to earn any.

"It's Deja-vu all over again". Yogi Berra

That Thanksgiving we went to Colorado. Opec had just had a meeting and it was clear Saudi Arabia was not going to support the oil price and it was going to collapse. I had seen this scenario play out before in 1986 and I knew my oil investments were going to get hammered. Perhaps most telling was how the Saudis had recently discounted their crude oil to Asia in order to "guarantee Asian refiners a positive margin". This was eerily similar to the era of netback crude pricing in 1986 that saw the Gulf Producers sell their crude at a fixed differential to a basket of products and guaranteeing the refiner a profit. Clearly we were in for a serious and perhaps prolonged price fall: it was all but certain. However, as was always agonisingly the case, when I was effectively certain of something, I was unable to act, for whatever reason. I had no problem acting when it was probably a mistake. I could not bring myself to sell. My mind was a knot of torment and anguish. I was afraid of losing my monthly dividends plus the old demons of thinking that whatever I did would go wrong came to the fore: if I sold I would never again be able to make another wise investment so why not just hold on. I simply never considered following my own rules and stopping out, such was the monthly dividend mania imprinted onto my mind. The "normal" me had wanted to exit but the "delusional" me controlled by the "creature" would not allow this act of self-preservation. When "the creature" had control every fibre of my body and every cell of my brain seemed to be dominated by destructive instinct and fearful impulses. It was as if I had lost the freedom of my own will, simply moving fatalistically towards my own terrible end.

And so I watched in pure mental agony as my portfolio lost about 30%. I was utterly distraught and inconsolable. Susan tried to pull me around but it was not possible. All I could talk about was killing myself. How desperately did I want this living hell to be over once and for all. I seriously thought about walking up to the nearby I-10 and jumping in front of a lorry: how appealing that seemed. Though there were the lorry driver's feelings to consider: I would write him a note of thanks, I thought.

Susan insisted on taking me to the Emergency Room where I was talked to by a doctor and a counsellor. The counsellor was sufficiently worried that he wanted to commit me unless I was able to convince him that I would keep myself safe. I did not want to be committed in Colorado as we were due to go back to Austin in three days but he was not convinced by what I said. Eventually I managed to convince him that I was ok and that I would go to the Emergency Room back in Austin when I returned.

That was the day of Thanksgiving. We had dinner with friends in the Westin that night and I barely managed to keep it together. Suicidal thoughts were never far from my mind. In Austin my financial situation continued to deteriorate, as expected. I was beside myself. Susan took me to the Brackenridge Mental Hospital ER where the doctor suggested I up my Effexor slightly and also prescribed Xanax. The Xanax did calm me for a while but I was prone to panic attacks and sheer mental devastation plus dangerously elevated blood pressure.

The following week Susan took me back to Brackenridge and the doctor persuaded me that for my own safety I needed to be admitted to the Shoal Creek hospital for a few days. I reluctantly agreed.

"The conflict between the will to deny horrible events and the will to proclaim them aloud is the central dialectic of psychological trauma" Judith Lewis Herman

The admissions nurse took note of my symptoms and I noticed that she assigned me a 7 on the scale of 1-10 for a likely suicide attempt. I was shown to my room which had two beds but that night I was alone. I lay on my bed and cried and cried for what seemed like an eternity. I just wanted to die. Nothing was going to save me. A nurse came in for quite a long chat. I explained that I had lost so much money that I would no longer be able to support my family and that I was therefore worthless and better off dead. She commented that it would be terribly sad if all my family looked to me for was money and she was sure that was not the case. That sadly was precisely how I felt and I had failed in my ability to provide sufficient money and therefore I felt that I no longer served any purpose: my family and the world would be better off without me.

"It always seemed that a fear of judgement is a mark of guilt and the burden of insecurity". Criss Jami

The hospital switched me from Xanax to valium, 30 mg per day, and also gave me 45 mg of Remeron (mirtazapine) at night. In the hospital I was calmer and was subjected to several psychological evaluations. Susan came to visit me each day and was very concerned. I mentioned that I simply could no longer tolerate the massive financial stress but Susan immediately angrily assumed this was a direct criticism of her which she vehemently rejected, telling me not to think of blaming her as it was all my own fault. The doctors confirmed what I already knew: I had major depression and severe anxiety disorder as well as elements of various other personality disorders notably narcissism. Now I was not deemed a classic narcissist in the traditional understanding of the term but more in the way that, "My insides did not match my outsides". In other words I was capable of projecting to the outside world a facade of happiness or calmness while inside my brain was being ripped apart by despair and thoughts of suicide. This was indeed how I had operated for most of the last 25 years. Perhaps the doctors did not wish to over burden me with negativity so they left their diagnosis there. I wish they had given me the whole picture. Susan desperately tried to persuade them to keep me for a couple more days as she knew I needed more treatment which undoubtedly I did. Sadly, and I believe at enormous cost, they did not relent to Susan's efforts at persuasion. The doctors did have a private chat with Susan where they mentioned that I had elements of a number of personality disorders including obsessive-compulsive disorder, maladaptive disorder and was a very complex case. They and Susan mentioned the narcissism to me but I would much later learn to my deepest regret and sadness that there was perhaps something there that concerned "the creature" and it was not shared with me until the "creature" had essentially won and destroyed my life

Haven't we met before?

After 4 nights I was allowed to go home but would have to take a five week DBT (dialectic behaviour therapy course) for three hours a morning, four days a week. During this course I learnt a great deal of mind control techniques but it is very difficult to put them into practice when your life continues to collapse all around you. One article I was presented with was especially heart-breaking to read. It was titled "Haven't we met before?" and described the classic borderline/narcissist couple. With all the false pieces of negative information about Susan that I had stored for years in my mental box I jumped to the conclusion that Susan had many of the borderline personality disorder (BPD) traits and that I those of the narcissist, as discussed. This article brought me to tears, such was its poignancy and profound effect on my mind. The article goes on to describe how the borderline will basically turn the narcissist's world upside down, such that he can lose his entire fortune and become a mere shadow of his former self. The narcissist so wants to win but has no chance to do so in this dangerous game in which the borderline is far more skilled. This article was written by Shari Schreiber and can be found at "gettingbetter.com". Susan obviously believes I am totally wrong in thinking that she suffers from BPD but I had disastrously clung to this false notion until late November when a much more frightening and devastating, and I believe correct, revelation came starkly to light.

One of Susan's' pet peeves, which is simply a total misunderstanding, is that I do not want her to work. This is totally untrue but she clings adamantly to the idea. Late last year she had an opportunity to work for a computer software company that sold Oracle database systems, under license from Oracle, to small companies. It really sounded like an ideal opportunity for Susan and I fully supported her efforts in this venture. After a few months she decided that it was not going to work: she needed more organisational support and she did not have a realistic set of potential customer leads. She said she wanted to quit. I suggested whatever she felt she should do was the right thing to do. She also would oddly suggest that I would try to "put her in a box". Quite what she referred to I have no idea. In my view, given her apparent resentment at my not working a regular job, I would think it more likely to think that I was the one being forced into a box. Susan would also claim that I reminded her of her father who she claims during her later childhood sat around doing nothing. Again the comparison appears totally invalid. Furthermore she would often quip that she did not wish to live like my parents who led an extremely frugal existence: I hardly feel our life in any way resembled theirs. I am not at all sure but perhaps my venture into more risky trading was a way of showing that I did not simply do nothing. If it were the case it was certainly a disastrous step.

After discharge, I was still prescribed the Effexor, Remeron and valium plus a blood pressure medication. My leaving hospital would coincide with when my mother was over for Christmas but she was quite understanding and did not probe too deeply. She and Susan agreed that I needed to stop trading the markets and instead to buy a business of some sort. I was in general agreement but I still had to pay the bills and I desperately wanted to see my portfolio recover from its down 40%. However, this was not to be. Had I been in full command of my mental faculties I could have cut my losses and turned my life in a totally new direction that would have removed the mental torment of trading and would have saved us all a year of hell. After my discharge Susan said she desperately wanted me to stop trading but tragically I simply would not listen though of course I knew it was dreadfully detrimental to my health. In contradiction of this, a mutual lady friend of ours told me that when I came out of hospital she told Susan that I absolutely had to stop trading. She went on to say that Susan said I had to trade as that was how we made money. Regardless and unfortunately, I could not accept taking the 40% loss and so I continued my futile efforts to salvage the sinking ship of my life. I firmly believe I was truly addicted and I would not listen to anyone, as I had also apparently been unbeknownst to me diagnosed with a disorder related to control issues. No-one could stop me from destroying myself, short of locking me away. There is no doubt in my mind that I could have done with a couple of days more in the hospital to more clearly define my numerous and complex personality disorders. My supposed control issues clearly manifested themselves over my desire to almost totally control our investing, but, I believe, the battle for control over our lives can be seen to be far more of a two way street, if not a one way street down which I was heading the wrong way.

My mother and Susan did agree that we, or primarily Susan, should start a business to remove some of my stress but frankly we needed to remove all of my trading stress, one hundred per cent.

Shortly afterwards we adopted a young orange (tabby) cat who I named Oscar as he was essentially wild. For several evenings I would sit for hours and wait for him to come to our back porch and spend hours getting him accustomed to me so that ultimately I could pet him with ease. However, in order to get him inside the house I had to resort to using a trap and once inside we housed him in Amelia's bedroom, complete with litter tray of course. Typically, after my DBT sessions I would lie on Amelia's bed and let Oscar jump up and sit next to me. I would often also sleep with him in Amelia's bed at night. He soon became very attached to me, and vice versa. After a few weeks he would happily wonder around the house and became increasingly comfortable. I felt that somehow he and I were going through a recovery together. We tried not to let him out in the evening as coyotes were often prowling around but we were not always successful. One evening, looking out the kitchen window, Susan saw Oscar in a "defensive posture". Before she could react the cat sprang into the air as a coyote, now visible, snapped at him. Susan ran outside and called for me. I picked up Oscar who was trembling and bleeding a little from his mouth but overall I thought he was ok. Susan took him to the emergency vet who called a few hours later to deliver the bad news: Oscar had suffered a punctured lung. Possibly emergency surgery, at a cost of about $2000, could have saved him but there was no guarantee. Given my money woes, I decided to have Oscar put to sleep. I had never been so attached to any pet even though I had only had him a few short months. I felt a part of me died that night too.

"An unexamined life is not worth living". Plato

Inevitably, as I had expected, the dividends on the stocks on my portfolio were cut in the New Year, and thus our monthly income was reduced. An obvious solution would have been to cut our monthly expenses but this did not occur to me such was the control I believe that the "creature" had over my mind and his determination to destroy me. I therefore bought more of the falling stocks on margin which was another fatal error. Our monthly income went up but my portfolio continued to fall, as anticipated, and I would often enter "margin hell" when I would have to carefully manage margin calls. The situation was utterly wretched and pure torment. I now see that I was basically locked into a delusional state thinking my investments which were clearly illogically based would miraculously turn around. Even when I knew they were going to fall I would, in a state I can only describe as delusional mania, buy more.

My wife tried all year after discharge to effectively save me from myself but I would not listen and simply and stubbornly allowed our lives to further and unnecessarily plummet to ever greater depths of despair and ruin. For my wife to watch this must have been absolute torture but only now am I able to see the pain, anguish and devastation that I caused. It was truly a tragedy.

**"The Truth does not change according to our ability to
stomach it".
Flannery O'Connor**

**"The truth will set you free but not until it is finished with you".
David Foster Wallace**

It is now December 2015 and I have struggled with this financial situation all year and I have lost 95% of my portfolio. The year has flashed by in a hellish haze. I wonder why this had to happen? Why did I not take evasive action when I sensed doom or at any time thereafter? Slowly over the year the stress of my depression and despair as well as my financial losses have further worn down an already depleted Susan and stretched our relationship to breaking point.

Our situation is utterly tragic: we had the ability to live a perfectly comfortable, stress-free life and I blew it. I have to take responsibility for the disastrous investing decisions. In my defence my mental makeup is not fit for this form of high risk, high stress trading which begs the question why did I do it, as I have known this for years. The only answer I can come up with is to self-destruct and damn the consequences. Well, the consequences have been truly damning, mentally and financially for both of us. Arguably, of course, I felt trapped by our massive monthly expenditures.

Until September I had continued to keep the dividends coming but as I did so my portfolio would decline far more. This summer we spent 10 days in our time share in Hawaii where I did little but watch and try to manage my portfolio. Susan told me to liquidate a portion and I ignored her. She had been correct and in fact my entire struggle with margin was utterly ridiculous, irresponsible and mentally devastating. As the end of September loomed I felt I had a good handle on my investments and I could somehow manage through this all be it in excruciating mental agony for as long as necessary. We have taken steps to take out a home equity loan in order to buy a business and plan to put the house up for sale, sadly, in the spring. The Colorado Condo is on the market and we will lose close to another $400k. My situation is desperate but in my weekly DBT therapy sessions that I have attended since February I agreed that I would "radically accept" my situation and strive to manage the portfolio as I felt I could. Sadly even this plan was derailed two weeks ago in a devastating fashion.

I had the strongest sense I could possibly have that my portfolio was going to run up nicely over the next 6-8 days, I would collect in excess of $20,000 in distributions and then exit my entire position in anticipation of a significant dip that I saw ten to 12 days ahead. I explained this to Susan and she appeared in agreement. My predictions were spot on.

However, on the following Monday morning in late September Susan came to see my at my computer and unleashed a tirade of hysterical abuse the likes of which I have never experienced. She told me repeatedly to "Fuck off" and that she wanted to divorce me. She screamed that I was an absolute idiot (not much argument there) and that I had to sell everything to preserve what little we had left. I was shaken to the core and did what she suggested. Two days later I had the golden chance to buy all that I had sold at a lower level and prepare for the inevitable rally that was about to come. I tried to explain my thinking via text to Susan but she responded that if I was unable to resist buying she would call our broker and have me frozen out from the account. I did not know what to do. I had reached the end of my rope. As my now non-existent portfolio rallied the next 3-4 days, as I said it would, and we left 40-50% of what we had left on the table, I broke down and cried as if I would never stop. I could not live with myself. My devastation was complete as indeed, Susan informed me via text, was hers. Susan said I should not have listened to her as I seldom did in the past but she had never reached these incredible heights of abuse and threatening behaviour. Obviously she wanted to stop the bleeding and to conserve what little we had left. My obsession over my investments, the massive losses and everything else had essentially driven our relationship beyond the breaking point. Throughout the spring and summer Susan had wanted to start a business and I was in total agreement but my constant wrestling with margin never gave me the chance to extract the money she needed. She felt at times I did not want her to have the money which is not true. The money kept slipping through my fingers like a bar of soap as my life spiralled down the plug hole. To this day she angrily berates me for deliberately not allowing her to start her business. I try to explain that I never deliberately did such a thing and that things were simply out of my control and I was enduring an absolute living hell. I absolutely wanted her to start the business and regret profoundly that I was not able to do so. Yes, I may have chosen to use the funds we had to defend margin, but I was not doing it out of spite or malice, but out of a desire to do what I felt was best for the family, something that I have always done, literally coming to the brink of death. Clearly I have not been capable of rational thinking for a very long time. I have always spent very little on myself because our outgoings have been exorbitant, especially these last four years: I have chosen to sacrifice. Yet I am berated mercilessly for something that is untrue, and would indeed have helped, but was not a panacea by any stretch of the imagination.

Susan was concerned at my mental state. I was inconsolable. She wanted to take me to the hospital but I refused and she was soon screaming and cursing ferociously once again and even took to beating me on the upper arm with a large, thick, Pottery Barn candle. I state this as a matter of fact. I am surprised Susan tolerated so much for so long such has been her, undeserved, dedication, to me. To be perfectly honest, I have, for the bulk of our marriage, arguably been a wretched husband. I do not think I even qualify as being like "The Curate's egg," that is, "good in parts".

The same exact situation presented itself at the end of October. However, I was paralysed with fear and unable to take advantage of it as I was still in a state of shock from the prior month. I watched another 30% plus go begging. I simply cannot go on like this. The pain of another golden opportunity that stared me in the face and was missed is totally devastating. The vicious verbal assault which I endured last month finally broke what little remained of my spirit, at precisely the time when I was about to salvage a modicum of relief from the mangled wreckage of my life. This opportunity was as close to risk free as you will ever see and I was not able to act. I was once again Dostoevsky's mouse. Not only have I long since abandoned all values I feel totally without value. My doctor just added lithium to my cocktail of drugs. Maybe it will reduce my mental torment a little. Who knows? Somehow I doubt it. However, had I successfully made some money over the last two months, yes, it would have been nice but it would just perpetuate the cycle of destruction, anguish and pain which is utterly futile, given my destiny. Unfortunately, for the third month in a row such a pattern became apparent. I felt compelled to act: after all, the same circumstances existed so why would it not work. Deep down I knew it would be a costly failure, but the only reason I could point to was that it was me and my destiny. That had always been a pretty reliable, if irrational indicator. It goes back to the fact that I should have accepted that I was truly that mouse: if only I never did or had done anything, much devastating heartache for me and others would have been avoided. And so some unexpected bad news was released and I got hammered again. Some things just do not change. I was beyond despair.

The lithium, somewhat to my surprise, has had a noticeably positive effect. I have been asked over the years if I have periods of mania and I have always very studiously answered in the negative. However, upon closer introspection, I called my psychiatrist recently to mention that I could indeed identify two powerful manic episodes, admittedly ten years apart. Of significance is the last episode which was when I frantically wrote the perhaps overly critical "Susan" section of an earlier draft of this work. With my newly acquired insights, this offensive section has been totally rewritten to more accurately reflect my story. Susan has often thought I was manic and I am only now beginning, not that it matters, frankly, to realise that there may be some merit to this. It may explain some of my history but in the overall scheme of things is trivial. I am quite open to as many psychiatric diagnoses as is appropriate: the more the merrier. As long as they are all valid of course.

"Every man is guilty of all the good he did not do". Voltaire

I now have no idea how we are going to pay our bills other than through spending savings which are quite minimal, especially after my latest disastrous and typical blunder. Interestingly this summer Susan's brother told her that her mother had rather cruelly commented that, "Susan was less uppity since she had lost all of her money". Susan had told me that years ago her mother had advised her to marry early, have a couple of kids, and then divorce her husband for all he was worth and to repeat the process until she was set. To Susan's credit she did not take this advice.
Fortunately, my best friend Alberto has offered to lend us some money to at least get us through the interim. To paraphrase Oscar Wilde, I hope Alberto is a pessimist as then he won't expect the money back.
Maybe our house and condo sell and we can somehow invest that but how. Maybe we buy the type of business that Susan thinks could work but will it? Nothing ever has worked. I am consumed by thoughts of suicide and only the fear of hurting my children stops me from following through on what I so dearly want to do. Susan and I barely talk. The only positive is our expenses are dramatically reduced, as they have to be. No one is to blame for this tragic situation, other than me, if it really matters: as Dega in "Papillon" said, "Blame is for God and small children". I have reached my appointed date with destiny as I fly over the cliff into the bottomless abyss of pain, suffering, agonising despair and financial ruin.

"Good writing excites me and makes life worth living". Harold Pinter

I would like to point out that I received somewhat of an inspiration to write this book after attending a book reading and signing by Jonathan Franzen here in Austin. We exchanged a few brief, but to me, quite meaningful words. Additionally, such was my despair after the incident above that I desperately needed a distraction. As my writing draws to a close I can feel the dense, black fog of despair and hopelessness wrap around me and I wonder if this shall not turn out to be a rather long but heartfelt, sincere, and, as far as I can recall, totally truthful, suicide note. No-one is to blame but myself and anyone who I may have suggested has done me harm is totally forgiven, especially my parents who I know loved my brother and me absolutely and did their very best. I can only pray that the inevitable sadness and sense of loss that my actions will create will, with time, fade away and ultimately be understood and indeed perhaps, maybe I can be forgiven.

I must say unequivocally that both of my wives have been excellent mothers to my children during what for them, too, has been an unbelievably trying time. It cannot have been easy living with such a tortured, seemingly unempathetic and conflicted soul as myself. I can see how Susan can view herself as being caught in the middle of a terrific, unpredictable tempest, throughout many of our trials and tribulations. She has done extremely well giving my children an excellent upbringing during these past, turbulent, chaotic years.

Conclusion: Towards my Destiny and the
Final Horrific Realisation

"Hell hath no fury like a woman scorned".
William Congreve

Well, if not scorned, sarcastically and condescendingly maligned. Perhaps not surprisingly, Susan has read an earlier version of this work in which I criticise her greatly and unjustly, claiming that she absolutely suffers from Borderline Personality Disorder, which I believe she does not, and is delusional. What I had written in terms of incidents was factually correct but dripped with sarcasm and condescension and most importantly it lacked context. I have subsequently amended these factors. Truth be told, I think Susan already knew all that I had written but seeing it in black and white and fearing the humiliation it could cause should her friends read it, thoroughly incensed her. Perhaps equally she had decided it was time to cash in on her losing investment in me. Of course I wrote it in a state of extreme shock and anger, having just received an incredibly vicious verbal and physical assault. Obviously she was outraged and has understandably but sadly filed for divorce. She angrily claimed that my writing revealed the true me and that my "mask" had finally come off. I found that comment interesting and wondered who indeed had been wearing a mask and for how long and when. This of course is very sad for many reasons, but not least because of our wonderful 8 and 11 year old children. Arguably it is a path down which I have previously journeyed but I certainly never wanted to take that path again. I did not want to divorce Susan as I love her yet I knew my writings would precipitate our divorce. Why did I wilfully do this? The answer is destiny. With "the creature" firmly in control having successfully destroyed me financially it was now time for the next necessary step before delivering the final coup de gras. And so I had to force Susan to divorce me.

"It ain't what you know that gets you into trouble. It's what you know for sure that just ain't so". Attributed to Mark Twain

Being served with divorce papers, as inevitable as it was, was still a sickening blow to the stomach and in this case it was made more so, perhaps not surprisingly, by the shocking and false allegations made in the court papers. Foolishly perhaps, I thought some lawyers had some ethics but clearly this was not the case with Kristi, a supposed friend, who Susan was using. I confronted Kristi over the phone for filing what she knew was a farrago of twisted facts and lies, and she, lying again, said this was standard. Well, she was intent on getting the judge to issue dramatically restrictive motions against me so she had to stand in front of the judge and fabricate her case. She claimed domestic violence, the only instance of which was when my wife hit me with the rather large candle detailed earlier. However, most egregiously, she had the judge issue an order stating that I was a menace to my children and should only see them under supervision. This infuriated me, understandably, and I hardly think that it is standard let alone anywhere near the truth. As Criss Jami eloquently says, "Just because something isn't a lie does not mean that it isn't deceptive. A liar knows that she is a liar, but one who speaks mere portions of truth in order to deceive is a craftsmen of destruction." Much of their desire to concoct a maliciously false case was borne out of revenge for my having written this book. The only thing, however, that concerned me were the legal obligations: the actual laughable allegations were of no concern primarily as the authors lacked any credibility. Maybe four or five days later, Kristi, doubtless proud of duping the judge with her lies, took my wife out to dinner, of course checking that I, the menace, was available to watch the children, as normal. I suppose Kristi and Susan felt that even an obvious fabrication was of some comfort when they had so few others. Fortunately, within less than two weeks, Susan saw sense and had the nonsensical motions set aside or negated, in non-legal parlance, with the help of my attorney.

"The Lady doth Protest too much, me thinks"
Shakespeare's Hamlet

One of Susan's favourite words, used of course by her lawyer, is abuse. She uses it so frequently that the above quote seems entirely apt. Almost everything I say and do is apparently some sort of abuse. Susan even stunned me recently with the accusation that I was "mentally abusive" to the children. This of course is most odd. Apparently by working outside, as I like to do, I am neglecting the children with whom I never do anything: other than, for example, swim, mess around, play games, cycle in Colorado, watch movies, help with homework, take to school and put to bed, go to school functions, attend boy scouts, and many other things that a typical father does.

Throughout my life thoughts of death have never been far from my struggling mind. For years, and indeed as stated to Sarna, I have felt that my destiny was to lose everything and then do away with myself. Perhaps because my mind was especially vulnerable in September of last year I allowed my destiny to begin to unfold. As earlier described, I basically shut down emotionally and physically and wilfully allowed the boulder of financial destruction to strike me, knowing I could easily side-step it but for whatever reason I chose not to. I believe I thought my time had come. Now I confess I did not expect the financial disaster to be quite as bad as it has been and I have spent this year in futile and obsessively disastrous efforts to salvage the situation, most of which have made matters worse. So losing everything has been achieved.

"The Secret of change is to focus all of your energy, not on fighting, but on building the new". Socrates

Haven't we met before: Revisited: a Mind at War with Itself

So if Susan does not have BPD how can my narcissistic true self be destroyed by the Borderline person. It was only a couple of days ago that Susan shared with me that the hospital last year had told her that I had BPD (on top of narcissistic disorder and maladaptive behavioural traits as well as obsessive-compulsive disorder). As I have said I thought this initially was total nonsense. However, I began to reflect a little upon this and came to a very hard and frankly horrifying conclusion but one that to me explains much of my self-destructive and mind crushing behaviour: both the narcissist and the borderline are me! The "Creature" is the Borderline me and it has destroyed my life. The "Creature" has been at War all these years inside my mind with my relatively normal, if narcissistic, self. My primary delusion was possibly thinking Susan was delusional. Perhaps my belief in "destiny" is a delusion. But I now see things so much more clearly, of course having lost my fortune and family. My destructive compulsion was to manically trade knowing that it destroyed me. I have often stated that were I not a trader I would choose to be an alcoholic and ideally drink myself to death. The final step is all too clear and will likely occur shortly after we have sorted out the legal necessities. As much as I don't want to lose Susan and my family I am not sure I could stay with them in good faith as I do not believe it is in their best interests. I have successfully destroyed myself and have no doubt that the world and indeed I will be better off without me. As discussed, over the years I convinced myself that Susan had BPD and even narcissism which is, I think, shamefully false. Perhaps this is simple projection on my part but the effects are not simple. I have dragged Susan, as strong as she is, down with me into my bottomless pit of despair and disaster, and that is not easily forgiven. Sadly, until now, I believe I have been devoid of empathy: these realisations have hit me like a sledgehammer. When I am in a particularly active borderline state my poor wife has the classic feeling of "walking on egg shells" and has explained that she has difficulty focusing on the most basic of tasks. At these times I could be extremely demeaning, accusing and controlling which had seriously negative implications for Susan such that she felt she was losing her own identity. For instance, on one occasion when trying to clear out the house she actually threw away a $4500 uncashed cheque. Luckily I happened to see it lying on top of the rubbish bin. Now of course I used this to fuel my delusion that she had BPD but in actuality, perhaps, she was so badly crushed by my behaviours that she could not perform the most basic of tasks with a clear mind. This is truly tragic. To her credit Susan has always been a tireless worker whenever we have had occasion to move house.

The only issue I have with her work is that very little attention is paid to what is important and what is not. It almost appears that her process is random. Over the years we have lost many important things including a large imitation Christmas tree but Susan has always blamed the movers or a maid. Just recently a small desk safe I had on my desk for four years disappeared. The safe had sat open and contained social security cards, voter registration cards and other important documents. It seemed to me obvious to simply close the safe and transport it as it was but when I finally found it, the contents had been ditched, goodness knows where, and the safe transported empty, but for a lone scuba diving card of Susan's. I cannot for the life of me understand this. Her lack of attention to important things had first come to light just before we were married. The church required proof that I was truly a member of the Church of England or Episcopal Church. I therefore gave Susan my confirmation certificate that I had kept safely for over 25 years: the certificate never made it to the church. Susan blamed the maid. I must confess I generally keep out of the way when we are packing up a house but not just because of laziness. Primarily, I avoid the issue because it would be too painful to confront the massive amount of superfluous stuff that we would have invariably, expensively accumulated since the last, mass clear out.

It is only now, with a heavy heart, that I see I have for years lied to myself and my delusions lied to me also. While at Vitol and Hess, though I laboured in absolute mental agony, through my respect for the corporate systems and my colleagues I managed, unknowingly, to keep my destructive, borderline-self under control. He would cause me untold pain but he was not able to wreak outright havoc.

Essentially, I see my mind being at war with itself. The two parties are my borderline self and my narcissistic self, neither particularly healthy but I believe the latter is the truer version of me that the borderline is out to kill. My narcissistic self can project a happy, out-going exterior whilst being torn apart with torment internally. It is terrified of failure and filled with debilitating anxiety. It detests trading and is prone to serious, prolonged periods of deep depression. My borderline self is utterly addicted to trading knowing it is a sure path to the destruction of my fragile narcissistic self. The borderline will get angry with others, for instance Susan, when really the anger should be pointed at myself. It is also very judgmental and critical which can clearly be tied back to my childhood experiences with my mother. My borderline self, as I have stated, is very quick to spot an opportunity to take control, usually when I am depressed or under stress. With control, it will typically throw me into a period of mania and delusion that will lead to massively negative consequences whether in relation to my wife or to my finances. With hindsight I even see now how my borderline self got me overly involved in the movie fiasco. I invested far too much but I was without a doubt deluded. I was actually, almost to spite myself, going to invest more but luckily my friend Alberto told me not to. Susan has told me that she felt helpless to stop me from doing what I wanted which I can see now with absolute, teary-eyed, clarity. My borderline self is essentially a prisoner of my own mind, as indeed is my truer narcissistic self, that suffers from severe depression, extreme anxiety, PTSD and a variety of other personality disorders. I can deal with the latter self and learn to live with and treat my conditions but it is the borderline self that must be defeated.

"Knowing your own darkness is the best method for dealing with the darknesses of other people".   C.G.Jung

It is actually frightening to have come to these understandings. I feel I am afflicted with dual, warring personalities, and will never be at peace and I should not inflict myself upon anyone. Susan has come to appreciate my insights but we have agreed to amicably divorce: she needs time, she says, to heal herself and to be free of the tortured, destructive lunatic that she has lived with for 14 years. Maybe with new understanding I can recognise when the borderline or "creature" is threatening to take over but my other, truer self, is hardly a barrel of laughs: the depressed, anxious, obsessive compulsive, fragile narcissist.

"The meaning of life is that it stops"   Franz Kafka

I do not yet know for sure where the "creature" came from but I have a suspicion. I think he is that incredibly sullen and angry little boy who grew into an angry adult. After my first marriage he was basically shoved aside and shut out. Except he wasn't. Although, as stated, my angry outbursts virtually stopped after my first marriage, I think the anger morphed into something far more dangerous and insidious. I have for years believed it was simply turned inwards and manifested itself as depression. This may be partly true. However, I believe the sad, angry little boy actually turned himself into a cunning, quiet, deadly creature determined to eventually destroy me and to deprive me of everything of value and then to kill me. It may be nearly 50 years ago but that little boy lying on the kitchen floor is about to plunge the knife. I was meant to look after that little boy but I let him down, I blew it. I made wrong decisions at bad times and turned him into me. No wonder he is still so angry (nod to Nick Hornby).

As previously discussed I have struggled greatly with the effects my suicide will have on my family. Again, recently, with my mind being in an especially fragile state, I believe I entered a manic state under the control of the "creature" when I wrote all about Susan in a deliberate effort to precipitate divorce, a divorce I did not want, but one which my destiny demands.

"A man devoid of hope and conscious of being so has ceased to belong to the future". Albert Camus

I have long since lost all confidence or sense of worth. I struggle greatly with the will to live. Maybe I am being a coward but I am following my destiny and carefully taking steps to see that it is fulfilled now that is it so clearly taking shape.

Susan and the children are about to head off to San Diego for the week of Thanksgiving. I very much hope they will have a terrific time without me that will ultimately lead to them having a wonderful life together without me.

I had dinner with Camille recently: I had given her a draft of my book. She asked me to assure her that the "suicide note" comment was not true. I hope I did not falsely assure her. I also saw my eldest son last week who is now 22 and well on his way in life. Camille commented that both she and her brother were now adults and would inevitably see their parents less. I actually asked her if she would be upset if I were to drop dead. She said of course, and that is was 20-30 years too early to go through that. One must do one's research.

When the family return from San Diego I plan to tell Susan that I agree the best course of action is to divorce amicably and quickly. I want Amelia and William to live happily with Susan and realise that I am actually surplus to requirements. I know there will be a period of grief but I plan to set the stage to minimise this and enable them to see that their lives are perfectly fine without me. Financially, I am at my lowest ebb for over 25 years with no realistic chances of meaningful employment, partly due my mental state. For Susan, she is actually emerging with a reasonable sum of money, greater than she would have received had I never lost a cent but had kept more accurate separate property records, given that our marital estate actually lost money during our marriage.

Looking back, which I am trying to do less frequently, I can see that I spent the last four years or so in a state of hyper anxiety and near panic. I was engaged in a permanent and obsessive campaign of trading or investing and bill paying. I am amazed I did not explode in some fashion or other. My obsessions extended to frantically recycling, seeking out and using restaurant coupons, and almost permanently burning wood in a fire pit outside, regardless of the temperature. Much of this wood was obtained by my obsessively digging out old cedar roots on our land. It was as if I was in a crusade, which ultimately I lost.

I am following my destiny and will use this coming week at home to put a lot of my affairs in order. Interestingly, when I mentioned to Susan that I would write a book she commented that I should try to write one in the vein of "A Confederacy of Dunces" by John Kennedy Toole. I am flattered by her belief in my writing abilities but I am far more realistic, and in no way could I match his Pulitzer prize winning genius. However, there does appear to be a looming, potential similarity in the fate of the two authors.

Perhaps, with all this new knowledge, if I can defeat and contain my borderline self, there is hope for me to regain some mental stability and even some semblance of financial stability and security. Susan and I have actually been getting along much better of late and talking more frankly than ever. Whether it is in my best interest's or not, I firmly believe that we could make a better go of it, equipped with my new self-understanding but Susan disagrees and is resolved to divorce in spite of my sincere apologies and newly acquired insight. I deeply regret the profoundly sad effect this is going to have on my two wonderful young children but I feel in good conscience that I have done everything possible to avoid it.

> **"Of all the words of mice and men,**
> **the saddest are,**
> **"It might have been"".**
> **Kurt Vonnegut**

Sadly for me, it appears that John Steinbeck was correct, as indeed were the words of **Sigmund Freud:**
"Yes, America is gigantic, but a gigantic mistake".

So, with divorce looming
I will close with some words of **Lisa Schroeder:**
"OK. I will go. But only if you will give me
your guilt to take with me".

Jonathan Ford